Llewellyn's

2008

Witches'

Spell-A-Day

Almanac

Holidays & Lore   Spells & Recipes

Rituals & Meditations

Copyright 2007 Llewellyn Worldwide.
Editing: K. M. Brielmaier; Design: Michael Fallon
Cover Design: Lisa Novak; Background Photo: © PhotoDisc
Monthly Introductions by James Kambos; Interior Art: © 2005, Terry Miura
(illustrations: pp. 9, 29, 49, 71, 91, 111, 129, 151, 171, 191, 211, 231);
© 2005 Eris Klein (holiday and day icons)

You can order Llewellyn books and annuals from *New Worlds*, Llewellyn's
magazine catalog. To request a free copy of the catalog, call toll-free
1-877-NEW WRLD, or visit our website at http://subscriptions.llewellyn.com.

ISBN-10: 0-7387-0559-4; ISBN-13: 978-0-7387-0559-0
Llewellyn is a registered trademark of Llewellyn Worldwide, Ltd.
2143 Wooddale Drive, Dept. 0-7387-0559-4
Woodbury, MN 55125

Table of Contents

About the Authors

Elizabeth Barrette serves as the managing editor of *PanGaia*. She has been involved with the Pagan community for more than eighteen years. Her other writing fields include speculative fiction and gender studies. She lives in central Illinois in a house with a woodstove and plenty of firewood. Visit her website at: www.worthlink.net/~ysabet/sitemap.html.

Nancy Bennett has had her work published in various places, including Llewellyn's annuals, We'moon, Circle network, and many mainstream publications. Her pet projects include reading and writing about history and creating ethnic dinners to test on her family. She lives near a protected salmon stream where the deer and the bears often play.

Ellen Dugan, the "Garden Witch," is a psychic-clairvoyant and has been a practicing Witch for twenty years. Ellen is the author of several Llewellyn books, *Garden Witchery, Elements of Witchcraft, 7 Days of Magic, Cottage Witchery, Autumn Equinox, The Enchanted Cat, Herb Magic for Beginners, Natural Witchery*, and *How to Enchant a Man* (2008).

Ember is a freelance writer, poet, and regular contributor to Llewellyn annuals. Her interests include collecting rocks and minerals, gardening, and nature photography. She lives in Missouri with her husband and two feline companions.

Lily Gardner is a lifelong student of folklore and mythology. In addition to writing for Llewellyn, she is working on a murder mystery and a book of saint folklore and spells. Lily has been practicing witchcraft in Portland, Oregon for fourteen years.

Igraine is a lifelong progressive Witch. She lives with her non-Pagan husband of twenty-seven years in Bucks County, Pennsylvania, where she is a high priestess of the coven PanGaia. An accomplished astrologer, tarotist, herbalist, writer, and teacher, she intertwines all of these arts into her professional practice. She is officially a Maiden, Mother, and Crone.

James Kambos wrote the introductions to each month as well as many daily spells. He is a folk artist and writer who makes his home in the beautiful hill country of southern Ohio. A regular contributor to Llewellyn annuals, he has a degree in history and geography. He has authored numerous articles on the folk magic traditions of Appalachia, Greece, and the Near East.

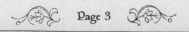

Deborah Lipp has been Wiccan since 1981 and teaching Wicca since 1986. She is the author of *The Elements of Ritual*, *The Way of Four*, and *The Way of Four Spellbook*.

Kristin Madden is a bestselling author of several books on parenting, shamanism, and Paganism, including the Llewellyn books *The Book of Shamanic Healing* and *Dancing the Goddess Incarnate*. A Druid and tutor in the Order of Bards, Ovates, and Druids, she is also Dean of the Ardantane School of Shamanic Studies.

Sharynne MacLeod NicMhacha is a Celtic priestess, bard, and scholar, and a faculty member of the Celtic Institute of North America. She has studied Celtic mythology through Harvard University, and has taught widely in the United States and the British Isles.

Diana Rajchel finds herself developing—somewhat to her alarm—into a Pagan critic, social commentator, and curmudgeon feminist. She has practiced Wicca for the last ten years, and even as she prods at the practices and culture associated with her religion, she loves her dedicated gods all the more fiercely. At present, she is working on a book about handparting.

Laurel Reufner has been a solitary Pagan for over a decade. She is active in the local CUUPS chapter, Circle of Gaia Dreaming, and is often attracted to bright and shiny ideas. Southeastern Ohio has always been home, and she currently lives in lovely Athens County with her wonderful husband and two adorable heathens, er, daughters.

Cerridwen Iris Shea longs for a garden. She writes, teaches tarot, cooks, is owned by several cats, and is a fan of ice hockey and thoroughbred racing. Visit her tarot blog, Kemmyrk (tarotkemmyrk.blogspot.com) and her website, Cerridwen's Cottage (www.cerridwenscottage.com).

Gail Wood has been a Witch and Wiccan priestess for more than twenty years, practicing a shamanic path celebrating the Dark Moon. She is clergy, teacher, ritual leader, tarot reader, and Reiki Master. She is the author of *Rituals of the Dark Moon: 13 Lunar Rites for a Magical Path* and *The Wild God: Meditations and Rituals on the Sacred Masculine*.

Winter Wren is the founding priestess of the Temple of the Sacred Lady of Avalon and the former Illinois director for Witches Against Religious Discrimination. She now resides in southeastern Michigan where she makes a living reading tarot and creating art. She is owned by a Maine coon cat.

A Note on Magic and Spells

The spells in the *Witches' Spell-A-Day Almanac* evoke everyday magic designed to improve our lives and homes. You needn't be an expert on magic to follow these simple rites and spells; as you will see if you use these spells through the year, magic, once mastered, is easy to perform. The only advanced technique required of you is the art of visualization.

Visualization is an act of controlled imagination. If you can call up in your mind a picture of your best friend's face or a flag flapping in the breeze, you can visualize. In magic, visualizations are used to direct and control magical energies. Basically, the spell-caster creates a visual image of the spell's desired goal, whether it be perfect health, a safe house, or a protected pet.

Visualization is the basis of all good spells, and as such it is a tool that should be properly used. Visualization must be real in the mind of the spell-caster so that it allows him or her to raise, concentrate, and send forth energy to accomplish the spell.

Perhaps when visualizing you'll find that you're doing everything right, but you don't feel anything. This is common, for we haven't been trained to acknowledge—let alone utilize—our magical abilities. Keep practicing, however, for your spells can "take" even if you're not the most experienced natural magician.

You will notice also that many spells in this collection have a somewhat "light" tone. They are seemingly fun and frivolous, filled with rhyme and colloquial speech. This is not to diminish the seriousness of the purpose, but rather to create a relaxed atmosphere for the practitioner. Lightness of spirit helps focus energy; rhyme and common language help the spell-caster remember the words and train the mind where it is needed. The intent of this magic is indeed very serious at times; and magic is never to be trifled with.

Even when your spells are effective, magic won't usually sparkle before your very eyes. The test of magic's success is time, not immediate eye-popping results. But you can feel magic's energy for yourself by rubbing your palms together briskly for ten seconds, then holding them a few inches apart. Sense the energy passing through them, the warm tingle

in your palms. This is the power raised and used in magic. It comes from within and is perfectly natural.

Among the features of the *Witches' Spell-A-Day Almanac* are an easy-to-use "book of days" format; new spells specifically tailored for each day of the year (and its particular magical, astrological, and historical energies); and additional tips and lore for various days throughout the year—including color correspondences based on planetary influences, obscure and forgotten holidays and festivals, and an incense-of-the-day to help you waft magical energies from the ether into your space.

In creating this product, we were inspired by the ancient almanac traditions and the layout of the classic nineteenth-century almanac *Chamber's Book of Days*, which is subtitled *A Miscellany of Popular Antiquities in connection with the Calendar*. As you will see, our fifteen authors this year made history a theme of their spells, and we hope that by knowing something of the magic of past years we may make our current year all the better.

Enjoy your days, and have a magical year!

2008
Year of Spells

 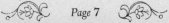

January is the first month of the Gregorian calendar. Its name comes from the two-faced Roman god Janus, ruler of gates and doorways. Its astrological sign Capricorn, the goat (December 21–January 20), is a cardinal earth sign ruled by Saturn. Once again our Earth begins its journey around Father Sun. From the ashes of the past January appears as a steady flame, lighting our way toward the future. For the ancients, New Year's Day was a time of gift-giving; for Christians, January 6 is Epiphany, the last night of the Christmas season. In northern Europe, January 7 was observed as a day to honor the return of the strengthening Sun—and as the old saying goes, "As the daylight lengthens, the cold strengthens." In many areas a layer of snow softens the barren landscape, and the light of both the Sun and January's Full Moon, the Wolf Moon, shimmers on snow-covered rooftops. The night air is crisp—almost brittle—and the evening sky shimmers with starlight. For a January ceremony, follow Pagan tradition and place two pine branches in the form of a solar cross upon a ritual fire. As they burn, they will release their magical power of everlasting life. To bring a wish into your life, charge an ice cube or a bowl of fresh snow with your intent. Place the ice or snow outdoors; as it melts, your wish will be absorbed by Mother Earth.

January 1
Tuesday

New Year's Day – Kwanzaa ends

 4th ♎

☽ → ♏ 8:32 pm

Color of the day: Maroon
Incense of the day: Geranium

Luck Spell

Eating cabbage on New Year's Day will bring you luck in the coming year. Try this family recipe for Lucky Sauerkraut and see how your new year goes. You'll need one jar of sauerkraut, ¼ cup brown sugar, firmly packed, and 1½ teaspoons caraway seed. Dump the sauerkraut into a saucepan and, using a low-medium heat, bring to a boil. Add the brown sugar and caraway seeds. Stir to thoroughly mix together, envisioning luck for the entire year. For best results, serve with the pork or ham dish of your choice. Cabbage is one of the fastest growing vegetables in the garden, making it plentiful as well as lucky. Caraway seeds also represent plenty and prosperity. Have a healthy, lucky New Year!

Laurel Reufner

Notes:

Holiday lore: New Year's Day calls for safeguards, augurs, charms, and proclamations. All over the world on this day, people kiss strangers, shoot guns into the air, toll bells, and exchange gifts. Preferred gifts are herring, bread, and fuel for the fire.

January 2
Wednesday

 4th ♏

Color of the day: White
Incense of the day: Lavender

Subtle Spell

Sometimes you need to work magic in public, without attracting attention. In that case, you can do everything through visualization instead of setting up a whole ritual with tools, gestures, chants, etc. In order to contain the energy so that it won't be detectable to nearby people, you can ward the spell. Here is a simple warding charm to say silently before you begin:

> Only in my mind,
> The spell takes shape.
> Power lies still,
> And can't escape.

Elizabeth Barrette

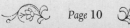

Notes:

won't be found—near an entryway if you can. Perform this spell again in one year.

James Kambos

Notes:

January 3
Thursday

 4th ♏

Color of the day: Purple
Incense of the day: Nutmeg

A House Blessing Spell

In ancient times this was one of the days households offered small sweets as a thank you to the gods, and to ask for their blessing. Honey was one of the traditional flavors found in these sacrificial cakes. An easy way to do this is to buy a piece of honey-soaked pastry, such as baklava, and bless it according to your spiritual path. The pastry must be taken to a crossroads and left as an offering to one of your deities. To gain more prosperity, you may also add a coin by inserting it into the pastry. Another way to protect and bless the household is to take a small piece of wool fabric and sprinkle a bit of cinnamon, or other protective herb, in the center. Bring the corners of the fabric together and tie them. Hide the protective bundle where it

January 4
Friday

4th ♏

☽ → ♐ 9:13 am

Color of the day: Coral
Incense of the day: Orchid

Winter Abundance Spell

As the winter winds howl around your door, light a flame to ensure prosperity and well-being throughout the dark half of the year. Bake small, unleavened cakes from oat and barley flour to work a spell of abundance. Steep magical herbs in a vessel of melted snow: heather for remembrance of the ancestors, mistletoe for healing, and juniper to clear unwanted energies. Sprinkle the ritual cakes gently with the herbed water and pass them over the flame while repeating this charm:

O gods and goddesses of the sacred Earth,

I thank you for your many
blessings.
Protect me and guide me
from step to step.
I seek the abundance of the
seventh bread
And the chalice of the drink
of immortality.
In respect and honour, may I
live in peace and plenty.
In the name of the Old Ones
With the power of those
unseen,
This winter charm is done.

Sharynne NicMhacha

Notes:

January 5
Saturday

4ℏ ♐
Color of the day: Indigo
Incense of the day: Magnolia

Twelfth Night Spell

In Christian tradition, today is Twelfth Night or Twelfth Day Eve. This marks the beginning of Epiphany and kicks off the start of the Carnivale season, which lasts through Mardis Gras. In some old English festivities, a Lord of Misrule would be elected to preside over both feasting and debauchery, while the normal social customs were suspended or reversed in a spirit similar to the Roman holiday Saturnalia. Twelfth Night is an excellent time to disperse stagnant energy and to upend rigid customs. Begin by cleaning your home and dumping material goods that you do not need or want. Then get crazy. Put your clothes on inside out to repel evil spells. Give a gift to a total stranger. Write with the opposite hand. Spend this day doing things out of the ordinary, and see what epiphany it brings you.

Diana Rajchel

Notes:

January 6
Sunday

 4th ♐
D → ♑ 8:43 pm

Color of the day: Orange
Incense of the day: Eucalyptus

Protection Spell

Traditionally on this day, known as Three Kings, a spell of protection was performed in the home to insure safety for those who dwelled within. Dried herbs were blessed and burned in the name of the Three Kings or Magi—Caspar, Melchior, and Balthasar—and holy water was sprinkled at the doorways. With a piece of chalk the initials CMB were inscribed over the doorway along with the current year. The master of the house would then say: "Caspar, Melchior, Balthasar, protect us this year from the dangers of fire and water." Adapting this ritual for present day Pagans, invoke the Three Kings or pick three of your favorite gods and/or goddesses to protect your home. Inscribe their names or initials on a wooden plaque along with the year, 2008. Burn frankincense and myrrh in a gold bowl at your altar, as these were the gifts of the three Magi. Gold will draw the light of the Sun and invoke wealth, vitality, and joy. Frankincense and myrrh have similar magical properties of purification, banishing negativity. Sprinkle consecrated salt water around your entranceway and hang the plaque above your door to protect your house for the coming year.

Igraine

Notes:

Holiday lore: Twelfth Night and the night following it are when wassailing used to take place. The word "wassail" comes from the Anglo-Saxon words *waes heil*, meaning "to be whole or healthy." People drank to each other's health from a large bowl filled with drink such as "lamb's wool," which was made of hot ale or cider, nutmeg, and sugar with roasted crab apples. In some parts of Britain, trees and bees are still wassailed to ensure a healthy crop. Having drunk to the tree's health, people fire shotguns into the branches. Different regions sing different wassail songs to the tree. Here's one from Worcestershire:

> Here's to thee, old apple tree,
> Whence thou mayest bud,
> Whence thou mayest blow,
> Whence thou mayest bear
>   apples enow.

January 7
Monday

 4th ♑

Color of the day: Gray
Incense of the day: Hyssop

Moonbeam Spell

Breathe into relaxation and imagine that you are standing outside under the Moon. Notice the phase of the Moon. Is it full, dark, or crescent? Is it waning or waxing? Feel the light of the Moon on your body as it begins to sink into your skin, filling your being. Give thanks for the presence of the Moon and its energy. Allow the experience to unfold as it will, trusting that you will learn what you need to at this time. You may meet with a god or goddess of the Moon. You may be drawn up to the Moon itself or ride the moonbeams to another world. When you feel you have received what you will in this session, thank those present for their guidance and return to your physical body.

Kristin Madden

Notes:

January 8
Tuesday

 4th ♑

New Moon 6:37 am

Color of the day: White
Incense of the day: Cedar

Moon Rune Spell

In Scotland, a charm known as a "rune" was uttered when first catching a glimpse of the New Moon. This word differs from the one used to describe the Norse runes, and comes from the Scottish Gaelic word *rún*, which means "a secret" or "a mystery." It was also used to refer to someone who was beloved. It was traditional to turn over a piece of silver in the pocket when seeing the New Moon for the first time. Hold a silver vessel of sacred water in your hands as you scan the skies for the first appearance of the crescent Moon. When you see her, pour three circles of water on the ground and repeat this rune:

> When I see the new crescent
> It becomes me to say my
>   rune.
> May the Moon of Moons
> Be coming through the
>   clouds,
> And be my knee bent down
> To the queen of loveliness.

Sharynne NicMhacha

Notes:

Notes:

January 9
Wednesday

 1st ♑

☽ → ♒ 6:13 am

Color of the day: Yellow
Incense of the day: Honeysuckle

Write a Wish

This is a spell to manifest a desire. This will be private: no one else will see your secret wish. Write it down on a sheet of yellow paper. Take as much time as you need and elaborate as much as you can. Be specific! Always consider the consequences of what you ask for: be sure you really want it, and that it's not an attempt to control or manipulate another person. Then, fold the paper three times and say with each fold:

> For the good of all,
> With harm to none,
> As I wish,
> So it be done.

Place the folded paper in a special, secret location while you wait for your wish to manifest.

Ember

January 10
Thursday

Islamic New Year

1st ♒

Color of the day: Green
Incense of the day: Mulberry

Resolution Spell

Today marks the Islamic new year, the first of two that will happen this year. Because the Muslim calendar falls eleven to twelve days short of the solar calendar, all Islamic holidays migrate through the seasons over the years. While Muslims do not officially celebrate the new year, some exchange gifts and cards in memory of the emigration of the prophet Muhammed, while others mourn martyr Imam Hussein, and still others commemorate the death of the first Caliph, Abu Bakr. There are two things to contemplate for all people of faith: death and life. Choose a loved one or a role model who is deceased. Write a letter to that person, telling him or her how you intend to live your life

in honor of what that person taught you. Put this in a bottle and hide it in a space sacred to you. Check your letter in a year.

Diana Rajchel

Notes:

of paper with "_____ is flying" over and over. Leave room at the end for "So mote it be!" and sign your name. Go to a high spot; your roof will work. Fold the paper into a paper airplane. Say "_____ is flying! So mote it be!" and let 'er rip!

Deborah Lipp

Notes:

January 11
Friday

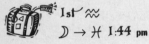 1st ♒
☽ → ♓ 1:44 pm

Color of the day: Pink
Incense of the day: Vanilla

Spell for Flight

Today is Amelia Earhart Day. In honor of the first woman to fly across the Atlantic, an airplane spell is in order! Imagine things taking flight. Something in your life is grounded, or stable, or slow and steady, and you want it to fly. Your career is steady, but you'd like it to take off. Your relationship is pleasant, but hasn't hit the heights. You communicate well with your friends, but never have adventures. Come up with a short, simple, statement about what you want to fly, like "my career" or "Joe & Me." Fill a clean, new piece

January 12
Saturday

1st ♓

Color of the day: Blue
Incense of the day: Pine

Give Birth to Prophecy Spell

Today is a good day to begin developing your own prophetic powers. January 11 through 15 is the Festival of Carmenta, the Roman birth goddess. Carmenta beheld the future of each child born. In her temple, it was forbidden to wear leather, so it's best not to wear any while working this spell. Choose a tool such as tarot cards, runes, or a new crystal. Place them on a mirrored surface and form a circle of salt around them on your altar. Say:

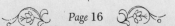
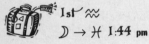

*Oh goddess Carmenta! Giver
of birth, seer of safe beginnings and future directions,
I bid thee to grace this object
with true prophecies and to
bless me with the knowledge
to use it well. So reflect back
upon me, this power.
Blessed be.*

If possible, leave the mirror in place
for one full day. After twenty-four
hours, begin to use your tool to
guide you in your future.

Nancy Bennett

Notes:

January 13
Sunday

 1st ♓

☽ → ♈ 7:23 pm

Color of the day: Yellow
Incense of the day: Almond

Spell for Committed Relationships

St. Hilary was said to have been
a happily married man, and his
feast day marks the traditional beginning of the wedding season. Using
St. Hilary's energies and traditional
wedding symbols, this spell will help
bring more intimacy and commit-
ment into your relationship. Writing
has a way of focusing one's thoughts,
so begin the spell by making four
lists. On your first list, write down
the qualities in your mate that con-
tribute to feelings of intimacy the two
of you already share. Now, write on
your second list whatever is missing in your relationship. On your
third list, write down the qualities
you bring to the relationship, and on
the fourth list write any actions you
could take to deepen your relationship. Fold your lists in half, tie them
with a blue bow, and slip them in the
toe of one of your shoes. Add several
grains of rice for fertility, a penny
for prosperity, and a ring for eternal
love. Place the shoe under the bed on
your partner's side. If you don't have
a partner and desire one, place the
shoe under your altar.

Lily Gardner

Notes:

January 14
Monday

 1st ♈

Color of the day: Lavender
Incense of the day: Clary sage

Psychic Spell

Monday is the day of the week dedicated to the Moon and all of her magics. This waxing Moon could be used to increase your intuition and psychic abilities. Light a silver candle for the Moon goddess Selene, and a purple candle to increase your own psychic powers. Call on Selene and ask for her assistance. She is known to be very fond of Witches and magic users, and offers practical and quick solutions.

> Under the waxing
> January Moon,
> Selene hear my call
> And grant me a boon.
> Increase my intuition
> And psychic powers,
> My thanks I send to you,
> In this magic hour.

> Ellen Dugan

Notes:

January 15
Tuesday

 1st ♈

2nd quarter 2:46 pm

☽ → ♉ 11:13 pm

Color of the day: Black
Incense of the day: Bayberry

Invoking Creativity

Today is one of the days of Carmentalia, the festival honoring the Roman goddess Carmenta. Each of us has some spark of creativity within. Some are more aware of it than others, but it is there to be awakened. During this time of the waxing Moon, focus your thoughts on your own creativity. What do you wish to bring forth from within your being? What beauty can the muse awaken in your soul? What inspiration do you seek? When you have meditated on these thoughts for a bit, light a lavender candle and place it before a bowl of clear, fresh water. Settle yourself before the candle and invoke Carmenta with the following chant:

> Carmenta, Carmenta,
> Goddess so fair,
> I invoke of you
> Your wisdom to share.
> I come to thee,
> As have others before,
> Seeking your aid,
> So my creative visions
> May pour—

Flowing forth in the world
Like the waters
Of your spring,
Carmenta, Carmenta,
Please, your guidance bring.

Meditate for a time before the candle and remember to thank Carmenta for her blessings.

Winter Wren

Notes:

from harm while you travel. Keep the toy car in a safe place. You could even stash it in the glove box of your car. If you wish, use a toy model of whatever car you drive. A similar spell could be used for commuting via public transportation.

Laurel Reufner

Notes:

January 16
Wednesday

 2nd ♉

Color of the day: Topaz
Incense of the day: Marjoram

Auto Charm

For this little car protection charm, you'll need a small red toy car and some oil of rosemary. Sit calmly, grounding yourself. Hold the toy car in your dominant hand. While visualizing the car being surrounded by a swirling circle of white protective energy, anoint the car's hood, roof, and wheels with dabs of the rosemary oil. Close your other hand over the car and tell yourself that it is done. Your car will be safe

January 17
Thursday

2nd ♉

Color of the day: Turquoise
Incense of the day: Myrrh

Blessing Our Pets Spell

Today honors St. Anthony, the patron saint of domestic animals. We can magically ask divine protection for the health and safety of our pets. Create sacred space for you and your pet. Bring together representations of air, fire, water, and earth. Call in appropriate deities to be patrons of your animals. Wafting the elements over the pet, say:

By air I seek the knowledge
to keep these creatures
healthy and safe, by fire I

 Page 19

will the power to do what must be done, by water I call love throughout their life, by earth I give their safety and health to you. Protect and bless them all their life. Blessed be.

Bow and thank the elements and gods and hug your pet.

Gail Wood

Notes:

January 18
Friday

 2nd ♉

☽ → ♊ 1:30 am

Color of the day: Rose
Incense of the day: Pine

Meditation on Clear Intent

In our very hectic world, it can be quite easy to lose sight of our focus. In order to be truly effective and in balance within ourselves, it is necessary to maintain sight of our intent in all areas of our lives. This simple meditation can assist in regaining one's intent. Sit easily, spine straight, and breathe deeply in and out. Slow your thoughts and allow your mind to become quiet. Visualize yourself receiving light through the top of your head and earth energy through the soles of your feet. Be aware of these two beams of light meeting within your being. Observe the flowing stream of awareness, light giving birth to the manifestation of energy within you. Attune yourself to the light of a clear mind leading to thought and action in harmony with your divine purpose, which will allow you to shape your life in right relationship with yourself, with others, and with our Earth Mother. Dedicate your thoughts and actions to peace. Absorb light into yourself and put a vision of a peaceful planet into your heart. Let rose-colored light expand outward from your heart and reach all realms of your thought. Let your mind become quiet once more and then go out into your day in peace.

Winter Wren

Notes:

 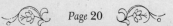

January 19
Saturday

2nd ♊

Color of the day: Brown
Incense of the day: Patchouli

First Day Spell

Today is January 19. To figure out the numerology of the day (not the date, but the day), do the math. $1 + 9 = 10$. $1 + 0 = 1$. Today is the first day of the rest of your life. Literally. It is about you. It is early in the New Year, an opportunity for a fresh start, without the pressure and subsequent disappointment of New Year's resolutions. Meditate on your goals and dreams for the year. Write them down, and under each list small, manageable steps to achieve them. Pamper yourself and face the future with optimism. Think of the World tarot card: everything is open to you. Now it's up to you to decide what that "everything" includes!

Cerridwen Iris Shea

Notes:

January 20
Sunday

2nd ♊

☽ → ♋ 3:05 am
☉ → ♒ 11:43 am

Color of the day: Gold
Incense of the day: Marigold

A Rosemary Dream Spell

Long ago at this time of year, the herb rosemary was used to conjure prophetic dreams. You'll need two sprigs of rosemary and some spring water—bottled is fine. Before you go to bed, relax and inhale the scent of the rosemary. Sprinkle each sprig with three drops of the water. Place the sprigs near your pillow. Traditionally, a sprig was placed in each shoe or slipper you wore that day. Without thinking of anything or anyone specific, drift off to sleep. Clear your mind of all thoughts or worries. Let the dreams come. If you happen to dream of a romantic partner, it's said he or she will speak to you during the dream. Record anything you see or hear in your dream journal. See if it comes to pass.

James Kambos

Notes:

January 21
Monday

Martin Luther King, Jr. Day

 2nd ☉

Color of the day: White

Incense of the day: Rosemary

Magic for the heck of It

Sometimes we get too serious about our magical working, forgetting that working magic puts us in connection with our deities and the wonderful energies of the universe. To reconnect our magic to our sense of wonder and joy, go to your sacred space. Breathe in all the magic that you have done in that space. Close your eyes and continue to breathe deeply. Send your awareness to the element of air and ask for its knowledge. Listen. Send your awareness to the element of fire and ask for its vitality. Listen. Send your awareness to the element of water and ask for its heart. Listen. Send your awareness to the element of earth and ask for its wisdom. Send your awareness to the Goddess and God and ask them to show you your inner divinity. Listen. Ask them to show you their own divine selves. Listen. When you are done, reconnect to your grounding. Thank all the elements and deities.

Gail Wood

Holiday lore: Feast Day of Saint Agnes of Rome. Since the fourth century, the primitive church held Saint Agnes in high honor above all the other virgin martyrs of Rome. Church fathers and Christian poets sang her praises, and they extolled her virginity and heroism under torture. The feast day for Saint Agnes was assigned to January 21. Early records gave the same date for her feast, and the Catholic Church continues to keep her memory sacred.

January 22
Tuesday

2nd ♋

☽ → ♌ 5:20 am

Full Moon 8:35 am

Color of the day: Scarlet
Incense of the day: Ylang-ylang

Wolf Song Spell

Deep in the winter, the world wears a white coat of snow. The Full Moon shines through bare branches, casting its brilliant light across the glittering landscape. There! A shadow slipping through shadows, a wisp of snow blowing low over the frozen ground. Suddenly they take form, and figment becomes fact: a pack of wolves serenading the sky. Native American tribes name the Full Moons based on natural events. The Algonquin and other eastern peoples refer to the January Full Moon as the Wolf Moon. During this time, wolf packs howl hungrily in the forests and roam widely in search of food. Wolves have always been linked closely with lunar symbolism. In Pagan traditions, they are creatures of the maiden goddess, and strong heroines are "women who run with the wolves." Now is an appropriate time to work with wolf energy for family loyalty, teamwork, hunting magic, and mystery. Help the species by "adopting" a wolf at a zoo or wolf park. Honor the spirit with wolf stories or praise poetry, such as:

> Wolf song in winter wind
> Wide tracks in the deep snow
> Hunter at the deer's heels—
> In you lives the wildness
> At the heart of the world.

Elizabeth Barrette

Notes:

January 23
Wednesday

3rd ♌

Color of the day: Brown
Incense of the day: Lilac

Release Negative Energy

For this spell you will need incense of your choice. You will focus on the element of air to take away negative thoughts or energy. You can use this to remove negative and self-limiting thoughts about yourself and increase self-confidence and happiness. This spell can also be used to cleanse negativity from a room, such as after an argument or conflicting emotions have been expressed. First, focus on the negative

 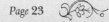

energy to be cleared. If it's in a room, go to that room. Light the incense and say:

> Smoke that rises take away
> Negative energy—
> These thoughts can't stay.
> Anger, misery,
> Worry and doubt,
> Smoke, please carry them
> Out, out, out!

Sit for a few moments and watch the smoke rise. Visualize it capturing the negativity and dissolving it, carrying it higher and higher until it completely disappears.

Ember

Notes:

January 24
Thursday

 3rd ♌
☽ → ♏ 9:48 am

Color of the day: Purple
Incense of the day: Clove

A Melting Spell
Is there a chill between you and a friend? Are things in your life frozen and you long for a thaw? A

winter day in the waning Moon is the time to create warmth from the cold. If there's snow outside, get about a tablespoonful of it. Otherwise, prepare ice chips from the freezer. As you gather your snow or ice, visualize the thing that is frozen. Set up your altar with a cauldron or other fire-safe container over a flame. The snow or ice is in the cauldron. The flame is not yet lit. Have a fire extinguisher handy. Ground and center. Make a statement of intent; something like, "This is the coldness between Joe and me. This coldness melts away." Light the fire. Tone or chant, "Warming! Heating! Melting!" or similar words. When the snow is melted, send a final wave of power into the cauldron. Say, "So mote it be!" Allow the water to evaporate.

Deborah Lipp

Notes:

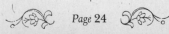

January 25
Friday

 3rd ♏

Color of the day: Coral
Incense of the day: Thyme

Burns' Night

Burns' Night suppers, honoring the birthday of Scottish poet Robert Burns, have been held on this night for over two hundred years. This is a wonderful time to celebrate not only the well-known poet, but also your friends and family with a delicious meal, good drink, and great fun. Your supper need not be traditional. Make it a potluck or have a few friends over to cook your favorite foods. Be sure that beverages for toasting are plentiful and include a truly fabulous dessert. It is traditional for bagpiping to accompany the arrival of guests and the main dish. A formal welcome to the guests opens the supper. Follow this with toasts to everyone and everything, including the meal. The toast to the "lassies" by the men and the reply to that by the "lassies" is usually full of joking and teasing. And remember to end by singing "Auld Lang Syne."

Kristin Madden

Notes:

Holiday lore: Burns' Night is a key event in Scotland that has been observed for about 200 years in honor of Robert Burns, who was born on this day. One of Scotland's most beloved bards, Burns immortalized haggis in a famous poem. This is a Scottish dish of animal organs boiled in a sheep's stomach with suet and oatmeal. "Burns' Suppers" are celebrated not only in Scotland but wherever patriotic Scots or those of Scottish descent live.

January 26
Saturday

 3rd ♏
☽ → ♎ 5:35 pm

Color of the day: Indigo
Incense of the day: Sandalwood

Mind–Body–Spirit Exercise

Witches work well in the realms of mind and spirit but often neglect their physical bodies. Shapeshifting is a magical way to balance mind, body, and spirit. You can perform this exercise outside or at the gym on the treadmill. Begin by warming up for a few minutes, moving gently but with intent. Focus your eyes directly in front of you, keeping your gaze very soft. Find yourself beginning to lose awareness of your surroundings. Don't

allow distractions to throw you off. Increase your pace and start to breathe rhythmically. Imagine you are on an African savannah. The air around you is thick, hot, and moist. You can feel the heat rising as the Sun travels overhead. You begin to quicken your run as you spot a gazelle just ahead, leaping through the tall, dry grass. Your heart pumps harder as you move like a hunting lioness, taut and streamlined. Concentrate on the movement of this awesome cat, elegant, graceful, agile, and strong. Visualize its well-muscled body. Become one with her powerful form as you run faster now in pursuit of your prey. You can see the gazelle bounding, springing high into the air. Run, breathing deeply into the belly. Let the power of your breath carry you as far as you want to go.

Igraine

Notes:

Just have Fun Ritual

According to the Roman calendar, today is the *Sementivae Feria*. All labor and legal finagling are suspended. Since today is Sunday, many of you will have the day off from your regular work life. In addition, take the day off from your "have-tos" at home. Leave the laundry, stack the dishes. Gather the family and do something fun. Dig out old family board games. Pull out large sheets of paper and paint or crayons and create a mural together that you can tape on the wall. Cook a meal together, or go out for pizza. Enjoy each other's company. Remember to laugh, and remember the importance of impromptu family "holy days."

Cerridwen Iris Shea

Notes:

January 27
Sunday

 3rd ♎

Color of the day: Amber
Incense of the day: Juniper

January 28
Monday

 3rd ♎

Color of the day: Silver
Incense of the day: Lily

National Fun at Work Day

It's over a month past Yule, the weather is blah, and so is your job.

Page 26

So what do you do? A spell to re-energize your work space! Buy some colorful pens, a fun calendar, and some wacky office toys (my favorite is the stuffed voodoo computer). Gather them up on a colorful scarf and say:

> No more the dull
> And dreary days
> Of mundane work,
> No time to play.
> With this spell
> I bring a change.
> Let fun infuse
> And rearrange!
> Smiles I bring
> And laughter be,
> This spell is cast,
> So mote it be!

Tie the items in the scarf. Now get into your most colorful clothes, put on a smile and head to work. Sweep your space clean and arrange the items from the scarf around you. This works for home as well, if you work from there.

Nancy Bennett

Notes:

January 29
Tuesday

 3rd ♎
☽ → ♏ 4:35 am

Color of the day: Gray
Incense of the day: Basil

Inner Child Altar

One way to cure the winter blues is to make an inner child altar. In the center of your altar, place a framed photo of yourself as a child. Write on a piece of paper, "I nurture the child within me," and place it in front of your photo. Decorate the altar with childhood toys or your favorite objects and use your favorite colors for cloth and candles. Light your candle and quiet your mind. As you sit before your altar, check in with your inner child. Does he or she feel listened to and heeded? Many of us in our everyday life are too busy working and doing chores to take the time to be kind to ourselves. Ask yourself what you could do on a weekly basis that would take care of your inner child. It could be anything from a long bubble bath, a neighborhood game of basketball, or a painting class. Whatever you decide, make sure it's fun.

Lily Gardner

Notes:

January 30
Wednesday

 3rd ♏

4th quarter 12:03 am

Color of the day: Yellow
Incense of the day: Bay laurel

Hecate's Day

The thirtieth of each month is the sacred day of the triple goddess of crossroads and the patroness of Witches, Hecate. Hecate had many names and titles: Hecate Trevia, "of the three ways"; Hecate Phosphoros, "the light bringer"; Hecate Nykterian "of the night"; and Hecate Basileia, "Hecate Queen." On this night of the waning Moon we have a perfect opportunity to work with this goddess and ask for her blessing to illuminate our darkest times, and grant us her protection.

> Hecate, goddess of the
> crossroads, hear my cry,
> Protect and guard me under
> your midnight sky.
> Hecate Phosphoros "she who
> brings the light,"
> Hecate Trevia bless me with
> your wisdom tonight.

Ellen Dugan

Notes:

January 31
Thursday

 4th ♏

☽ → ♐ 5:08 pm

Color of the day: Crimson
Incense of the day: Jasmine

Banish Criticism Spell

It is human to be critical of ourselves. What we fail to realize is that our self-criticism can be harmful. Often, we fail to understand that self-criticism is not self-assessment. Self-assessment is positive, as it allows us to see paths for change and improvement. During this time of the waning Moon, focus on letting go of self-criticism. On a piece of paper, write down all the ways you criticize yourself. Fold the paper into quarters and, while folding, think about never addressing yourself in those negative ways again. Light a white candle by your burning dish. Tear the folded paper seven times, drop it into your burning dish, and ignite it. As the paper goes up in flames, see your criticism of yourself going with it. As the ashes cool, meditate in the light of the candle on the following mantra: "It is not what I am that holds me back; it is what I think I am not."

Winter Wren

Notes:

February is the second month of the Gregorian calendar, and the year's shortest month. Its astrological sign is Aquarius, the water-bearer (January 20–February 18), a fixed air sign ruled by unpredictable Uranus. In colder regions, February is a month of deep snow and fierce storms. February's Full Moon was known as the Snow Moon. Frost may etch the window panes and icy winds may howl, but Mother Earth begins to stir with new life. You can see it as the buds on trees begin to swell, and the tips of green daffodil foliage pierce the frozen Earth. In old England it was believed that the Sun awoke in February. The Pagan holiday of Imbolc on February 2 is a day of purification and a time to honor the turning of the year toward spring. Corn dollies or an ear of corn from last year's harvest may be placed on the hearth to draw fertility and protection. For Christians this day is Candlemas, a time when all Yule greenery must be removed and burned. Valentine's Day on February 14 is a day for flowers, candies, and love magic. February days may appear gray and bleak, but new life is pulsing deep within the Earth. To call forth the promise of abundance, place a new houseplant or potted crocus near a window. Light a solitary white candle while meditating on the coming warmth.

February 1
Friday

 4th ♐

Color of the day: Purple
Incense of the day: Violet

New Friends Spell

We all like to make new friends, but for some of us it's hard. This spell should help banish fears and other obstacles we place in our way. You will need a favorite cologne or scent, some dried basil to use as an incense (plus the materials necessary for burning it), and a pink candle. Light the candle and incense. Pass the cologne through the incense smoke, imagining the smoke cleansing the cologne and carrying away some of what stands between you and making new friends. Set the bottle near the candle and allow it to burn out. Try to wear the cologne when you go out and keep yourself open to the possibility of meeting someone new.

Laurel Reufner

Notes:

February 2
Saturday
Imbolc – Groundhog Day

 4th ♐

Color of the day: Black
Incense of the day: Sage

Awaken Inspiration

This is the time of year when life begins to stir. Although winter may still appear to hold the land, spring approaches. This is a wonderful time to celebrate the awakening of a creative endeavor or creativity in general. If you're an artist, writer, musician, etc., use this ritual to invite inspiration. If you don't have an interest in a particular creative art, simply ask to be inspired in any way that will enrich your life. On your altar or a table, arrange as many white candles as you can find into a circle. In the center of the circle, place a clean glass dish or bowl of crushed ice. (If you like, use clean snow instead, or just use drinking water.) As you light the candles, imagine the fires of inspiration flowing into the bowl of water. Visualize the water collecting this creative power.

> Nut to tree, seed to flower,
> Nurture my creative power,
> Growing as it fills this dish,
> Inspiration is my wish.

Allow the candles to burn as long as you can, then snuff them out.

 Page 30

Imagine that the bowl contains water from the mythical spring Hippocrene, the waters of creative inspiration. Drink the water.

Ember

Notes:

Holiday lore: On Imbolc, a bundle of corn from the harvest is dressed in ribbons and becomes the Corn Bride. On February 2, the Corn Bride is placed on the hearth or hung on the door to bring prosperity, fertility, and protection to the home.

February 3
Sunday

4th ♐
☽ → ♑ 4:52 am

Color of the day: Gold
Incense of the day: Hyacinth

Winter Zip Spell

Winter can make you sluggish, even after three cups of coffee. This spell can help you toss off that groggy feeling and take on those projects you're too tired to do. Take a brisk bath, and add a few drops of a citrus essential oil or some mint. Inhale deeply. These stimulate circulation and brain activity. When you step out of the tub, give yourself a brisk rubdown with your towel, or use a body brush to stimulate circulation. After you have done this, take ten short sharp breaths, inhaling through your nose and blowing out through your mouth. As you do this, picture a ray of Sun shining on you and inside you, heating you at your core. When warm from head to toe, visualize a bubble sealing you in with that solar energy. You should feel energized and ready to take on the next project.

Diana Rajchel

Notes:

February 4
Monday

 4th ♑

Color of the day: Lavender
Incense of the day: Narcissus

King Frost Day

The Celtic calendar denotes today as King Frost Day, who reigned with the Queen of the Snowflakes. Decorate your home and work spaces with representations of winter, icicles, and snowflakes. If you're in a cold climate, go ice skating, attend a hockey game, build a snowman, or go cross-country skiing—or sit inside by the fire with a cup of cocoa and watch the snow fall outside. If you're in a warm climate, eat ice cream or build an ice sculpture and watch it melt. Take joy in the cold, clean attributes of King Frost.

Cerridwen Iris Shea

Notes:

February 5
Tuesday
Mardi Gras

 4th ♑
☽ → ♒ 2:10 pm

Color of the day: Red
Incense of the day: Ginger

Mardi Gras Celebration

Today is Mardi Gras, a fandangous festival most famously celebrated in New Orleans. Although originally inspired by Christianity, Mardi Gras is really an interfaith celebration, combining motifs from many different religious and magical traditions. Customs include parades with a king and queen, parties, masked balls, and the eating of cinnamon "king cakes" topped with tricolored sugars. The three colors associated with Mardi Gras represent justice (purple), faith (green), and power (gold). Tap into the tremendous energy of this festival by wearing one or more of the colors. To manifest all three qualities, braid together three ribbons or cords; the resulting braid can be used to wear a pendant, or hung over your altar. If you want to go all out, throw a Mardi Gras party for your magical friends and raise energy for justice, faith, and power.

Elizabeth Barrette

Notes:

When the Full Moon is reached, return the stones to your altar and thank the goddess for her help. This spell can be done whenever healing is needed, but is best near the New Moon for a fresh start.

Nancy Bennett

Notes:

February 6
Wednesday
Ash Wednesday

 4th ≈

New Moon 10:44 pm

Color of the day: Topaz
Incense of the day: Lilac

A Spell for Personal Healing

In the dark of night, place a candle on a blue cloth. Call upon the four directions and then center yourself. Take a handful of reflective stones (such as rhinestones, small white quartz, or other clear crystals) and place them round on the altar. Say,

> As the Moon returns from darkness, so shall my healing begin tonight. By the power of Sirona, goddess of the stars. You who shine upon the world with healing, shine upon me now.

Place the stones in a small dark bag and carry them with you as a charm.

February 7
Thursday
Chinese New Year (rat)

 1st ≈

$\mathcal{D} \to \mathcal{H}$ 8:46 pm

Color of the day: Turquoise
Incense of the day: Apricot

Accumulating Wealth Spell

The New Moon in February marks the beginning of the Chinese New Year. This year is the Year of the Rat, which is the first sign in the twelve-year cycle of the Chinese zodiac. In ancient times, the rat was welcomed as a bringer of prosperity. In Chinese folklore they are a symbol of good luck and wealth. It is deemed an honor to be born in the Year of the Rat according to Chinese astrology. Though it corresponds to the cold of winter and the dark of night, it is considered to be a year of bounty. This is a fortuitous year for accumulating wealth, as Rats have a knack with money and they know how to make something out of nothing. Status and monetary satisfaction are their greatest motivators. The New Moon is the best time for spells involving gain and Jupiter, the planet of expansion and good fortune. Working with the attributes and associations of the Year of the Rat, perform this spell today to accumulate wealth over the coming year. At 11 pm, light white, black, and red candles. Place a raw wooden treasure chest (you can buy them at the craft store) on your altar. Wrap a garnet in a dollar bill and, holding it in your hand, chant:

> With the cunning of the Rat
> and Jupiter's good fortune,
> I charge this garnet with
> money magic! May this year
> bring me wealth in the form
> of _____.

Place the garnet in the chest and seal the magic by drawing a rat and the symbol for Jupiter on the chest.

Igraine

Notes:

February 8
Friday

 1st ♓

Color of the day: Coral
Incense of the day: Cypress

Dissolving Illness Spell

Traditional healers often work with the powers of the natural world to perform healing work. Make an offering to the spirits of nature, asking them to protect you and your loved ones from wintertime ailments. In Scotland, healers envisioned an illness breaking up into parts that were sent out to be healed and transmuted by the energies of the Earth. Here is a charm you can use to dissolve illness:

> I will heal thee, and may
> Bridget be with me.
>
> The first third of your
> illness, may it be upon the
> grey clouds, since they have
> the best power to move.
>
> May the second third be upon
> the watery land, since it has
> the best power to absorb.

 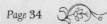

*The last third upon the
bountiful meadows, since
they have the best power to
carry.*

*I make this charm with my
two palms on the ground*

In the name of the old ones.

Sharynne NicMhacha

Notes:

H oliday lore: Today is the Buddhist
Needle Memorial. On this
day, as part of the principle of endless compassion espoused by the
Buddhist faith for all sentient and
nonsentient beings, all the sewing needles that have been retired during the
year are honored. That is, needles are
brought to the shrine and pushed into
a slab of tofu that rests on the second
tier of a three-tiered altar. Priests sing
sutras to comfort the needles and heal
their injured spirits.

1st ♓

Color of the day: Brown
Incense of the day: Rue

Bumping the Grind Spell

T oday is Gypsy Rose Lee's birthday, one of the most famous
ecdysiasts (striptease artists) of her
day. Sometimes our lives become
routine and we need something to
kick-start us enjoying life again. In
your sacred space, bring things that
excite you. Bring a multivitamin and
a cookie spiced with ginger. Stand
up and say, "It's the same story told,
I am tired of the old." Take the vita-
min and eat the spicy ginger food and
chant several times until energy is
raised:

> *Bless this pill as I do will:*
> *See my life as a great thrill,*
> *Taking life in one huge slice;*
> *Full of love and full of spice.*

Give yourself a hug, thank your deities and dance out into your great big
fat life!

Gail Wood

Notes:

February 10
Sunday

 1st ♓
☽ → ♈ 1:17 am

Color of the day: Yellow
Incense of the day: Frankincense

Lifting Your Spirits

In the dreary days of late winter, this spell will give your spirit a lift. Cut several stems from a forsythia shrub. Select stems that have a large number of swollen leaf buds. Remove the buds and crush them to form a paste. Sprinkle the substance upon a small brass tray and let it dry in a sunny window. Once dry, light eight candles in colors representing the Sun—yellow, orange, or gold. Standing before the burning candles, crumble the dried buds into a small box or dish. Add a sprinkle of gold glitter and say: "The spirit never dies. The spirit lives." This magical powder which you have prepared can be added to any growth or prosperity spell. Leave the powder on your altar during the winter to remind you that during the dark season, the life-force of Mother Earth is not dead—only resting.

James Kambos

Notes:

February 11
Monday

 1st ♈

Color of the day: Ivory
Incense of the day: Hyssop

Vasant Panchami

Today is *Vasant Panchami*— Saraswati Day. Saraswati is the Hindu goddess of learning and knowledge. Beloved of students and teachers, her image appears in schools (from kindergarten through university) throughout India. Saraswati is also a goddess of the arts, and is often depicted playing the sitar. Her sacred animal is the swan. Vasant Panchami is Saraswati's birthday. The sacred color of the day is yellow. Today, her images and altars are draped in yellow, her worshippers wear yellow clothing, and yellow-tinged foods are given as gifts. Today is an excellent day to begin learning something new. In India, today is the day to teach children their first words. You can start a book club or a study group on Vasant Panchami.

Deborah Lipp

Notes:

February 12
Tuesday

 1st ♈
☽ → ♉ 4:34 am

Color of the day: White
Incense of the day: Cinnamon

Festival of Artemis

On this night of the waxing Moon and on this festival day of Artemis, call on this tough and fiercely independent deity. Visualize her as a trim and athletic woman wearing a light-colored tunic and hunting with her silver bow. She is accompanied by her faithful hounds and her stride is light and sure. Artemis will help to boost your sense of self, to remind you to be both brave and daring, while you walk your own unique spiritual path.

> Artemis Maiden Huntress,
> With your silver bow,
> Grant me independence,
> Let my bravery show.
> Help me follow my dreams
> And to do what's right,
> I am not afraid to walk
> My own path in this life.

>   Ellen Dugan

Notes:

Holiday lore: Lincoln is called the Great Emancipator and is thought of as one of our greatest presidents. Know this, however: Lincoln was an almost unknown figure until the age of forty, when he first entered the Illinois state legislature. His later assassination threw the country into widespread mourning, inspiring Walt Whitman to write:

> Coffin that passes
> through lanes and street,
> through day and night
> with the great cloud
> darkening the land . . .
> I mourned, and yet shall
> mourn with ever-
> returning spring.

February 13
Wednesday

 1st ♉

2nd quarter 10:33 pm

Color of the day: Brown
Incense of the day: Lavender

Parentalia Divination

On this day, the Romans celebrated Parentalia by honoring their deceased ancestors. Honor your dead by visiting their graves with gifts of food and flowers, or by making an ancestral altar with photos of your departed relatives. Whether you're at the gravesite or at your altar, light a new candle and quiet your mind. Begin with a prayer to your ancestors, asking them if they have a message for you. Meditate for twenty minutes. When you finish meditating, throw a tarot card spread. Your reading should be especially meaningful. Then, just for fun, try this traditional love divination performed on Valentine's Eve. Write the names of three potential lovers on separate slips of paper. Roll the slips of paper in clay balls and drop them in a bowl of water. Your lover will be the first clay ball to rise to the surface.

Lily Gardner

Notes:

February 14
Thursday
Valentine's Day

 2nd ♉

☽ → ♊ 7:19 am

Color of the day: Purple
Incense of the day: Carnation

A Night of Love

If you wish to use it, this love spell contains the Middle Eastern lust-spell ingredient mastic, which can be purchased at Greek and Middle Eastern grocers. Scent a room with a sensuality incense such as patchouli, rose, or vanilla. Have a bottle of sweet red wine, a red cloth, crushed almonds, and a bowl of sweet red cherries on hand. For a real lust enhancer you may also obtain some mastic-flavored chewing gum. When you and your romantic partner are in the mood, pour each other a glass of wine. Sip slowly and feed each other the cherries. Save the cherry seeds and place them on the red cloth. Add the crushed almonds and tie this bundle up with red thread and keep for future love spells. Before love-making, chew the mastic gum. During the days of the Ottoman Empire mastic was thought to be a powerful aphrodisiac. The women of the Sultan's harem would always chew it before a romantic encounter with the Sultan. The cherry seeds you've saved may be used in a love or fertility spell, or planted to ensure an enduring love.

James Kambos

Notes:

the wolf for its guidance. Return through the woods and back to your physical body.

Kristin Madden

Notes:

February 15
Friday

 2nd ♊

Color of the day: Pink
Incense of the day: Yarrow

Lupercalia

In honor of the Lupercalia, why not explore the wolf energy in your life? Imagine that you are walking in the woods. In the distance, you hear the howling of wolves. You hear a rustle in the leaves nearby and suddenly a lone wolf stands before you. Notice the color of its fur, its eyes, and the presence of any other beings. As you look at the wolf's eyes, it throws back its head and howls before looking back at you. Hear the others answer from a distance. Then ask your question or voice your concern. Be open to any messages, feelings, or symbols that you experience. When you feel you have received what you will in this session, thank

February 16
Saturday

 2nd ♊
☽ → ♋ 10:12 am

Color of the day: Gray
Incense of the day: Ivy

Fitness Spell

A good day to promote any healthy change in your lifestyle is today, for it celebrates the Roman goddess Victoria, who was also known as "Nike" in Greek mythology. First, decide on a sport or physical challenge you wish to pursue in the coming months. Then gather a few small things to represent it. Are you a swimmer? Then bring to your altar a nose plug, or shells from the sea. Perhaps you wish to be a runner. Then place on your altar laces and feathers to inspire swiftness. Once you have gathered your "charms," call upon the directions. Then say:

Goddess Victoria, hear me pray,
Let me start a healthier way.
In times to come, a future fair,
A fitter me in every way.

Dear Nike, dear Nike.
Bless these charms, I pray,
Fleet of foot, healthy and free,
Through the goddess,
Mote it be.

Nancy Bennett

Notes:

and tense your feet. Hold that for a second and then relax. Feel the relaxation in your toes, your soles, your arches, and your ankles. Continue up through your entire body. Be sure to include areas you might not ordinarily think of, like your ears, lips, and jaw. Breathe deeply, filling your lungs as you relax. Just be with that experience of complete relaxation for a time.

Kristin Madden

Notes:

February 17
Sunday

 2nd ♋

Color of the day: Orange
Incense of the day: Almond

Bathroom Break

Most of us live fairly stressful, overscheduled lives, and we need to find time to relax. But in the time you get for a bathroom break at work, you can achieve a healthy state of relaxation that will benefit your mind, body, and soul. First, take a deep breath. Bend your neck forward and circle it around, stretching the muscles. Circle your wrists and feet. Take another deep breath

February 18
Monday
Presidents' Day (observed)

 2nd ♋
☽ → ♌ 1:51 pm

Color of the day: Silver
Incense of the day: Neroli

A Dream Spell

Care to see the future or the past? Well here's your big chance. As we are a few days away from a Full Moon, let's try a little dream magic tonight. Call on the Moon goddess Selene and ask for her help in sending you a magical dream. Before you

retire for the evening, set a pen and notebook by your bed. When you wake in the morning you are ready to jot down your memories from your dreams.

> As the waxing Moon rises,
> I call on beautiful Selene,
> As I retire for the night,
> Send me a magical dream.
> Show me what may be, or
> Grant knowledge of the past,
> As I wake, the images will
> Hold true and fast.

Ellen Dugan

Notes:

February 19
Tuesday

 2nd ♌
☉ → ♓ 1:49 am

Color of the day: Gray
Incense of the day: Bayberry

Winter Fires

Winter is a good season to perform fire magic. Fire has long been used to purify and protect magical tools, and it can activate or intensify magical workings. Walk around the perimeter of your house in a widdershins direction, burning herbs like sage or juniper to clear negative energies. Take a lit candle inscribed with magical symbols of good fortune and protection, and walk around the house in a sunwise direction. Pass your magical tools over the flame three times in a widdershins circle to clear any non-beneficial energy that has accumulated, re-energizing and consecrating them in a sunwise direction, while chanting these words:

> Yours be the power of fire,
> Yours be the might of ocean,
> Yours be the energy
> Of wind and mist,
> And the unending
> Powers of the Earth.
> The magic of the serpent
> Be yours,
> The magic of the flame
> Be yours,
> And the might
> Of all the elements.

Sharynne NicMhacha

Notes:

February 20
Wednesday

2nd ♌

☽ → ♍ 7:06 pm

Full Moon 10:30 pm

Color of the day: Yellow
Incense of the day: Honeysuckle

Full Moon Ritual

Here, on the night of the Full Moon, the Moon Mother shines in her brightest glory. In addition to being a time of protection magic and the dismissing of unwanted energies in our lives, Full Moons offer us a chance to say "thank you" for things accomplished during the previous lunar cycle. Giving thanks for completed work is part of the cycle of balance that we work toward achieving in our lives. Create your sacred space, invoke your guardians, and light a red candle and some frankincense. Quiet your mind for a few moments, reflecting back over the workings you have completed in the past month. When you are ready, speak with the Lady in her guise as Moon Mother:

> Lady Mother, I, who am your child, stand between the worlds in sacred space under your light. Once more I affirm my joy in life and in my union with you upon your path. I honor you, Lady Goddess, for the favors and energy you bring to my life, and ask your blessings upon me.

> Beautiful Lady, thank you for the light and beauty you bring to my life. Thank you for the energy and wisdom you give to me to walk in balance in your world.

> So mote it be.

Winter Wren

Notes:

February 21
Thursday

3rd ♍

Color of the day: Green
Incense of the day: Balsam

Honor Your Ancestors

This is the last day of *Feralia*, an ancestor-worship festival; it's the ancient Roman version of the Day of the Dead. Prepare your altar or other special place by arranging votive candles and flowers to honor a loved one who has passed on. If you have no physical reminder of the ancestor you wish to honor, use a photo or simply write the person's name on a piece of paper. Arrange the candles and flowers around the item, photo, or name. Use as many items of remembrance as you like. Or, you can honor several people at the same time by using an object to represent each of them. If you don't have a specific ancestor you wish to honor, meditate on unknown ancestors of your past. Offer thanks to them for the good qualities you possess and ask for strength and courage to overcome or understand any less-than-desirable qualities.

Ember

Notes:

Ƒebruary 22
Friday

 3rd ♏

Color of the day: White
Incense of the day: Alder

The Empathy Mirror

When we're surrounded by complex people, we may not understand their motivations. When you work or live with someone who might seem impenetrable, try this simple mirror spell to gain some empathy. Look into a mirror, and visualize the person you want to understand reflected back at you. Be as visceral as possible. Say three times as you gaze into the glass:

> Open me, open mind,
> Open us, in kind.
> To see similarity,
> To treat all with charity
> Open me, open mind,
> Mystery unwind.

As you gaze into the glass, holding the other person's picture in your mind, imagine how that person feels when looking back at you. What do you imagine the thought processes to be? What motivations does this person have? What does the person need to say that you perhaps have not yet heard? See if this helps you behave with empathy toward your co-worker or friend.

Diana Rajchel

Notes:

Holiday lore: We all know the lore about our first president—cherry tree, silver dollar, wooden teeth—but the truth behind this most legendary of American figures is sometimes more entertaining than the folklore. For instance, did you know that once when young George went for a dip in the Rappahannock River, two Fredericksburg women stole his clothes? This story was recorded in the Spotsylvania County records. Picture then the young man scampering home flustered and naked, and the icon of the dollar bill becomes just a bit more real.

factors make Saturday an ideal day to deal with any mundane or magical tangles that have come up during the week. Light a stick of cypress or cinnamon incense, or wear wintergreen oil. Wear a Saturn stone such as onyx, jet, or garnet for added support. Then meditate on recent challenges and how you met them. If you got into a disagreement that hurt someone's feelings, or otherwise wronged someone, try to make amends. Even better than a verbal apology is a practical demonstration of caring, such as the gift of a favorite food or other treat. You might offer to do a chore that's usually someone else's responsibility—or even just do it without saying anything. Repeat weekly.

Elizabeth Barrette

Notes:

February 23
Saturday

 3rd ♍
☽ → ♎ 2:44 am

Color of the day: Blue
Incense of the day: Sandalwood

Saturday Resolutions

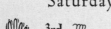 Saturday is ruled by the planet Saturn, associated with such concepts as time and karma. As the last day of the week, it also corresponds to completion and resolution. These

 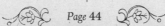

February 24
Sunday

 3rd ♎

Color of the day: Amber
Incense of the day: Heliotrope

Improvising with the Elements

When space is limited or your practice is solitary, a wise Witch will invest in a five pillar candelabra. This special piece is all you need to perform rituals effectively. Place your candelabra in the center of your altar. Put a yellow candle in the east (air), red in the south (fire), blue in the west (water), green in the north (earth), and a white candle in the center representing spirit. These are your quarters or directions. You can call them into your circle by simply lighting each candle in turn and perhaps saying a word or a phrase that corresponds with each element. Improvise, saying whatever comes to mind such as: East: "Wind" or "Birds in flight"; South: "Blaze" or "Dragon's breath"; West: "River" or "Swimming in sapphire pools"; North: "Rock" or "Dunes of sand." You can build on this improvisation by adding instruments. Play the recorder for the east, sing for the south, ring a bell for the west, and beat a drum for the north. If you have four people to circle with, this creative play can turn into an entire ritual improvising with the elements as you go.

Igraine

Notes:

February 25
Monday

 3rd ♎
☽ → ♏ 1:05 pm

Color of the day: White
Incense of the day: Clary sage

Grant Me Patience

Family getting the better of you? Draw upon your reserves and more easily banish that impatience. Find some quiet time where you can be by yourself. Sit comfortably, a small piece of obsidian in your hands. Breathe deep breaths and become aware of how you feel relaxed and at ease. Imprint that feeling upon yourself. Imagine shaking off the anger and impatience, the energy dissipating harmlessly in the air. Pour those feelings of calmness into the obsidian. During the day, when you feel your calm slipping, reach for your calming stone and mentally shake off the impatient energy trying to consume you and make you lose control.

Laurel Reufner

Notes:

his right foot to his left hand and cut. From his left hand to his right hand, measure the string and cut. Run the string from his right hand to his left foot and cut. Run the final length of string from his left foot back to his chin and cut. Burn the string in your cauldron.

Lily Gardner

Notes:

February 26
Tuesday

 3rd ♏

Color of the day: Black
Incense of the day: Geranium

Gypsy healing Spell
February 26 is Pentagram Night. The Babylonians, the Egyptians, and the ancient Greeks worshipped the pentacle as the womb of the Mother goddess. The Greek meaning for pentacle was "life" or "health," a symbol sacred to Hygeia, goddess of healing. The gypsies use the figure of the pentacle in this healing spell called "measuring the pentacle." With your patient lying spread-eagled on his back, use a long piece of string to trace a length from his chin to his right foot. Cut the string. By cutting the string you're severing the illness from his body. Run the string from

February 27
Wednesday

 3rd ♏

Color of the day: Topaz
Incense of the day: Marjoram

Let the Good Times Roll Spell
The first Mardi Gras was celebrated on this day in Mobile Alabama in 1703. Mardi Gras is the big party before the season of Lent and, as the Cajuns say, "Laissez les bon temps rouler." Gather together a piece of paper, a black pen, a necklace of shiny beads, rosemary, basil, and a small container or box with a tight seal or lock. List all the things that hold you back from having a good time, including money wor-

ries, health concerns, or just time management. Write them down with concentration and intention. Sprinkle the list with rosemary for intention. Fold the paper and rosemary in half with the blank side facing out. Write BE QUIET NOW on the outside and put it in the container. Sprinkle with basil for strength and success. Seal the container and place it on your altar. Go and have a good time. Remember to come back and deal with your list later. Right now, put on the beads and let the good times roll!

Gail Wood

Notes:

smokers love smoking and are comforted by lighting up. In order to successfully and permanently quit, it's important to acknowledge and release these feelings. Make an altar to your smoking habit. Have cigarettes, your favorite ashtray, matches or lighter, etc. Invoke the gods to witness. Speak freely to your cigarettes. Personify them. Say something like, "Whenever I've been afraid, you've been there for me. Smoking you has calmed me in those moments." Just let it all out. Now speak about letting go. "I'm saying goodbye to you now. It's time to move on." Speak words that are meaningful and as honest as you can make them. End with something like, "I no longer smoke." Say, "So mote it be."

Deborah Lipp

Notes:

February 28
Thursday

3rd ♏

☽ → ♐ 1:22 am

4th quarter 9:18 pm

Color of the day: Crimson
Incense of the day: Mulberry

Spell to Quit Smoking

One reason quitting smoking is so hard is that we don't complete our relationship with cigarettes. We may hate to admit it, but most

February 29
Friday
Leap Day

 4th ↗

Color of the day: Rose
Incense of the day: Mint

Leap Day

Today is an extraordinary day! It
only happens once every four years.
That is enough cause to jump for
joy—a precious day that rarely
makes an appearance. An extra day!
Traditionally, this is the day where
women are "allowed" to propose
to men. In the twenty-first century,
that's possible every day. Instead,
take full advantage of "Leap Day."
Today is the day for you to take a
leap in your life—a Life Leap Day!
What is something you always
wanted to try? Do it today. Open
up a new vista. Invoke Nicevenn, a
Scottish goddess often equated with
Diana, to bless your new venture.
Take the day off from your "normal"
life and do something unusual and
extraordinary in honor of the day.

Cerridwen Iris Shea

Notes:

March is the third month of the Gregorian calendar, and it was the first month of the Roman calendar. The month is named for the Roman god of agriculture and war, Mars. Its astrological sign is Pisces, the fish (February 18–March 20), a mutable water sign ruled by Neptune. In March we witness the power of the life-force. Plants begin to emerge from the cold Earth; from the bud will come the leaf. The winds still roar, but now they bring the promise of life renewed. In the old days March's Full Moon was called the Storm Moon, a time when the icy grip of winter began to weaken. Ostara is the major Pagan celebration of the month, when we pause to celebrate the Goddess as she arises from her winter sleep. And now the light begins to overtake the darkness at the Vernal Equinox—the first day of spring. Signs of the season are everywhere. Robins begin building their nests and rabbits frolic in the grass. Daffodils brighten suburban lawns, and garden centers are stocked with soil, mulch, and new plants. For fertility magic, try dyeing eggs in pastel colors, or decorating them with magical symbols. For a little March magic, grate some fresh ginger root and bless it by holding it beneath the rays of the Storm Moon. Then incorporate it into any love or success spell.

March 1
Saturday

 4th ♐
☽ → ♑ 1:33 pm

Color of the day: Pine
Incense of the day: Cedar

Juno Ritual

On this day, the primary festival of Juno was held. Juno was a Greek goddess with many titles and duties: Juno Matronalia, the goddess of marriage, and Juno Lucina, the goddess of light and prosperity in marriage. This goddess is a powerful matriarch and a patron deity to both married women and pregnant women. This is the deity to call on when working magic to strengthen the emotional bonds of your loving marriage, and to celebrate a happy, fertile, and prosperous union.

> Juno Matronalia,
> My marriage please bless,
> Help strengthen our love
> And grant us success.
>
> Juno Lucina,
> The goddess of light,
> May the flame of love
> Brighten our life.

Ellen Dugan

Notes:

Holiday lore: On March 1, Roman matrons held a festival known as Matronalia in honor of Juno Lucina, an aspect of the goddess Juno associated with light and childbirth. Some records indicated that her name was derived from a grove on the Esquiline Hill where a temple was dedicated to her in 375 BC. Whenever a baby entered the world in Roman times, it was believed that the infant was "brought to light." Women who worshipped Juno Lucina untied knots and unbraided their hair to release any entanglements that might block safe delivery.

March 2
Sunday

 4th ♑

Color of the day: Yellow
Incense of the day: Juniper

Singing Spell

Music and singing can raise your energy and make you feel happy. No matter where you are today, find a place to sing. It doesn't matter if you sing well or not, this

is just for you. Sing in the shower, in your car—anywhere. Sing anything—a lullaby, advertising jingle, a song from the radio, or something you made up yourself. While you sing, visualize your best and most confident self. You can pretend to be a rock star and play air guitar, or maybe you're on Broadway starring in a musical production, or serenading a loved one. Sometimes we forget that these kinds of fantasy acts are good for us. Magically, you can use this time to focus on fulfillment of a need. As you sing, express your heart's desire and draw it close to you. Do more than merely sing— sing with intent.

Ember

Notes:

March 3
Monday

 4th ♑

☽ → ♒ 11:24 pm

Color of the day: Lavender
Incense of the day: Neroli

Releasing Tensions

Life has a way of becoming hectic, and our energies quickly become stressed and jumpy. To soothe the tensions in a stressed-out household, put a ceramic pan, with some water in it, on the back burner. Add in small handfuls of lavender, roses, and cedar. Toss in some cinnamon sticks. Add a generous pinch of oak moss. For the spring or summer, use some bits of lemon peel. Allow to simmer on the back burner for as long as needed, refreshing the ingredients as necessary. (You can also use this formula in the fall and winter by switching the lemon peel to orange peel.)

Laurel Reufner

Notes:

March 4
Tuesday

 4th ≈

Color of the day: Maroon
Incense of the day: Basil

Spell for Undoing Falsehoods

Feeling like you have been unjustly accused of something you did not do? Have you had the finger pointed at you by coworkers or friends? Call upon Rhiannon to work in your defense. You will need stones, horsehair (or picture of a horse), bird feathers, a white candle, and a cauldron. Outside your home or in a special place, make a stone circle. Gather together the horsehair (or picture) and some bird feathers and place these inside the stone circle. Light the candle. Say:

> Rhiannon, thou who was
> falsely accused. Rhiannon,
> share with me thy strength.
> To stand firm in the face of
> injustice. To let the truth be
> known.

Move the stones and enter the circle. Place the horsehair and feathers in the cauldron and light them. As they burn, visualize yourself accepting apologies from those who accused you. When the ashes have cooled they can be carried as a talisman in a bag.

Nancy Bennett

March 5
Wednesday

 4th ≈

Color of the day: Yellow
Incense of the day: Marjoram

Taking a Bold Step Spell

On this day in 1783 the parachute was first demonstrated. There are times in our lives when we need to shore up our courage and do the thing we fear. To tap into our own valiant nature, gather together a red candle and a yellow candle, an object such as a charm, pendant, rock, or shell to serve as a talisman, and rose incense. Light the incense, breathe, and say, "Courage be in me!" Light the red candle and say, "Banish fear, boldness be in me!" Light the yellow candle and say, "Sunlit power and success be in me!" Call in the deities and elements according to your practice and ask the deities and elements to focus their blessings of courage and boldness into it. Then encircle the talisman with the incense, and the candles. Close your hands around it and say, "Empower this reminder to say I am powerful, bold, courageous, and strong. I have the words and I have the guts to do what must be done. As I will it so mote it be!" Extinguish the candles, say goodbye to the powers, and carry the talisman as a reminder.

Gail Wood

Notes:

on it. Hold it as you visualize your wallet filling with cash. Tell yourself that you deserve this money—and believe it. Take a deep breath and, as you exhale, blow this intent onto the almond. Taking all the dollars out of your wallet, fold them in half toward you with the almond in the center of the fold. As you fold, chant,

> *Money, money, plentiful,*
> *Make my wallet mighty full.*
> *Money, money overflowing,*
> *Keep my cashflow ever growing.*

Place the almond billfold in your wallet and expect that cash to continue to multiply.

Kristin Madden

Notes:

March 6
Thursday

4th ♒
☽ → ♓ 5:53 am

Color of the day: Green
Incense of the day: Clove

Attracting Money Spell

Almonds hold the power to attract money and prosperity. Keeping one in your wallet just might bring you more cash. Take one sliced almond and carve three dollar signs

March 7
Friday

 4th ♓
New Moon 12:14 pm

Color of the day: Purple
Incense of the day: Rose

Self-Confidence Working

According to surveys, public speaking is the number one fear of Americans. Still, it's required of most people at least once, whether presenting at a meeting or toasting a friend's wedding. Rather than letting the fear make you wobble and mutter "Um" too often, try this spell to stay cool and confident while all eyes are on you. Set aside some time to practice your speech. Even thirty-second speeches require practice. Take a piece of paper large enough to stand on, and draw the Sun and the glyphs for Mercury and Jupiter. See each symbol glowing as you place your feet on the paper; let that glow climb up your body and through the crown of your head. Practice your speech a few times, and allow the glow to flow through you and out your mouth. On the day of the speech, feel yourself glow on stage, knowing you're prepared.

Diana Rajchel

Notes:

Holiday lore: Although the month of June is named for Juno, principal goddess of the Roman pantheon, major festivals dedicated to her are scattered throughout the year. For instance, today marks Junoalia, a festival in honor of Juno celebrated in solemnity by matrons. Two images of Juno made of cypress were borne in a procession of twenty-seven girls dressed in long robes, singing a hymn to the goddess composed by the poet Livius. Along the way, the procession would dance in the great field of Rome before proceeding ahead to the temple of Juno.

March 8
Saturday

 1st ♓

☽ → ♈ 9:23 am

Color of the day: Brown
Incense of the day: Magnolia

A Meditation for Change

*See in your mind the last
injustice you witnessed;
See how you can right that
injustice;
See yourself doing so.*

*See in your mind the last
hurt you witnessed;
See how you can heal that
hurt;
See yourself doing so.*

*See in your mind the last
abuse you witnessed;
See how you can undo that
abuse;
See yourself doing so.*

*See in your mind the last
uncompleted task you
witnessed;
See how you can complete
that task;
See yourself doing so.*

*See in your mind the last
person in need you
witnessed;*

*See how you can alleviate
that need;
See yourself doing so.*

Change begins with each of us. Each step we take makes a difference. Remember the words of Gandhi: "Be the change you want to see in the world."

Winter Wren

Notes:

Holiday lore: While most holidays across the world celebrate the lives and achievement of men, March 8 is one day wholly dedicated to the achievement and work of women. Originally inspired by a pair of mid-nineteenth-century ladies' garment workers' strikes, today the holiday is little known in its country of origin; though this day's legacy is clear in March's designation by the U.S. Congress as Women's History Month. Throughout the month, women's groups in American towns hold celebrations and events, concerts, exhibitions, and rituals that recall heroic and gifted women of every stripe.

March 9
Sunday

Daylight Saving Time begins 2 am

 1st ♈

Color of the day: Gold
Incense of the day: Eucalyptus

Draw Your Desire

Even if you're not an artist, you can draw or sketch. This kind of focus is almost like meditation. Lose yourself in creating a work of art that expresses something you need, or just let go and be creative. You can use pencil or ink, or try paint. Use paper, cardboard, whatever you have on hand. Have fun. Color in a kid's coloring book if you want. Lose yourself in the experience, but focus: doodling while you're on the phone doesn't count. You must devote all your attention to the task, and in this way forget about stress. It's a great rest for the mind and a boost for creative energy. Light some gold or yellow candles around your work space and listen to music that inspires you.

Ember

Notes:

March 10
Monday

 1st ♈
🌙 → ♉ 12:13 pm

Color of the day: Ivory
Incense of the day: Lily

Protection Spell

If you feel you're the subject of a curse or psychic attack, or if you've had a run of bad luck, try this spell. On a piece of plain paper write out the problem. If you suspect a specific person of causing you harm, keep the individual in mind. Write an affirmation declaring you'll no longer be a victim. After writing your affirmation, smudge the paper with soot and crumple the paper. Build a ritual fire or light a work candle. As the flames grow, sprinkle ground cloves over the fire for purification. Toss the crumpled paper into the flames. Watch it be consumed and speak these words in a firm voice:

> From paper to fire,
> From fire to ash,
> From ash to ember,
> This curse must surrender.
> So mote it be!

James Kambos

Notes:

 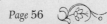

March 11
Tuesday

1st ♉
Color of the day: Gray
Incense of the day: Cedar

Mars Day Spell

Hey, it's Mars day! This day of the week is loaded with passionate and courageous energies. Mars was a major deity in the Roman pantheon, and it is believed that the month of March got its name from him. So let's put all this to good use by conjuring up a little magic that increases bravery and courage. Burn a red candle for Mars and an orange candle for energy and vitality.

> On this day of Mars,
> Passionate energy abounds,
> If you search inside yourself,
> Courage will be found.
> Mars send to me,
> The strength of a warrior true,
> To use this power wisely,
> In all that I do.

Ellen Dugan

Notes:

March 12
Wednesday

1st ♉
☽ → ♊ 1:54 pm

Color of the day: White
Incense of the day: Bay laurel

Crocus Divination

Crocus flowers are among the earliest to bloom each spring. They represent perseverence and cheer amidst adversity, blooming even in the snow. According to Ovid, the crocus was named for a youth who was transformed into this flower. Here is a fun little divination you can do to see what the coming season holds. Find a park, botanical garden, or residential neighborhood where you can walk safely and enjoy the spring flowers. Watch for the first crocus you spot. Its color will give you a hint of what's to come. White: truth, safety, peace. Yellow: change, communication, joy. Purple: spirituality, psychic power, counteracting negativity.

Elizabeth Barrette

Notes:

March 13
Thursday

 1st ♊

Color of the day: Purple
Incense of the day: Myrrh

Dream Muse Magic

Venus moves into her exalted sign of Pisces today. Here she is free and uncontained. She swims in the mystic sea of fantasy and illusion. Her mood becomes romantic, lyrical, poetic, and dreamy. Elevated to the role of muse, she presents us with the gifts of idealized vision, devotion and self sacrifice. Flowing into Pisces she prompts us to discover our own inner muse through intuition and dreamwork. Before going to sleep, write a request on a piece of parchment for your muse to come to you. Ask to remember her. Place it in your pillowcase, accompanied by a moonstone. This will encourage lucid dreaming and enhance your psychic receptivity. If she doesn't present herself on the first night, try again. When she finally does greet you don't forget to ask her name! Call out to her whenever you need your muse.

Igraine

Notes:

March 14
Friday

 1st ♊

2nd quarter 6:45 am
☽ → ♋ 4:37 pm

Color of the day: Coral
Incense of the day: Thyme

May Your Wishes Come True

Known for gusty winds, March is the perfect time to use the powers of air. In this season of new beginnings, what do you wish to manifest? Once you're clear about what you are wishing for, take a bottle of soap bubbles outdoors. Blowing bubbles brings out the child in all of us. Our inner child sees wonder and possibility. It's only in adulthood that we grow skeptical. As you blow bubbles, open yourself to the belief that your wish can and will come true. Ask the element of air to empower your wish. When you go back indoors, use the creative channel you've opened for yourself during this spell to brainstorm ways to achieve your wish. As with all spells, you need to do the work on the physical plane in order to manifest your wish.

Lily Gardner

Notes:

March 15
Saturday

2nd ♋

Color of the day: Blue
Incense of the day: Patchouli

Talisman for Fertility

This day is famous as the Ides of March; however, it's also the date of an important Japanese fertility festival. Tap in to the energy of the day by casting a spell for fertility or abundance. This could be used to increase fertility, a personal goal, career advancement, or garden bounty. Place a smooth oval rock upon your altar. With paint or permanent marker, draw the shape of an egg. Around the egg shape draw flames to represent the Sun. Breathe onto the rock and say, "With stone, egg and Sun this spell for abundance has begun." You've just made what is known as a talisman. Hold the rock and imbue it with your personal power. Keep it hidden until you need to invoke its power again. For a future spell, use your talisman as the centerpiece for a fertility or prosperity charm.

James Kambos

Notes

Holiday lore: Why is March 15 so notorious? On this date in 226 BC, an earthquake brought the Colossus of Rhodes—one of the Seven Wonders of the Ancient World—to its knees. But a more famous event likely accounts for the notoriety of the "Ides of March." Julius Caesar's rule, somewhere along the way, became tyrannical. In February of 44 BC, Caesar had himself named Dictator Perpetuus—Dictator for Life. Brutus assassinated him on March 15. Caesar's murder was foretold by soothsayers and even by his wife, Calpurnia, who had a nightmare in which Caesar was being butchered like an animal. Caesar chose to ignore these portents and the rest, of course, is history.

March 16
Sunday
Palm Sunday

 2nd ♋

☽ → ♌ 9:04 pm

Color of the day: Orange
Incense of the day: Marigold

Personal Deities

The goddess has ten thousand names. She is invoked with different names for different aspects of her – and our – personalities. Since our religion is a living, ever-evolving energy, sometimes we have to name a new aspect to get the right shade of meaning for a particular situation. What aspect do you need in your life? Name it. Build an altar to that new god or goddess and celebrate the aspect of both deity and yourself. Create rituals, a feast day, tokens, and talismans specific to this creation. Add it to your personal pantheon.

Cerridwen Iris Shea

Notes:

March 17
Monday
St. Patrick's Day

 2nd ♌

Color of the day: Silver
Incense of the day: Rosemary

Invitational Spell

St. Patrick's Day is a big day for partying, and this spell will attract social invitations. Get six to ten party invitations. Don't use sets; each invitation you use should be unique. Make some, buy some pre-printed, or write some, as you like. Fill out each one, inviting yourself to a party in a different location on a different date. Use occasions like birthdays, anniversaries, holidays, the Oscars, etc. Put each in a stamped envelope addressed to yourself (no return address). As you fill each out, think, "I am invited" while imagining yourself receiving an invitation. Feel the happiness of being invited, and send that happiness into your spell. When they're done, use your athame, wand, or hand to send power into the envelopes, saying, "I bring invitations to me. So mote it be." Mail each one from a different location. When the invitations arrive, allow yourself to be delighted to receive them.

Deborah Lipp

Notes:

March 18
Tuesday

2nd ♌

Color of the day: Black
Incense of the day: Bayberry

Personal Protection Zone

Create a personal protection zone around yourself as needed. You will need a bottle of your favorite shampoo and essential oil in one of the following scents: cedar, frankincense, lavender, or pine. All of these are not only protective, but also possess beneficial aromatherapy properties. You will also need a small tiger's-eye stone. Add seven drops of your chosen essential oil to the shampoo bottle and anoint the tiger's-eye as well. Tilt the bottle back and forth to combine the essential oil and the shampoo. Imbue the bottle with gentle protective energies, then place it on a windowsill where it will hopefully catch the Moon's nighttime rays. On days you need to feel more protected, use this special bottle of shampoo.

Laurel Reufner

Notes:

Holiday lore: Much folklore surrounds St. Patrick's Day. Though originally a Catholic holy day, St. Patrick's Day has evolved into more of a secular holiday today. One traditional icon of the day is the shamrock. This stems from an Irish tale that tells how Patrick used the three-leafed shamrock to explain the Trinity of Christian dogma. His followers adopted the custom of wearing a shamrock on his feast day; though why we wear green on this day is less clear. St. Patrick's Day came to America in 1737, the date of the first public celebration of the holiday in Boston.

March 19
Wednesday

2nd ♌
☽ → ♍ 3:25 am

Color of the day: Brown
Incense of the day: Honeysuckle

Festival of Quinquatria

The old Roman festival of Quinquatria honors the goddess Minerva. Minerva is the goddess of wisdom and learning. She is often seen accompanied by an owl. She is also the goddess of arts and crafts, and is especially fond of weaving. Make today a day of weaving in your own festival of Quinquatria. Even if you are not a weaver, you can create some form of weaving: weave your words into small charms of blessings as your greet your friends and co-workers; weave together a few stems of fresh flowers or a few strips of colored paper to create a small item of color and beauty; weave together some strands of dough to create a tasty treat or even some strands of your own hair to give you a touch-able reminder of the wisdom and beauty of Minerva.

Winter Wren

Notes:

March 20
Thursday

Ostara – Spring Equinox –
International Astrology Day

2nd ♍
☉ → ♈ 1:48 am

Color of the day: Turquoise
Incense of the day: Jasmine

Ostara Creation Spell

This joyous holiday honors the spring goddess, Ostara, whose name means "movement toward the rising Sun." Just as Imbolc signals the return of light, Ostara signals the awakening of the Earth. Trees are blooming, bulbs are pushing up out of the ground, birds are nesting, and animals are mating. The creative energy is at its strongest during this season. If you haven't decided what you wish to manifest this year, do so now. To empower your goal, write it on a hard-boiled egg with a wax crayon. The egg is a powerful symbol representing the universe in embryo. Your goal lives within you in the same way that creation lives within its egg, and like the egg, your goal has everything it needs to manifest. Now, draw two interlocking triangles to form a six-pointed star on your egg. This star symbolizes one of the most important keys in magic: as above, so below. What you can create in your imagination, you can manifest

on the physical plane. Dye your egg a deep red to symbolize the goddess and life itself. Using your egg as a focus, work in the days ahead with the interplay of imagination and physical striving to achieve your desire.

Lily Gardner

Notes:

March 21
Friday
Good Friday – Purim

 2nd ♏︎
☽ → ♎︎ 11:45 am
Full Moon 2:40 pm

Color of the day: Pink
Incense of the day: Orchid

Rhythm Web Game

The Rhythm Web Game is about each person's own special voice and how, when we all share our true voices, we can make beautiful things happen. This game allows you and your community to share your heart's voices and feel how you are all connected in a beautiful web of energy. Drums and rattles are ideal for this game but people should be encouraged to clap hands, stomp feet,

sing, make noises, or do whatever is right for them. The leader starts by playing a rhythm he or she wants to play. Then the leader passes the sound randomly to someone else in the circle. That person should then play whatever rhythm comes from the heart and then pass it on randomly to someone else in the circle. Continue to randomly pass on the rhythm, creating a web of connected strands of sound. When the leader feels the time is right, he or she tells everyone to join in and play together. Allow the group enough time to harmonize and feel the joy in the playing.

Kristin Madden

Notes:

 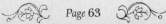

March 22
Saturday

3rd ♎

Color of the day: Gray
Incense of the day: Sage

Workspace Blessing Spell

This is a nice general blessing that can be done on your computer when you clean your office space or get a new piece of hardware/software. All this new technology can be intimidating. Minerva understands, and she will be there to help. Once you have installed something new or cleaned up your space, sit for a moment in front of your computer. Breathe in and ground yourself. Say:

> *Minerva, great goddess,*
> *Let this space be*
> *Productive, constructive,*
> *And trouble free.*
>
> *Let spam be gone,*
> *Let no virus invade,*
>
> *Nor hardware falter*
> *Or problems plague.*
>
> *I ask for your blessing,*
> *Three times three,*
> *Minerva, Minerva,*
> *Please let it be.*

Chant this twice more. It's good for whenever you feel your work space needs a reboot.

— Nancy Bennett

Notes:

Holiday lore: Cybele was the Great Mother of the gods in Ida, and she was taken to Rome from Phrygia in 204 BC. She was also considered the Great Mother of all Asia Minor. Her festivals were known as *ludi*, or "games," and were solemnized with various mysterious rites. Along with Hecate and Demeter of Eleusis, Cybele was one of the leading deities of Rome when mystery cults were at their prime. Hila'aria, or "Hilaria," originally seemed to have been a name given to any day or season of rejoicing that was either private or public. Such days were devoted to general rejoicing and people were not allowed to show signs of grief or sorrow. The Hilaria actually falls on March 25 and is the last day of a festival of Cybele that commences today. However, the Hilaria was not mentioned in the Roman calendar or in Ovid's *Fasti*.

 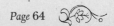

March 23
Sunday
Easter

 3rd ♎
☽ → ♏ 10:06 pm

Color of the day: Amber
Incense of the day: Frankincense

Eostre Invocation

The Christian feast of Easter, which is held in the spring, has retained the name of an Anglo-Saxon goddess who may have been associated with the spring season. This is the goddess Eostre, whose name is connected to the word for "east," and probably also to the concept of dawn. Springtime, dawn, and the New Moon are often associated with growth and new beginnings. Elsewhere in the Germanic world, a goddess known as Erce was invoked for the abundance of the land, and these two goddesses may be connected. Here is part of an ancient magical invocation to the Earth goddess in spring:

> Erce, Erce, Erce,
> Mother of Earth,
> Fields growing and
>   flourishing,
> Bringing forth and
>   strengthening
> Bright fruits and wide
>   barley-crops.

> Hail to you, Earth,
> Mother of human beings.
> May you spring up in the
> Embrace of the Sky God
> And be filled with food
> For the use of mortals.

> Sharynne NicMhacha

Notes:

March 24
Monday

 3rd ♏

Color of the day: Gray
Incense of the day: Narcissus

Moonbeam Illusion Spell

Monday is ruled by the Moon. Lunar energy concerns such things as mystery, illusion, and dreams. Too often, people think of illusion as a bad thing—deceitful, misleading, and false. Yet many of nature's grandest displays are illusions: a rainbow, a ring around the Moon, the bending of light through water. Here is a simple spell to make yourself seem more beautiful through the power of illusion. Fill a white or silver bowl with pure water, and leave it overnight where moonlight can reach it. Wash your hands and face in the water, visualizing yourself gaining the elusive beauty of the Moon. Then dress up as you ordinarily would, wearing lunar colors of white, silver, or pale blue. Moonstone jewelry and perfume from night-blooming flowers like jasmine will enhance the effects. When you go out, the illusion will enhance your natural assets and minimize flaws.

Elizabeth Barrette

Notes:

natural sparkle, gather together glitter, a square of brightly colored cloth, a birthday candle, and a couple of safety pins. Pour a generous amount of glitter on the cloth and then fold it into an envelope and pin it securely. Place it on your altar for a day. Then take the glitter packet in your hands and say, "Off with the old, sparkle like gold" three times. Place the packet close to the birthday candle, light the candle, and let it burn all the way down. The next time you feel a little depressed or down, take out the packet, open it up and throw the glitter all over yourself. Remember it is your time to shine.

Gail Wood

Notes:

March 25
Tuesday

3rd ♏

Color of the day: Red
Incense of the day: Ylang-ylang

Time to Glitter Spell

In the early days of spring, especially if winter's grip is still a tight fist, it's hard to remember that we are beings of shining light. To regain our

March 26
Wednesday

 3rd ♏
☽ → ♐ 10:11 am

Color of the day: Topaz
Incense of the day: Lilac

Seed-Sowing Ritual

March is the traditional month for sowing seeds. Therefore, it is a perfect time to plant the magical seeds of things we would like to see grow in the coming season. Fill a small iron cauldron with soil, and moisten the soil with sacred water. Make three small indentations in the soil. Quiet your mind, and clearly visualize the magical wish you would like to create. Take flower seeds, nuts, beans, or kernels of grain, and breathe your prayers and intentions into them. When you are ready, repeat this traditional spell for consecrating the seed as you plant your wishes:

> I sow these seeds
> In the name of those
> Who give them growth.
> Every seed that lay in sleep
> Will take root
> Deep in the Earth
> As the gods of the elements
>   desire.
>
> The plant will come forth
> With the dew.

> It will inhale life
> From the wind.

Sharynne NicMhacha

Notes:

March 27
Thursday

 3rd ♐

Color of the day: Crimson
Incense of the day: Clove

Bull by the horns Spell

If your shopping habits sometimes get you in trouble, try this binding spell to keep yourself out of trouble. Take the credit cards that you use and abuse the most, a pair of scissors, an envelope, and some twine. Set up a sacred space for yourself where you can sit comfortably. Take a length of twine about as long as your leg, and wrap the credit card in the string while saying,

> I bind myself from
>   overspending,
> And overlook what tempts
>   too much.

*My cash flow sees a happy
    ending,
I learn to look and not to
    touch
As further debt is bound.*

Seal the credit card in the envelope and then put it in your freezer. When your credit card bills come, after you've reviewed them and paid them each month, tuck each statement in the freezer next to your credit cards as a symbolic freeze on your account.

Diana Rajchel

Notes:

March 28
Friday

 3rd ♐
☽ → ♑ 10:43 pm

Color of the day: White
Incense of the day: Vanilla

Invoke Mars Spell

Before Mars was a god of war, he was a god of agriculture and protection. March is his month and an ideal time to call upon his powers of protection. In a small dish combine any three of the following: cinnamon, ginger, allspice, the thorns of a hawthorn, or the root of bloodroot. Concentrate on protection and free will as you blend your spell ingredients. If possible, perform this ritual outdoors, and if it's windy that's even better. In a private place, face south, letting the wind cleanse any negativity you may be feeling. Breathe deeply and begin turning clockwise. As you do so, sprinkle your protection powder. Stop when you return to your south-facing direction. Even if it's cloudy, visualize the Sun burning through. Imagine you're accomplishing all your goals. If it's windy, end this ritual by pretending you can hear the howling of a wolf; wolves are one of Mars' power animals. Walk away feeling empowered. You can reach any goal you aim for.

James Kambos

Notes:

March 29
Saturday

3rd ♑
4th quarter 5:47 pm

Color of the day: Black
Incense of the day: Rue

Spell to Banish Clutter

A waning Moon in early spring—what better time to banish junk? By making the de-cluttering process magical, we have a powerful tool to overcome procrastination and resistance. Do one room or closet at a time. In each, ground and center, smudge with sage, and visualize cleanness and orderliness. Say, "Clutter be gone!" Then get to work. When finished, smudge that spot again, saying, "Clutter is gone and shall not return. So mote it be." You'll be making three piles: "garbage," "donate," and "keep." Things that you're keeping should be put away at once—if they don't have a spot, make one now. Things that you're donating should be handled when the whole house/apartment is done; choose a charity you like, but don't stall over picking one! As for garbage, be firm with yourself—no changing your mind!

Deborah Lipp

Notes:

March 30
Sunday

4th ♑

Color of the day: Orange
Incense of the day: Hyacinth

Charm to Prevent Sickness

The Festival of Hygeia was celebrated on this day in ancient Greece. In Greek mythology, Hygeia was the goddess of health, hygiene, and later the Moon. Her father Asclepius was considered the giver of health while she was more closely associated with the prevention of sickness. The caduceus, our symbol for medicine, resembles the rod of Asclepius entwined by the snake of his daughter Hygeia, who was often depicted wrapped in a huge snake. Her cults flourished in the seventh century BC after the catastrophic plagues of Athens. In her temples, offerings were made by covering her statues with women's hair and clothing. To keep yourself well this spring, take a lock of your hair and wrap it in a silk cord of gold for vitality. Place it outside when the Sun is at its highest. Offer your hair to Hygeia, saying, "Goddess of health and well being, keep me as strong as the Sun!"

Igraine

Notes:

March 31
Monday

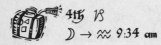 4th ♑
☽ → ≈ 9:34 am

Color of the day: Lavender
Incense of the day: Hyssop

Feast of Luna

The Roman goddess Luna was not just the Moon goddess. She was also the goddess of the charioteers. Today, in honor of Luna, get into your chariot (your car, your bicycle, your horse, your roller skates) and take a day trip. If you're near a harness race track, spend some time watching the horses run. Ask Luna for her blessing. Pour her a libation of milk or wine at your destination. Enjoy yourself! Upon your safe return in the evening, go outside into the moonlight and give thanks. Take a Moon bath, hang up images of the Moon, and wear clothes that make you feel luminous.

Cerridwen Iris Shea

Notes:

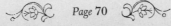

April is the fourth month of the Gregorian calendar and the first month of the astrological calendar. Its astrological sign is Aries, the ram (March 20–April 20), a cardinal fire sign ruled by Mars. The name of the month comes from the Latin *aprilis*, which derives from *aper*, or "boar," as April was thought to be the month of the boar. The sights and scents of April lift our spirits. Lawns are lush again, and tulips of every color dazzle the eye. Pink and white flowering trees burst into bloom, and the air is sweet with the fragrance of crab apple and freshly mown grass. It is easy to understand why colonial Americans referred to April's Full Moon as the Pink Moon. The month begins with April Fools' Day—a day of practical jokes, but also a day to honor the Trickster. Earth Day is observed on April 22 to help make us more aware of our environment and how we can better care for it. In the countryside, farmers return to their fields as plowing begins. At home, gardeners begin to plant early crops such as lettuce, onions, and spinach. During April in ancient Rome, Cybele the great mother goddess was honored in one of the most important celebrations of the Roman calendar. She was regarded as the creator of everything and the ruler of the eternal cycle of life, death, and rebirth. To honor her, bring fragrant cut flowers into your home. They'll cleanse your living space.

April 1
Tuesday
April Fools' Day

 4th ♒
Color of the day: White
Incense of the day: Ginger

Spell for Relationships

Even though today is quite well known as April Fool's Day, in Roman times it was known as Veneralia, the festival of Venus Verticordia, the changer of hearts. On this day, Romans went to the temples of Venus seeking divine aid in their relationships. Prepare your sacred space with flowers in pastel colors and a mirror. Place pink candles in the candleholders and lavender incense in the burner. Light your candles and incense and settle yourself comfortably before the mirror. While looking in the mirror, say:

*May my relationships be
filled with beauty and joy.
May those I love know peace
in their hearts.*

*May my love be healing and
helpful to those I send it to.
Let my love be given freely
with no strings.*

*And let me receive love
graciously in my heart.*

— Winter Wren

April 2
Wednesday

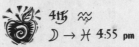 4th ♒
☽ → ♓ 4:55 pm

Color of the day: Brown
Incense of the day: Lavender

Get Over It Spell

Sometimes we just mess up. To stop that inner harangue, go to your sacred space. Play some soothing music and let your body move softly to the music. Burn lemon balm or lavender incense. As you breathe in the harmony of the space, see the mistake as a solid piece of stone. Visualize it resting in your hand and look at it dispassionately. Ask yourself if you have done everything you can to resolve the situation. If the answer is no, ask for the wisdom to solve it. If the answer is yes, see the stone dissolve in your hand, leaving nothing behind except a few drops of water. You awareness tells you that this water is the soothing balm of forgiveness. The water melts into

your palm and you feel that soothing forgiveness spread throughout your body. If there is something you must do to resolve the situation, go and do it, and then repeat the meditation.

Gail Wood

Notes:

and then release them into running water outside or flush them down the drain, letting whatever remains of your problem follow the ashes away from your life.

Laurel Reufner

Notes:

April 3
Thursday

 4ᵗʰ ♓

Color of the day: Green
Incense of the day: Apricot

Money Troubles Banishing

Have a money problem that won't go away? Banish it with this spell. Write out what you need removed from your financial life on a blank piece of paper. If it's an old bill you need to get rid of, use an old copy of that instead. Light a black candle and ignite the paper. Make sure you've a fire/heat proof container on hand in which to let it burn. As the smoke rises, visualize your problems going with it, dissipating in the air. After the paper is done burning, soak the ashes in water,

April 4
Friday

 4ᵗʰ ♓
☽ → ♈ 8:27 pm

Color of the day: Pink
Incense of the day: Mint

Planting Spell for Abundance

There's something very satisfying about planting a seed and watching it grow. In honor of the new spring season, buy a packet of flower seeds and some potting soil. Find a suitable container and plant the seeds according to the package directions. You can just plant a few of them, if you wish. As you plant the seeds, consider the life contained in such a tiny object. Send your nurturing intent to the seed and soil and enjoy the process of watching the seed or seeds germinate and begin to grow. Focus on wherever you need growth and abundance in your life.

> Little plants, thrive and grow
> Reach toward the Sun,
> Bring abundance to my life,
> As I will so it be done.

Ember

Notes:

April 5
Saturday

 4th ♈
New Moon 11:55 pm

Color of the day: Blue
Incense of the day: Ivy

New Moon Closing Charm

New Moons are effective as a way of closing the business of the last month and opening the business of the new month. As a monthly time between times, it's fitting to petition gods that are dark archetypes or between-time gods. Thresholds and windows are of particular importance: sweep them out as a symbol of "sweeping out the old" in your home. One ritual you can perform honors the Roman god of the past and future. The Roman god Janus is portrayed as two faces positioned in opposite directions; he appears on coins and other pieces of iconography. He helps end stagnation and bring vitality. To make sure that old business is out and new business is in, stand in a doorway (make sure the neighbors don't see) with a key in your hand:

> The door shuts behind me.
> The door opens before me.
> Janus, the old chance is done.
> Janus, the new chance comes.

Tap the key twice each on the threshold and the lintel, then go about your day. If endeavors go well, leave a plate of bread out on your stove as an offering, and then bury it outside the next day.

Diana Rajchel

Notes:

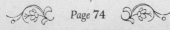

April 6
Sunday

1st ♈

☽ → ♉ 9:19 pm

Color of the day: Yellow
Incense of the day: Almond

Mars Independence Meditation

The first formal declaration of independence took place this day in 1320 in Scotland, as the Sun was traveling through Aries, the sign of independent action. Today both the Sun and the Moon are conjoined in Aries, making it a powerful day for declaring your "I" versus "We." Mars is the ruling planet of Aries. By engaging his fiery energy we will find the power to transmit our call to freedom. He will lead us boldly, blazing new trails of initiative and courage. So I ask you to close your eyes, centering, quieting. Engage Muladhara, the root chakra at the base of the spine. Embrace the radiant red energy of this first chakra. Feel its vibrancy grow within you. When you have vividly connected to the sense of stability and groundedness that Muladhara brings, allow the energy to rise up within you like a shaft of ruby light connecting Earth to the heavens. Radiate outward, reaching for the red planet. Attempt to connect your ray of light to the frequency that Mars is emanating. Earth unites with fire. When you feel the link, be open to the messages that come through as you declare "I am free!

Igraine

Notes:

April 7
Monday

1st ♉

Color of the day: Gray
Incense of the day: Rosemary

Rune Defense Spell

Spring brings tempestuous weather. As the world warms, air and water lash themselves into a frenzy of storms. In some places, this brings nothing worse than thundershowers. In others, tornadoes may result. Mundane precautions against violent weather are necessary, but all aim at surviving it, not at diverting it. Rune magic is more direct. It is one of the oldest and most powerful magical traditions. The rune algiz looks like a crow's foot pointing up. It grants defense, warding off harm. To use algiz as a shield, carve the rune into wood—for instance, the door of a house, or a wooden fencepost—and paint the carved lines red. The rune should face in the direction from which danger threatens—in the case of storms, usually north, northwest, or west.

Elizabeth Barrette

Notes:

April 8
Tuesday

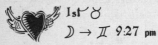 1st ♉
☽ → ♊ 9:27 pm

Color of the day: Black
Incense of the day: Cinnamon

Spell for Loving Kindness

What better way to celebrate the Buddha's birthday then to do a Loving Kindness meditation, also known as Meta meditation. Sit before your altar, take three full

breaths, and center. Say in your mind:

I am protected and safe.
I am free from fear and danger.
I am loved and I am loving.
I am pleased and content.
I am happy in my mind.
I am happy in my body.
*My life unfolds smoothly
   and with ease.*
*I awaken to my
   higher nature.*

Repeat this Meta for your spiritual teacher, each of your parents, your mate, your children, your friends, your enemies, all the people in the world, all the animals in the world. This meditation does wonders for healing bad feelings and gives the meditator a feeling of inner peace.

Lily Gardner

Notes:

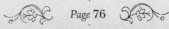

April 9
Wednesday

 1st ♊
Color of the day: Yellow
Incense of the day: Lilac

Mercury Message Spell

Today let's put those spring winds to work along with the help of Mercury the messenger god. Here is a communication spell. Is there someone you are trying to get in touch with, but all your attempts at email and phone calls have failed? Well, try this out. Gather a few flower blossoms or fresh leaves and hold them up to the breeze. As the breeze catches them and they fly away, repeat the following charm.

> I send you a message
> On the four winds
> With the greatest of ease.
>
> You will feel the urge to
> Contact me, as these petals
> Catch the breeze.
>
> For the good of all,
> As it brings no harm,
>
> In Mercury's name
> I do spin this charm.

> Ellen Dugan

Notes:

April 10
Thursday

 1st ♊
☽ → ♋ 10:43 pm

Color of the day: Turquoise
Incense of the day: Balsam

Fairy Cheer Charm

Although folklore often portrays them as tricksters, the fairies are generous to those who befriend them. They are especially fond of things they can't easily make or obtain themselves, such as cream and butter. Rich yellow butter also draws on the power of the Sun. For this spell, you need a small piece of real butter—organic butter, if you can get it. Put the butter on a plate, and set it outside in the morning. (If you don't want to leave good dishware outside, use a leaf as a plate.) Then say:

> Fairy folk, so full of cheer,
> Bring a happy presence here.
>
> Grant to me a sunny fate,
> As the butter on this plate.

The fairies will consume the essence of the butter and grant you a joyful day. In the evening, bring the plate back indoors.

> Elizabeth Barrette

Notes:

April 11
Friday

 1st ♋

Color of the day: White
Incense of the day: Yarrow

Find Your Love Match

Have your altar set up with symbols of the four elements. You'll need a pink candle and an ashtray or fireproof tile. Draw a picture of yourself (or whomever you're doing the spell for) and a picture of your ideal lover (someone you haven't yet met). Cut each picture out in a heart shape. Place the two pictures one on top of the other, facing each other. Roll the two pieces of paper up together, and tie the bundle with pink or red thread or ribbon. Consecrate the bundle by the four elements, sending power into it. Visualize love, attraction, and magnetism. Say, "This love match is soon to be!" while sending more energy into the bundle. Light the pictures on the candle and burn them in the ashtray. See the energy released into the world to do its work. Scatter the ashes outdoors.

Deborah Lipp

Notes:

April 12
Saturday

 1st ♋

2nd quarter 2:32 pm

Color of the day: Indigo
Incense of the day: Sage

A Tree Power Spell

Trees are ancient beings. They are keepers of the life force. They receive nourishment from Mother Earth and Father Sun. To gain power from a tree and to receive the same magical energy which they possess, remove three hairs from your head and tie them together with ordinary garden twine. Go to a wooded area where you won't be disturbed. Walk around until you find a tree you're attracted to. It should represent the powers you're looking for: a pine tree for longevity, or an oak tree for strength, etc. Tie your bundle of hair to a longer piece of twine. Wrap the twine about the tree trunk and tie as you say, "With hair and twine, my strength is yours, and your strength is mine." You and your sacred tree are now bound, from toe to crown.

James Kambos

Notes:

 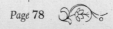

Historical note: On April 12, 1961, Yuri Gagarin piloted the first manned spaceship to leave the pull of our planet's gravity. This achievement is given much less attention than it deserves. Part of that is politics, since Gagarin was a cosmonaut for the Soviet Union. Part of it, too, is time; today, space pilots live and work for months aboard space stations, so a simple space flight seems routine. Still, Yuri Gagarin's 108-minute flight in space represented a triumph of science and engineering, and also broke a psychological barrier. It was literally a flight into the unknown. "Am I happy to be setting off on a cosmic flight?" said Yuri Gagarin in an interview before the launch. "Of course. In all ages and epochs people have experienced the greatest happiness in embarking upon new voyages of discovery . . . I say 'until we meet again' to you, dear friends, as we always say to each other when setting off on a long journey."

April 13
Sunday

2nd ♋

☽ → ♌ 2:29 am

Color of the day: Amber
Incense of the day: Juniper

Festival of Libertas

Libertas began her career as a goddess of freedom and later became the goddess of the Commonwealth of Rome. On this day, to honor Libertas, take a stand to protect your personal freedoms and the freedoms of those around you. Do you see an injustice? Sit down and write a letter to the newspaper, your political representatives, or blog about it. If you're fortunate enough to live in a place of freedom and tolerance, do something to help those who don't. Log on to PEN (www.pen.org) and write a letter in support of an artist whose freedoms are compromised. Honor Libertas with action.

Cerridwen Iris Shea

Notes:

April 14
Monday

2nd ♌

Color of the day: Lavender
Incense of the day: Clary sage

Rama Navami

Today is *Rama Navami*, the Hindu celebration of the god Rama, who embodies cherished characteristics like courage, kindness, sense of justice and duty, patience, and compassion. This is a good day to consider how much you practice what you preach. Across the top of a yellow sheet of paper turned sideways, make a column for each of the top nine personal characteristics you feel are truly important. In each column, note how you embody this characteristic and specific ways that you can better integrate it. Light sandalwood incense, thank the god Rama for setting such a powerful example, and call upon your deities for their blessings. Imagine how you would look and feel if you truly embodied all nine characteristics. Imagine your life as that person and vow to take the steps necessary to create that. Light a candle to yourself. Begin your journey of becoming that very day.

Kristin Madden

Notes:

April 15
Tuesday

2nd ♌
☽ → ♏ 9:06 am

Color of the day: Gray
Incense of the day: Basil

Feline Blessing

For this spell you will need an envelope decorated with Egyptian symbols of good luck and blessing, some clippings of your cat's hair and your own, and a picture of your most beloved feline familiar. Set up this altar in the Sun, near an area where your cat likes to bask. Spread your altar with cat stuff—her favorite toys, catnip, etc. Place the picture and hair in the middle and say:

> Beloved cat, beloved friend,
> May our friendship
> Never end.
> From whiskers' edge
> To tip of tail,
> May Bast protect

Without fail.
Nine times nine
Your life and mine,
In Bast's blessing,
Intertwined.

Seal the envelope with both sets of hair and picture inside. Place it high on your mantle or shelf near the heart of your home (or somewhere special to your cat). Open the catnip, invite your cat up for a cuddle, and have a purrfect ending to this spell.

Nancy Bennett

Notes:

April 16
Wednesday

2nd ♏

Color of the day: White
Incense of the day: Honeysuckle

Journey Prayer to the Gods

As the weather becomes warmer and the world of nature comes to life, we are powerfully drawn to the outside world. Once spring has come, we are able to travel around much more than during the long months of winter. When setting out for a nature walk or a long journey, call upon the old gods with this magical charm and prayer:

> May the gods bless the pathway on which I pass, and the Earth beneath my feet.
>
> Bless the things of my desire every step of the journey on which I go.
>
> May the gods be with me on every mountain and the goddesses in every stream, the spirits be with me in every meadow, on sea and land, on crest and wave.
>
> Be a smooth path before me,
> Be a guiding star above me,
> Be a keen eye behind me,
> Bless my journey
> Each step of the way.

Sharynne NicMhacha

Notes:

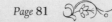

April 17
Thursday

2nd ♏
☽ → ♎ 6:10 pm

Color of the day: Purple
Incense of the day: Carnation

In Celebration of Caffeinia

Ah, the blessed goddess Caffeinia, a grand lady whose blessing is required by many to get through the day. Today, let your morning brew, whether it is coffee or tea, be an act of blessing and thanksgiving. As you fill your pot, take a few moments to meditate over the water. Focus your intentions for the day into the flowing, clear water. Think about what you wish to accomplish, how you wish to feel, how you want the day to flow, how you want to be viewed as you move through your day. Brew your beverage. Take the time to savor your drink, drinking in once more all the intentions you set forth as you prepared the brew. Now go forth and greet your day with your energy focused for the positive accomplishments ahead.

Winter Wren

Notes:

April 18
Friday

2nd ♎

Color of the day: Rose
Incense of the day: Alder

Friday Night Love Spell

The lucent Libra Moon is close to full and Fridays promise romance. Venus is surely in attendance. It is a perfect evening for a little sex magic! In the Tantric tradition of yoga, couples practice postures to encourage a vibrational flow between them. They build a loving bond by engaging routinely in this very simple exchange of energy. To foster love and intimacy in your relationship, light a red candle next to your bed. Mist the sheets with lavender water to create a sense of calm. Lie down together side by side, facing in the same direction. Position your heart chakra next to your partner's. Visualize a ray of green light emanating from this heart center known as Anahata, uniting your bodies as one. As you lie quietly, silently chant:

> Lovers entwine,
> Combine, align,
> Our hearts like a poem pulse
> In rhythm and rhyme.
>
> Weaving our bodies
> Together like vine,

Binding forever
Our love for all time.

Igraine

Notes:

stone, cloud, or body of water calls to you, take the time to pick out a few images from that object and listen to their story. Open your mind and senses to the answers that are laid out before you. All you need to do is read the story.

Kristin Madden

Notes:

April 19
Saturday

 2nd ♎
☉ → ♉ 12:51 pm

Color of the day: Black
Incense of the day: Patchouli

Insight Story

Take a walk today to gain insight into any situation that concerns you. Find a natural place away from distraction where you will feel safe and can walk for at least thirty minutes. Stand with eyes closed for a moment, holding the situation or question in your mind. Then choose a direction, open your eyes, and begin to walk. As you walk, consider the images and symbols you see in the clouds, the trees, the stones, and more. What story do they tell about your question? If one tree,

April 20
Sunday
Passover begins

 2nd ♎
☽ → ♏ 5:00 am
Full Moon 6:25 am

Color of the day: Gold
Incense of the day: Heliotrope

Good Choices Spell

One of the best tricks for being healthy and losing weight involves making good choices about what goes into your mouth. While the occasional bad food choice probably won't kill you, and can certainly help keep you sane, too many bad

foods packs on the pounds and causes other problems. Controlling your portions and making good food choices are the keys to healthy eating. Try this affirmation to remind yourself of good food choices. In the morning, look in your mirror and tell yourself, "Today I will make good, healthy food choices." At the beginning of every meal, repeat the affirmation, reminding yourself that every bite brings you closer to your health goals. And remember, eating well doesn't have to be boring.

Laurel Reufner

Notes:

ebrating liberation, and will pray that all peoples will soon be free. At the same time, people in many parts of the world live in refugee camps. Their freedom to live safely in their homelands has been cut off. Put together a package of needed goods—clothes, medical supplies, bandages, sanitary products—and send it to a reputable charity. (If you're not sure what to send, ask the charity.) Before sending, imbue the package with freedom and safety. Visualizing a good life in a safe home, touch the package with each of the four elements, saying, "By [air, fire, water, earth] I fill this package with safety and freedom." Use markers to draw a happy family in a happy home on a discreet spot on the package.

Deborah Lipp

Notes:

April 21
Monday

 3rd ♏

Color of the day: White

Incense of the day: Lily

Spell for Refugees

Today is the second day of Passover. Jews all over the world will have a Seder, a feast cel-

 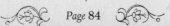

April 22
Tuesday
Earth Day

3rd ♏
☽ → ♐ 5:07 pm

Color of the day: Red
Incense of the day: Geranium

Planting Magic

Today is Earth Day, a day to raise consciousness about humanity's impact on the planet. More specifically, this day addresses how our day-to-day practices affect our long-term changes for survival. The single most appropriate action anyone can do on Earth Day is to plant a tree. Every freshly planted tree helps refresh the oxygen supply in the atmosphere, filters pollution, and undoes a portion of the damage that industrial toxins cause. Since not everyone can plant a tree, particularly those who live in apartments, the next best thing someone can do to honor this day and to honor the magical life is to start a small indoor garden. A small box and a plant light can help grow small herbs such as peppermint that you can use in tea and in regular practice—and the small plants still filter the air within your apartment, making your own space healthier.

Diana Rajchel

Notes:

April 23
Wednesday

3rd ♐

Color of the day: Topaz
Incense of the day: Bay laurel

Invoking Jupiter

According to the ancient Roman calendar, this was the day the previous year's wine production was served. The first wine poured was used to honor Jupiter, the greatest of their gods. Keeping this in mind, today would be a good day to seek Jupiter's aid in achieving your goals. Light a deep blue candle and scent the room with success-attracting herbs associated with Jupiter, such as clove or nutmeg. Write one goal in blue ink on clean white paper, and visualize it coming to fruition. Decorate the corners of the paper with symbols representing Jupiter— usually lightning bolts or eagle feathers. Save the paper and review it later

to see if things have started moving. Watch for any opportunities coming your way that would help you achieve your wish and follow through. When the spell has worked, leave an offering of wine or grape juice by your door.

James Kambos

Notes:

Wash your face with a clean cool cloth soaked in clear fresh water, and chant, "Soothing water wash care away, soothing water bring calm today." Wash your hands with cold water and then rub lavender-scented lotion on your hands and your face. Breathe in the calming, soothing, beautiful scent of lavender.

Gail Wood

Notes:

April 24
Thursday

 3rd ♐

Color of the day: White
Incense of the day: Nutmeg

Getting Over a Bad Day Spell

There are days when things just don't go right and we are feeling distressed and frustrated. To relax and refresh oneself and start over with a better frame of mind, take a few minutes to "get over it." This small ritual can be stripped to the bare bones and you can perform it quietly in the washroom at work or anywhere else. Take three deep breaths and renew your connection with Mother Earth and the universe.

April 25
Friday
Orthodox Good Friday

 3rd ♐
☽ → ♑ 5:47 am

Color of the day: Coral
Incense of the day: Violet

Chant to the Goddess

The world is in bloom, and the energies of the earth goddesses are alive at this very magical time of year. Step into a secluded natural place and breathe seven times into your heart chakra. Open yourself

fully to the beauty and the power of nature in its many guises and manifestations. Speak or sing aloud this invocation of the divine feminine in her magical flowering in spring:

> Flower-garland of the earth
> Flower-garland of the sea
> You are the bounty of the earth
> You are the treasure of the ocean
>
> Flower-garland of the stars
> Flower-garland of the skies
> You are the eye of morning
> You are the Sun of creation
>
> I call to you,
> In your flowering
> Queen-Maiden of compassion
> For you are
> The vessel of fullness
> And you are
> The cup of wisdom.
>
> As I revel in your beauty
> May I drink
> From your cauldron
> For you are the fulfillment
> Of all the world's desire.

Sharynne NicMhacha

Notes:

April 26
Saturday

 3rd ♑

Color of the day: Gray
Incense of the day: Ivy

Infinity Spell

Today is the twenty-sixth of April. Two plus six equals eight, and eight is the number of infinity. Take time today to contemplate infinity. What does the word mean to you? The dictionary defines "infinity" as "endless or unlimited space, time, distance, quantity, etc." What is the legacy you would like to leave to infinity? Are you living that life now? Consider the scope of your life within infinity. Even if you feel you're a tiny blip in the vastness of it all, shouldn't you live your path and leave your blip better than you found it? What changes do you need to make? Meditate on all the possibilities—which are also infinite—and make some positive choices for your life.

Cerridwen Iris Shea

Notes:

April 27
Sunday
Orthodox Easter – Passover ends

 3rd ♑
☽ → ♒ 5:27 pm

Color of the day: Orange
Incense of the day: Eucalyptus

A Fertility Spell

Whether you want to be fertile in body or in another aspect of your life, now is the time to call out and honor Flora and ask her for her blessing. For this spell you will need to purchase a plant that most represents your need. For instance, an orchid according to Chinese tradition is a symbol of many children. Poppy will bring fertility in money matters, while bachelor's buttons will assure you of "alone" time in abundance. Place the plant in an eastern window and say:

> New beginnings in the east,
> Bring fertile beginnings
> To my quest.
> Flora, please make
> My desires complete,
> Let them grow as I bequest.
> Here is my wish for fertility,
> Three times spoke,
> So mote it be!

Whisper to the plant your wish three times, and water it. Lovingly do this every time you tend it. As it grows, so will your wish be sown.

Nancy Bennett

Notes:

April 28
Monday

 3rd ♒
4th quarter 10:12 am

Color of the day: Silver
Incense of the day: Neroli

Charm for Beauty

Today's waning Moon in Aquarius is a perfect day for this beauty spell. The waning Moon, visible in the early hours of the morning, will help you let go of negative attitudes you have about your appearance. Choose a safe place outdoors where you can perform this spell. Prepare a vial of three drops of ylang-ylang mixed with almond or vegetable oil. In the pre-dawn hours, go to your safe place and invoke the goddess Flora. Ask her for the blessings of beauty and pleasure. Dip your fingertip in the vial and trace a flower on your forehead. Say: "The earth awakens to a new day, so my body." Repeat this, drawing an oil-soaked

finger on every part of your body that you formerly felt badly about. Pour the remaining oil onto the ground, visualizing your old feelings about yourself sinking into the earth.

Lily Gardner

Notes:

Consuming fire take away,
Obstacles that block my way;
Cleanse me with
The purest light,
Renew me,
Make my spirit bright.

Ember

Notes:

April 29
Tuesday

 4th ≈
Color of the day: Scarlet
Incense of the day: Cedar

Fresh Start Spell

Use this spell to create a fresh start whenever you feel the need. Light two candles, one red and one white, and keep them in a place where you can watch them burn. Visualize anything in your life that you want to change or be cleansed of—such as bad memories or a bad habit. Imagine the red candle consuming and the white re-energizing you with pure, white light.

April 30
Wednesday

4th ≈
☽ → ♓ 2:11 am

Color of the day: Brown
Incense of the day: Marjoram

Beltane Eve Fairy Spell

Tis the eve of Beltane and the fairies are out in force. Here is a fairy spell to work in your own garden or backyard. Gather together violets, St. John's wort, and clover. The violets are a fairy favorite. The St. John's wort will protect you from becoming fairy-led or tricked, and the clover is for prosperity and good luck. Gather these plants together, forming a little posy, and then tie it up with green ribbons. Blow the fairies a kiss and leave the posy as a gift. Now go and sit in the garden and try to meditate or to communicate with the fairies.

> *Fairies from far and wide,*
> *I offer you a gift,*
> *Tied up in green for luck,*
> *And sealed with a kiss.*
>
> *I can sense you*
> *If I'm pure of heart,*
> *Bless me with good luck*
> *To boost my Witch's art.*

Ellen Dugan

Notes:

 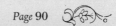

May is the fifth month of the year. Its astrological sign is Taurus, the bull (April 20–May 21), a fixed earth sign ruled by Venus. The month is named for Maia, a Roman goddess and mother of the god Hermes. May is a month of fertility and abundance. This theme is celebrated on May 1, which is Beltane or May Day. On Beltane the union of the Goddess and God is celebrated. Customs for this day include placing flowers outside your front door and erecting a maypole. Traditionally, a maypole was the trunk of a fir tree with the side branches removed—a symbol of fertility and the God aspect. The Earth that supports the maypole represents the Goddess. The beauty of May is like a spring tonic. We are surrounded by color and fragrance. Dogwood trees bloom, pansies add a cheery touch to flower beds, and wild blue violets carpet dooryards. In some regions black locust trees bloom with honey-scented clusters of white flowers. Early settlers honored the floral display of May by calling this Full Moon the Flower Moon. May is also a month to remember the ancient fertility symbol of the Green Man. He brings abundance back to nature after winter's rest. Fashion a small doll from twigs or grass, and release the figure into a body of water. By doing so you're giving thanks for the bounty Mother Earth returns to us.

May 1
Thursday

May Day – Beltane

 4℞ ♓

Color of the day: Purple
Incense of the day: Mulberry

Spiral into the Ecstatic

The Pagan holiday of Beltane celebrates the vibrant attraction and union of the Goddess with the God. This meditation can be done quietly or can be part of a large exuberant ritual of dancing and song. Take a deep breath and close your eyes. Take three more deep, cleansing breaths. As you breathe deeply, find yourself outdoors in a beautiful, wild place. As you stand there, you feel the heartbeat of the Earth. It sounds like a drumbeat, and your blood throbs in harmony. Before you stands the May Maiden and the Young God. Each takes one of your hands and leads you in a dance. You dance in a circle and then inward in a spiral. Inward you dance, as the heartbeat drums a rhythm. As you move into the drumbeat and feel the joyous laughter of the Maiden and the God, you let go of all inhibitions that hold you back from understanding a full connection to the ecstatic, loving universe. Time stops as you dance and spiral inward into the eternal. Your heart and blood beat in unison

with the dance as you move onward, inward, and fully into yourself and all-that-is. When it is time, come back fully to your time and place. Thank the Maiden and the Young God for the dance of heart and soul.

Gail Wood

Notes:

May 2
Friday

 4℞ ♓
☽ → ♈ 6:51 am

Color of the day: White
Incense of the day: Cypress

Aftermath Spell

After seasonal revelry, you may wake up one morning with that headache you can only get from too much of a really good party. While prevention is the best cure (drink lots of water), sometimes you forget that ounce of caution. Because of that, I present you with the purification-by-water cure. After stepping into the shower and breathing in the steam for about half an hour, stop for a moment and pay attention to

 Page 92

where the pain is located in your body. Does your head hurt? Is it your muscles? Do your joints ache? Focus on the pain and embody it, perhaps as black oil. Allow the water to wash over your body, particularly the affected area. See the water sweeping the pain off your body and swirling it down the drain. Inhale more of the steam, feeling the purifying water flow in through your pores.

Diana Rajchel

Notes:

distilled water in a dark glass bottle with spray top. Invert the bottle three times to mix the ingredients. Hold the bottle while the rest of the family stands around you, everyone touching a hand or shoulder so that you are all connected. Remind them of the feelings of love, comfort, and laughter that you have shared. Have everyone imagine your family bonds as strong and joyful. Then send that energy into the bottle. Whenever you feel the need to clear the air, spray this around and loving energy will fill your home.

Kristin Madden

Notes:

May 3
Saturday

 4th ♈

Color of the day: Black
Incense of the day: Sandalwood

Clearing the Air Charm

Sometimes family members just need to clear the air so we can move on and create healthier, happier relationships. To clear the energy in your home today, clear the air—literally. To make a cleansing spray you can use for several months, add eight to ten drops of the essential oil of orange or lemon to half a cup of

May 4
Sunday

 4th ♈
☽ → ♉ 7:58 am

Color of the day: Yellow
Incense of the day: Frankincense

Banishing Roadblocks

Sunday is the day of the week to promote wealth, fame, and success. Since we are in the darkest phase of the Moon, let's banish any

roadblocks that may be hampering your achievements. Burn a gold candle to promote prosperity and success. Burn a black candle to remove any blockage or troubles while on your journey. Light the candles and then repeat the spell verse.

> It is true that Sunday brings
> Success, wealth, and fame.
>
> A dark Moon removes
> Any blocks you'd care to name.
>
> Bring me change and joy to
> All facets of my life,
>
> As the candles burn away,
> On this darkest night.

Ellen Dugan

Notes:

May 5
Monday
Cinco de Mayo

 4th ♉
New Moon 8:18 am

Color of the day: Ivory
Incense of the day: Hyssop

Kitchen Spell

For this kitchen spell to promote harmony in the home, consider preparing a Mexican meal to honor Cinco de Mayo. Visualize harmony in the home as you cook, add ingredients, stir, bake, or even use the microwave. Imagine the food being infused with your intent; the feelings of peace and harmony will be passed along to those who consume the meal. Use this chant as you cook:

> Herbs and spices,
> Fruit of vines,
> Veggies, meat, water, wine,
> Sugar and bread,
> Salt and flour,
> Bring harmony to
> Every hour.
> Peace and love
> To fill our home,
> With each meal
> Let it be known.

Ember

Notes:

Holiday lore: Don't confuse Cinco de Mayo with Mexican Independence Day on September 16. Cinco de Mayo marks the victory of the brave Mexican army over the French at the Battle of Puebla. Although the Mexican army was eventually defeated, the *Batalla de Puebla* became a symbol of Mexican unity and patriotism. With this victory, Mexico demonstrated to the world that Mexico and all of Latin America were willing to defend themselves against any foreign or imperialist intervention.

May 6
Tuesday

 1st ♉

☽ → ♊ 7:17 am

Color of the day: Scarlet
Incense of the day: Bayberry

Divination Charm

In Celtic tradition, the seasons associated with Beltane (May) and Samhain (November) were considered the most powerful times to perform divination. While certain divinatory rites were performed directly on the quarter days, other auspicious days associated with the lunar cycle were also utilized in the quest to gain sacred wisdom. Seers often petitioned the divine powers to help them deepen and develop these abilities. Here is a traditional charm used to obtain the power to drink from the vessel of truth:

> The gods above me,
> The gods below me,
> The gods before me,
> The gods behind me.
>
> See that I am on your path
> And know that you
> Are in my footsteps.
>
> Give me eyes to see my quest
> With a power that will
> Never fail or dim.
>
> Knowledge of truth, not
> Knowledge of falsehood,
>
> That I may truly see
> All in my path.

Sharynne NicMhacha

Notes:

 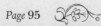

May 7
Wednesday

 1st ♊

Color of the day: Brown
Incense of the day: Lilac

Odin's Quickness Spell

Wednesday belongs to the god Odin, and is ruled by the planet Mercury. It concerns such matters as transformation, contradiction, cleverness, and creativity. To gain quickness of mind and tongue, you may call upon Odin. For this spell, you need a medallion with a symbol of Odin on it—such as a valknott, Odin's Horn, othala rune, or raven. Capture the energy of the day by reciting this charm over the medallion—once at dawn, once at noon, and once at dusk:

> Grey-bearded god
> Of Wednesday's wit,
> Lend me, when
> I have need of it,
>
> Raven's wondrously
> Clever tongue
> Of which the skalds
> Of old have sung.

Wear the medallion next to your skin when you need extra cleverness.

Elizabeth Barrette

Notes:

May 8
Thursday

 1st ♊

☽ → ♋ 7:02 am

Color of the day: Turquoise
Incense of the day: Myrrh

Salute to Taurus

The Sun is in Taurus now, and it's a good time to salute this aspect of sturdiness and steadfastness. Is there something in your life that needs stabilization? This is the time to work on it—especially since today is Thursday, a day of increase and prosperity. Check your astrological chart. Do any aspects fall in Taurus? Celebrate those parts of your personality. Wear solid colors. Eat substantial food. Drink a deep, red wine. Celebrate long-standing friendships (send a card, shoot off an email, make a phone call). Make long-term plans for your future. Celebrate stability! Celebrate Taurus!

Cerridwen Iris Shea

Notes:

 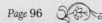

May 9
Friday

 1st ♋

      Color of the day: Rose
Incense of the day: Vanilla

Sweetening Spell

Sweeten up your love life with the following: Dress your altar with a white or silver candle for feminine energies and a yellow or gold candle for masculine energies. Place a red candle between the two, symbolizing their union. Light the candles and place a small canister before you. Fill it about halfway with sugar, and add a vanilla bean. Finish filling the canister. You should be able to notice the scent of vanilla in the sugar in about a week. Use this sugar when making sweets for your sweet or in any recipe calling for sugar. You could also try this with a good substitute sweetener, such as stevia.

                     Laurel Reufner

Notes:

May 10
Saturday

 1st ♋
      ☽ → ♌ 9:10 am

Color of the day: Blue
Incense of the day: Pine

Bird Divination

May 10 begins Bird Week in Japan. Many people bird-watch and build new habitats for birds, while others practice a system of divination using the sighting of birds or bird-calls. One way to perform this divination is to cast your magical circle outdoors. If you sight birds in the east, the matter concerns knowledge, new ventures, or communication. If you sight birds in the south, the matter concerns change, passion, or inspiration. In the west, the portent has to do with relationships or your emotions regarding an issue. Birds sighted in the north pertain to health, money matters, or property. As to the bird sighted, the following is a brief summary of what a bird symbolizes: a rooster means good fortune; wrens symbolize happiness; crows can mean change; doves portend love and peace; ducks represent union and beauty; eagles and hawks symbolize authority; geese symbolize inspiration or love; hummingbirds represent joy; jays represent trickster energies; owls

symbolize wisdom or death; robins represent resurrection.

Lily Gardner

Notes:

May 11
Sunday
Mother's Day

 1st ♍ ♌
2nd quarter 11:47 pm

Color of the day: Orange
Incense of the day: Marigold

Mother Goddess Invocation

Today is Mother's Day. Originally created as a holiday for promoting peace and tolerance over war and conflict, it later became a time to honor the state of motherhood and for people to show reverence for their own mothers. On this day, Pagans often revere the Mother Goddess in any or all of her many guises. A Mother's Day prayer or ritual might include words such as these:

> Tiamat, deep-sea womb of all
>   that lives,
> Inanna, queen of the first
>   city, Uruk,
> Danu, spirit of the
>   emerald isle,
> Isis, bright-winged Witch
>   of the river Nile,
> Sophia, fount of heavenly
>   wisdom,
> Freya, bearer of Brisingamen,
> Shakti, power of love
>   and creation,
> Gaia, broad belly of the
>   fertile Earth,
> Great Mother, we hail you by
>   all your names!

You may adorn your altar with flowers, fruit, candy, jewelry, or other delights such as might be presented to human mothers.

Elizabeth Barrette

Notes:

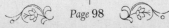

May 12
Monday

2nd ♌
☽ → ♏ 2:48 pm

Color of the day: Silver
Incense of the day: Narcissus

New Mom's Spell

Know a new or soon-to-be mom? Buy a mirror for her room or hallway and make or buy a baby blanket for her and her new child. Think of all the good wishes you want to bestow upon them both while purchasing or making it. When done, take the mirror, look into it, and say:

> In love, your reflection will
> echo back between the years,
> 'tween mother and a child.
> May precious memories,
> through this mirror, reflect
> all the blessings I have for
> you. Love, long life, and joys
> to discover: protect this bond
> between child and mother.

Wrap the mirror in the blanket and then present them both as gifts. Instruct her to hang it somewhere where she and her child will pass often.

Nancy Bennett

Notes:

May 13
Tuesday

2nd ♏

Color of the day: Gray
Incense of the day: Ginger

Exorcising Lemures

In ancient Rome, the feast of the Lemures was celebrated on this day, when rites were performed to exorcise the lingering, restless spirits of the dead. Romans offered beans and salt cakes to banish these malevolent ghosts known as the Lemures (or larvae) from their homes. To dispel negative energy that may be lingering in your home, begin by cleaning and clearing away all unnecessary clutter. Starting at the highest point and northern corner, sprinkle salt around the perimeter of every room, moving counterclockwise and downward. Say a prayer to your chosen gods and goddesses to eliminate any unwanted energy. Ending at your entranceway, draw a banishing pentagram on your front door to seal the magic.

Igraine

Notes:

May 14
Wednesday

 2nd ♏
☽ → ♎ 11:46 pm

Color of the day: Topaz
Incense of the day: Honeysuckle

Rosemary Rituals

Today is a good day to plant rosemary. Rosemary is a magical plant with a wide variety of uses. The perfect place for rosemary is near your front door, where it can bless your comings and goings. Pick a leaf to chew on your way out; rosemary awakens the senses, stimulates memory, and brings energy and a sense of well-being. It is said to fight illness and to bring love. Rosemary is considered a universal substitute; use it in any incense recipe where you're missing an ingredient. It benefits all magical and healing work. Carry a fresh rosemary leaf with you for good health. Rosemary is an evergreen that can be harvested year round. It cannot abide temperatures much below forty degrees and should be mulched over in a cold winter. It can be grown indoors in a sunny window. The plant should have good drainage and be watered frequently.

Deborah Lipp

Notes:

May 15
Thursday

 2nd ♎

Color of the day: White
Incense of the day: Clove

Embracing the Weird

All too often, we dismiss things that are harmless but different as "weird." Yet weird ideas, and harmless weird people, are intrinsic to the progress of our lives, and nowhere-near-the-box thinking is the only way some of the serious issues we face will be resolved. Use this spell to teach yourself to appreciate the creativity of others. Take a paper grocery bag and cut out the wide sides. Cut eyeholes in each sheet of paper, and take a pen or markers and create a mask. Make each mask resemble the person or type of person you want to understand better. When you have some time alone, look through the mask, imagining the world from that person's perspective, from behind that person's eyes. Imagine you are that person, and explore that. How do you feel? What has changed? Look at yourself in a mirror through the mask—how do you look to yourself?

Diana Rajchel

Notes:

 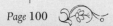

May 16
Friday

 2nd ♎

Color of the day: Coral
Incense of the day: Orchid

New Project Blessing

Whether they are the simple chores that keep the house functional, the crowning research of our educational path, the next expression of our creative selves, or the new major crisis the boss places on our desks at work, our lives are filled with projects. This is a little blessing for the start of a new project to get it off on the right foot.

> Maiden Goddess, spirit bright, who blossoms forth in spring, please share the emerging energy of the Earth.
>
> Mother Goddess, warming flame, who shines throughout the summer, please share the fertility of your fires.
>
> Ancient Goddess, vessel of wisdom, who holds us close in the season of slumber, please share the knowledge of the ages.
>
> Goddess, in all your forms, lend your guidance and support to this undertaking. Let it be my best work and the best expression of the gifts I possess.
>
> So mote it be.

Winter Wren

Notes:

May 17
Saturday

 2nd ♎
☽ → ♏ 10:59 am

Color of the day: Indigo
Incense of the day: Rue

Scrying by Water Spell

The old-timers of Appalachia believed May was the most potent time to scry with water to see future events. Seekers would scry into wells, ponds, or glasses of water to find the answers to their questions. To do this, sit or stand comfortably before your choice of water. Imagine being surrounded by a protective circle of white light. Focus on your question and gaze at the water. Soon the water will mist over and seem to swirl. As the mist clears, the vision will come. Symbols, animal shapes, numbers, or complete scenes will

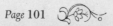

appear. Keep your gazing sessions short. To enhance your experience, you may place a silver coin in the water to serve as a focal point. When done, release your circle of protective light and thank the divine power.

James Kambos

Notes:

May 18
Sunday

 2nd ♏

Color of the day: Amber
Incense of the day: Hyacinth

Fairy Protection Spell

The month of May is tradition-ally associated with the fairies, and interactions between this world and the fairy realm are common at this time of year. In Celtic folklore, human beings venture forth to meet with both mortal and fairy lovers. If you desire this type of relationship, carry talismans of protection that will allow you to return to this world. These Scottish lyrics tell of a union with a fairy lover—use them if you dare!

Bannocks and cream
I'll give to thee,

Wine of the wort
I'll give to thee,
Well I'll love thee,
Under the plaid,
If you come home with me
To the fairy knoll.

I was last night
In the meadow,
Drinking ale with the
Beguiling one.
I left my love in the doorway
Of the fairy bower
With eyes like a star
And a voice like a
Stringed instrument.

My green-clad love
Of the mist.

Sharynne NicMhacha

Notes:

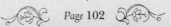

May 19
Monday

 2nd ♏
Full Moon 10:11 pm
☽ → ♐ 11:18 pm

Color of the day: Lavender
Incense of the day: Clary sage

Seeding Spell

May is a month of fertility, creativity, and productivity. The garden is abundant with new life. Flower bulbs force through the fecund earth, opening their petals to the Sun. Birds are nesting, animals are birthing, bees are beginning their buzz. The night's embrace feels cool and seductive, luring us outside to wonder at the beauty of the evening. Look up at the Moon, for she is full tonight and she will reveal the ripening fruit on the vine and grant us hidden desires. Stand skyclad (if that feels right) under the Full Moon. Reach your arms upward and recite:

Swollen belly beaming down,
Surround me
With your mantle.
Drape me in
A gossamer gown
And crown of golden apples.

That I may charm
The gods of seeds,
Enchant them
With my flower,

To grant me
My desire and need,
Impregnate me with power.

Ask for what you desire.

Notes:

Igraine

May 20
Tuesday

 3rd ♐
☉ → ♊ 12:01 pm

Color of the day: Red
Incense of the day: Ylang-Ylang

Ancestor Altar

Our ancestors are the root of who we are. One very special way to remember them and honor them is to create an ancestor altar. The ancestor altar can be a part of your personal altar or a separate one dedicated only to the ancestors. Gather pictures of the ancestors you wish to honor, as well as any little mementos of your loved ones you wish to add for an even deeper connection. Consider adding a doily crocheted by a loved grandmother for an altar cloth, a vase from an aunt's

dining room to hold flowers, or use a saucer from a cherished set of china for holding water. Assemble the altar with reverence and love, recalling fond memories of each of the ancestors you honor in this space. Continue to honor them with gifts of fresh flowers, incense, and candles, and thank them for the joy they brought to your life.

Winter Wren

Notes:

it's decaf or not. The important thing is the chicory. As you drink your coffee, imagine yourself on a relaxing vacation. Scatter the coffee grounds outside.

Laurel Reufner

Notes:

May 22
Thursday

 3rd ♐

☽ → ♑ 11:55 am

Color of the day: Green
Incense of the day: Jasmine

Cloud Gazing Inspiration

Have you ever picked out images from clouds? Cloud gazing can be great fun, but have you ever used it for divination? Like water and fire, clouds can be a wonderful canvas for the manifestation of divine inspiration. Close your eyes and take a deep breath. Form a clear question and hold that until you feel it fill your being, then blow the question out into the universe with your breath. Open your eyes and pick out three to five images from the clouds above. If you can hold the intent longer without your mind wandering, feel free to

May 21
Wednesday

3rd ♐

Color of the day: White
Incense of the day: Lavender

Take Me Away Ritual

Need to get away for a vacation, but obstacles keep jumping in your way? Try this simple ritual for the next seven days and see if your travel luck improves. Simply brew yourself a cup of coffee containing roasted chicory. It doesn't matter if the coffee is instant, ground, or whole bean, although whole bean that you grind yourself would pack more oomph. It also doesn't matter if

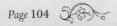

pick out more images. When you are done cloud gazing, put all the images together to find the pattern they share. What story do they tell you about your question?

Kristin Madden

Notes:

serve as your grounding stone. Use it to create a calm feeling whenever you feel anxious.

Ember

Notes:

May 23
Friday

 3rd ♑

Color of the day: Pink
Incense of the day: Thyme

Grounding Ritual

Developing a good grounding technique is essential in magical practice—and in everyday life it can help reduce stress and anxiety. Select a stone that you like and sit with it on the ground beneath a tree. If you don't have the chance to get outside, visualize the tree. Face north and close your eyes. Breathe deeply, and in your mind see all the green beauty around you—a thick forest embracing you. Hold the stone in your hands. Feel the weight of it anchoring you to the Earth. When you feel well-grounded, open your eyes. The stone can continue to

May 24
Saturday

 3rd ♑
☽ → ♒ 11:51 pm

Color of the day: Gray
Incense of the day: Magnolia

Breaking the Code Spell

The first Morse code message was sent on this day in 1884, going from Washington, D.C., to Baltimore, MD. There are times when we can't seem to fit in and we really want to find the knack or code for being part of a group. Find an old unused key and perform this small ritual as you get ready to join a gathering. Smudge yourself with sage. Holding the key in both hands, take a deep breath and connect to Mother Earth. Hold the key to your solar plexus, and as you breathe deeply say, "Key my power and energy to the vitality of the Sun." Hold the key to your heart and say, "Key my understanding to the wisdom of the heart," and hold the key to your throat and say, "Key my voice to speaking well." Hold the key to your third eye between your eyebrows and say, "Key my intuition to understanding rightly." Then breathe all this wisdom into the key. Keep the key in your pocket or around your person, and touch it if you need reminding of your own power to get what you need.

Gail Wood

Notes:

sies say that one way to make your wishes come true is to walk through a forest with the intention of finding a lucky talisman. When an object catches your eye, whether it is a twig, a stone, or a flower, hold it in your left hand. If it feels like your power object, put it in your putsi and carry it on your person until your wish comes true. When your wish comes true, bury your power object in the forest while saying a prayer of gratitude to St. Sara.

Lily Gardner

Notes:

May 25
Sunday

3rd ≈

Color of the day: Gold
Incense of the day: Almond

Gypsy Protection Amulet

The patron of the gypsies, St. Sara, is honored today. To make a gypsy amulet for good luck and protection, fill a black pouch, called a putsi, with a holed stone, a seashell, and a piece of fine paper on which you've drawn a spiral. Wear this putsi around your neck. The gyp-

May 26
Monday

Memorial Day (observed)

3rd ≈

Color of the day: White
Incense of the day: Lily

Remembering Our Ancestors

Fix an altar with pictures of your most beloved friends and family who have passed away. Light three white candles (one for past, one for present, one for future). Place them in front of the pictures. Study the flames and remember all the love you felt from those who came before you. Say:

> My family and my friends
> who have guided me, I bring
> you blessings and thanks on
> this day. Know that in my
> heart you will never be for-
> gotten. In everyday moments,
> I feel you close to me, and I
> am blessed for having had
> you touch my life.

Now study the pictures one by one, giving each a special thanks. You can at this point place favorite items of your ancestors on the table, such as food or flowers. Blow out the can-dles, but let the pictures remain for twenty-four hours. Smile each time you pass it.

Nancy Bennett

Notes:

May 27
Tuesday

3rd ≈≈
☽ → ♓ 9:38 am
4th quarter 10:56 pm

Color of the day: Black
Incense of the day: Cinnamon

Bury the hatchet Spell
Choose today to bury the hatchet with someone from your past. It's best if you can get a real hatchet for this, but one carved from balsa wood or made of paper will work too. Take as much time as you need to sit with this hatchet. Fill it with all the memories, judgments, and feelings that you associate with this person. Write all that on the hatchet, along with both your names. If you feel this person took power from you, then imagine yourself taking that back. Feel the power filling you. Use the hatchet to cut away any remaining cords that tie you to this person. Then take it outside and bury it. Place some sagebrush, pine, or cedar in the hole for additional purification. Ask the Earth to ground out these feelings and transform the energies.

Kristin Madden

Notes:

May 28
Wednesday

 4th ♓

Color of the day: Yellow
Incense of the day: Bay laurel

Shoo Fly Spell

Being hounded by junk mail, wrong numbers, and phone solicitors? Try this Mercury-themed night spell to make them leave you alone. This is a waning Moon phase, so it's a perfect time to banish and to make troublesome situations decrease. For this candle charm, burn an orange candle for Mercury and a black candle to remove bad vibes that have built up over the situation. Repeat the charm three times.

> By the winged feet
> Of Mercury,
> You shall bother me
> No more.
>
> All annoyance calls
> And junk mail
> Will be banished
> From our door.
>
> For the good of all
> With harm to none.
> Speak the spell and it is done.

Ellen Dugan

Notes:

Holiday lore: Opinions are divided concerning the origins of the holiday of Memorial Day in the United States. This is a day set aside for honoring the graves of American war dead. While most historians credit the origins of the custom to Southern women, there is also a rumor, historically speaking, of an anonymous German who fought in the American Civil War (no one is sure on which side). At the end of the war, this soldier was allegedly overheard commenting that in the Old World people scattered flowers on the graves of dead soldiers. In May of 1868, a Union army general suggested to Commander John A. Logan that a day be set aside each year to decorate Union graves. Logan agreed, and he set aside May 30 for this ritual. His proclamation acknowledged those "who died in defense of their country" and "whose bodies now lie in almost every city, village, or hamlet churchyard in the land." This patriotic holiday was later amended to include all the dead from all the wars, and its date was shifted to a convenient Monday late in May.

May 29
Thursday

 4th ♓
☽ → ♈ 3:52 pm

Color of the day: Crimson
Incense of the day: Carnation

An Oak Tree Spell

Ever since King Charles II of England hid in an oak tree to protect himself from political enemies during the 1600s, this day has been known as Oak Apple Day. Images of oak trees, acorns, oak leaves, and branches are displayed everywhere. The oak tree has had a long association with magic since the days of early Britain. Any part of an oak tree can be used in fertility, health, protection, or good luck spells. Here are two such spells. For good fortune, bind together two oak branches with red ribbon to form a cross and hang them outside your home. To bring a wish into your life, take three branches each of oak, hawthorn, and ash. Tie them together with raffia or twine. Think of your wish and cast them upon a fire to release the spell. Or keep your bundle of wood and burn it in a ritual fire at Litha, the Summer Solstice.

James Kambos

Notes:

May 30
Friday

 4th ♈

Color of the day: Purple
Incense of the day: Yarrow

Banish harm from the Garden

Where I live, late May is planting season, but in a waning Moon planting is not ideal. Instead, use this spell to drive away harmful plants, insects, and fungi from your garden. (Of course, you'll still have to weed and water and so on.) You'll need five cloves of garlic, peeled. Visualize the strong protective power of garlic. See it glowing with a bright energy that drives away all harm. With your athame, wand, or hand, send this power into the garlic, saying, "Harm be gone, harm be gone, harm be gone!" Place the garlic into the soil around your garden so that the five cloves form the points of a pentagram (a protective symbol). Say, "Harm be gone! So mote it be!" as you place each clove. Immediately water or pull a weed or otherwise tend the garden to seal the spell.

Deborah Lipp

Notes:

May 31
Saturday

 4th ♈
♌ → ♉ 6:18 pm

Color of the day: Indigo
Incense of the day: Patchouli

Feast of the Triple Goddess

According to a calendar of traditions marked only as "old European," today is the feast of the Triple Goddess. Specifically, it's a day to acknowledge and celebrate the turning wheel when Virgin becomes Mother. Celebrate the aspects of the goddess today, Maiden, Mother, and Crone, in everyone you meet. Smile. Radiate love and joy. See beyond clothing, religious representation, skin color, and surface accoutrements into the souls of those around you. Expect to experience the Goddess in everyone you meet, and you'll be pleasantly surprised.

Cerridwen Iris Shea

Notes:

June is the sixth month of the year. Its astrological sign is Gemini, the twins (May 21–June 21), a mutable air sign ruled by Mercury. It is named for Juno, the principal goddess of the Roman pantheon and wife of Jupiter. She is the patroness of marriage and the well-being of women. There is a sense of serenity as spring turns to summer and June settles softly over the countryside. Roses bloom heavily on garden fences; sweet clover sends out a heavenly fragrance. Dawn greets us with bird song and the sweet scent of honeysuckle. In rural areas, the afternoon is perfumed with one of the most ancient scents in the world—hay curing beneath the Sun. Country meadows are frosted with the white blooms of ox-eye daisies, and the orange flowers of wild daylilies star the roadsides. As nature reaches for maturity, the Sun ascends to its zenith, which brings us to the major holiday of the month, the Summer Solstice. The ancients lit bonfires for purification and to encourage the power of the life-giving Sun. Old-timers called June's Full Moon the Strong Sun Moon. And beneath the June Sun strawberries ripen, corn stretches for the sky, and bumblebees drift in the flower beds. Magical activities for the month may include charming away evil by hanging a sprig of valerian beneath a window or using some lemon balm in a love spell.

June 1
Sunday

4th ♉

Color of the day: Yellow
Incense of the day: Heliotrope

Make Your Own Sunshine Spell

We all need a little sunshine in our lives, and that joy can be found in surprisingly simple places, if we only remember to look. Try a few of these ideas this week and see how it affects your experience of life. You might be surprised to see how much happiness you can find by just spending two minutes, twice each day, on one of these suggestions. Take a deep breath, and be thankful that you are able to breathe. Thank the air, the trees, and the plants for breathing with you. Walk around your home and feel grateful that you have a place to live. Look at a weed, tree, bird, or cloud. Feel your connection to this natural object and give thanks that it is here for you now. Thank your friends and pets for sharing your life. Celebrate today, "just because."

Kristin Madden

Notes:

June 2
Monday

4th ♉
☽ → ♊ 6:06 pm

Color of the day: Gray
Incense of the day: Rosemary

Ritual Cleansing Bath

A good ritual bath can be an excellent lead-in to ritual or meditation. It is a good way to start getting yourself mentally, physically, and emotionally prepared to enter your sacred space and undertake the work at hand. This particular bath salt recipe is for cleansing and clearing. You will need a decent-sized ceramic or stone mortar and pestle to prepare this recipe. Combine 3 parts Epsom salts with 2 parts baking soda and 1 part sea salt. Grind these thoroughly in the mortar. When they are ground to a coarse powder, add one teaspoon sage essential oil and one teaspoon lavender essential oil. Mix thoroughly. Store in a tightly sealed jar until needed. Use these salts for a ritual bath prior to a public or private ritual to clear away any negative energies and tune in your mind and body to the work ahead.

Winter Wren

Notes:

June 3
Tuesday

 4th ♊
New Moon 3:22 pm

Color of the day: Red
Incense of the day: Cedar

Balancing Act

Sometimes it's difficult to find the balance between our inner and outer selves. While there are no quick fixes for feeling imbalanced, this little spell should help. You will need a piece of obsidian and blue, black, and white candles (or gold and silver). Find a quiet time when you can sit and concentrate. Light the candles, with the blue one in the middle representing the balance between light and dark, inner and outer. Sit quietly for a moment, watching the candle flame and allowing yourself to grow quiet. Picture the balance that is your existence. When you feel ready, pour that image and your current stillness into the obsidian. Extinguish the candles and carry the obsidian with you for times of need.

Laurel Reufner

Notes:

June 4
Wednesday

 1st ♊
☽ → ♋ 5:16 pm

Color of the day: Yellow
Incense of the day: Honeysuckle

To Release Worry

We each have stresses and worries we deal with each day. To release them and feel carefree, collect the following items: a fan (or you can do this outside on a windy day), a tray or cookie sheet, and enough sand to fill the tray. With your finger or a stick, write your worries in the sand. You can write a sentence or just a single word. Then, allow the wind to blow them away, or use a fan. Repeat as desired, with the following words:

> Element of air,
> Take away my cares,
> Blow them far away.
> Help me not worry
> About the little things
> Each day.
> Free my mind from stress,
> Set me free.
> As I will, so mote it be.

Ember

Notes:

June 5
Thursday

 1st ♋

Color of the day: Green
Incense of the day: Myrrh

Spell for a Late Bus

There's a simple spell you can do if you rely on public transportation. Carry paper and pencil with you. If the bus or train is late (or if you're running late, and it absolutely must come as soon as possible), take out your paper and pencil and draw the bus (or train) arriving. Get as detailed as possible. You can do a series of sketches, like cartoons; first the bus driving up, then stopping, then yourself getting on. Pour your concentration fully into your drawing. As you release energy into the drawing, you create a magical signal pulling the bus to you. Is this just a placebo effect? Did the bus come exactly when it would have anyway? No. Not only did your energy have an effect, but you also distracted yourself away from worried, unpleasant energy that might have been clogging things up.

Deborah Lipp

Notes:

June 6
Friday

1st ♋
☽ → ♌ 6:00 pm

Color of the day: White
Incense of the day: Alder

Ups and Downs Spell

The first roller coaster opened on this day in 1884 on Coney Island, New York. There are times when our lives seem like a roller coaster; it all makes a confusing mess. A little candle magic can help sort things out. Make a list of the things that are creating chaos in your life: a column of good things and a column of bad. Bring candles in an assortment of colors to your sacred space. Begin by centering and grounding. Start lighting candles, matching colors to issues, saying a wish as you light it. Reframe the bad things in your life as wishes. For example, light a red one and say "This is for the love and passion in my life; long may it continue." Another example is to light a blue candle and say, "This is for the broken water heater, may it be repaired." When you are done, admire the lighted candles. Then chant "All my wishes will come true" several times. Raise the energy by repeating the word "true" until the energy is sent into the universe. Thank the spirits for their blessings and extinguish all the candles with "blessed be."

Gail Wood

Notes:

best planning, take a ballpoint pen and draw the symbol of Mercury on your shoes. Mercury is the planet of travelers and of swift action. Picture the symbol infusing you with a silver glow, and send out this prayer to the god associated with travelers:

> From here to there,
> From A to B,
> Get me there,
> To see what I can see.

Diana Rajchel

Notes:

June 7
Saturday

 1st ♌

Color of the day: Brown
Incense of the day: Ivy

Smooth Summer Vacation Spell

We all look forward to that vacation day when we can relax, let go of it all, and have nothing to worry us for a short time. However, sometimes the foul-up fairy takes the trip with us, and missed flights and mixed-up reservations ruin the relaxation we're trying to achieve. Rather than melting down when travel plans go wrong, open yourself up to serendipity to make the trip an adventure. You'll lose stress while finding a way to more fun. When your plans are altered despite your

June 8
Sunday

 1st ♌
☽ → ♍ 10:01 pm

Color of the day: Orange
Incense of the day: Juniper

A Rain Spell

St. Medard's feast day is celebrated today. It was said that the saint could walk though the heaviest rainstorm without getting wet. June 8

is traditionally a weather marker for most of western Europe:

> If on the eighth of June it
>   rain,
> That foretells a wet harvest,
>   men sayen.

To cast a spell using the energies of rain, write your desire on a piece of rice paper. The next rainy day, hold the paper in your left hand. Visualize what your life will feel like once your desire is realized. "Feel" is the operative word; the more you can feel how your life will change, the better this spell will work. Take your paper out into the rain. Experience the rain as the blessings of the element of water. Hold the paper in your outstretched hand and watch the rain consume your wish. Leave the spell paper in a place where the rain can dissolve it into the earth. Your wish will come true.

Lily Gardner

Notes:

June 9
Monday

Shavuot

 1st ♍

Color of the day: Lavender
Incense of the day: Hyssop

Honoring Vesta

Today is the third day of Vestalia, a Roman festival devoted to Vesta, the virgin goddess of hearth and home. During this week-long period of festivities the women made sacrificial offerings at her altars throughout the city. The Virgo Moon invites us to enter the temple of Vesta today. We come before this goddess who embodies purity, duty, and order. Here we can learn the principles of health, self discipline, and the practical application of skills. We can honor these gifts by pledging to keep the hearth fire burning in our own holy dwelling, our physical bodies. She reminds us that compassion toward oneself fosters creativity. So adorn yourself with the veil of Vesta and acknowledge her with a personal sacrifice. Step forward and receive her blessing and surrender your offering into the sacred flame.

Igraine

Notes:

June 10
Tuesday

1st ♍
2nd quarter 11:03 am

Color of the day: White
Incense of the day: Basil

Sunwise Gathering Charm

Many magical practitioners are familiar with the concept of working in a sunwise direction. The term used to describe this motion is deosil, which comes from the Scottish Gaelic word *deisil* (or Irish *deiseal*), meaning "Sun-wise" or "toward the south." Widdershins, the opposite type of motion, was known as *tuaitheal*, "left-hand wise," or "northward." Right-hand movement was lucky or auspicious and left-hand motion unlucky (or associated with waning energies). For this reason, magical herbs were sometimes gathered with the right hand, as in this folk charm for gathering St. John's wort:

> St. John's wort,
> St. John's wort,
> My envy whoever has thee.
> I will pluck thee
> With my right hand
> And preserve thee
> With my left.
> I will gather my little plant
> So that mine may be
> Its power over all I see.

Sharynne NicMhacha

Notes:

June 11
Wednesday

2nd ♍
☽ → ♎ 5:55 am

Color of the day: Brown
Incense of the day: Marjoram

Children Blessing

The Matralia is the festival of the Italian goddess of the dawn, Mater Matuta. This day was for the safe birth and happiness of all children. Women traveled to the temple with their sister's children and prayed for their welfare. This would be a perfect day to work a charm for the happiness and health of the children of your friends and relatives who bless your life. List the names of these beloved children on a piece of paper. Then set a white candle in a holder on top of the paper. Light the candle and focus on the children. See them happy, healthy and strong. When you are ready, read the charm.

Mater Matuta,
Watch over these little ones
I pray.

Make them grow both strong
And true, gaining wisdom
Every day.

Ellen Dugan

Notes:

June 12
Thursday

2nd ♎

Color of the day: Turquoise
Incense of the day: Balsam

New home Blessing

When you move into a new home, it is a good time to welcome Hestia to your hearth. This spell is best done when your home is empty, but even if you moved in a while ago, this simple ritual will ignite her presence. In the "heart" of your home, take a broom and start to sweep, moving in a clockwise direction. Sweep around the area three times, chanting:

Hestia of the
Hearth and home,

Bless this space
I call my own.

Make my household
Trouble free,

Dearest Hestia,
Make it be.

Now brush the dust outside and bring in a table or chair to use as an altar. Place fresh flowers and baked goods on your altar. Sprinkle salt in each corner of the room in a clockwise direction (this keeps the negative spirits away). Open the windows and let the sunshine in.

Nancy Bennett

Notes:

 Page 118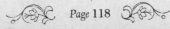

June 13
Friday

 2nd ♎︎

☽ → ♏︎ 4:53 pm

Color of the day: Pink
Incense of the day: Mint

Festival of Epona

Honored in the Celtic lands long before the coming of the Romans, Epona is known as the Celtic goddess of horses and the protector of all animals. With that in mind, this is an excellent day to honor our animal companions and friends. Spend extra time with your animal companions. They need quality attention and play time just as much as human friends. Invoke the blessing and guardianship of Epona upon them as they journey with you through life. For those who love animals and at this point in their life cannot have an animal friend of their own, consider this as an opportunity to spend time with animals who do not have human companions of their own. Consider spending volunteer time working with animals at the local animal shelter or doing fundraising in support of no-kill shelters to help animals find their home in this world. Epona will smile upon you.

Winter Wren

Notes:

June 14
Saturday
Flag Day

 2nd ♏︎

Color of the day: Gray
Incense of the day: Sage

A Wedding Spell

Use the wild grasses growing now to create this wedding spell. The couple who are going to be wed should perform this spell alone. The bride and groom should go into a field and each cut a small bouquet of grasses, clover, daisies, or whatever else is in season. Next, shape the bouquet of grasses into the form of a human figure—the bride shaping a woman; the groom a man. Using more grass, tie the figures together and say: "Hand to hand, heart to heart. Never shall we part." To complete the spell, dig a round hole amid the growing grass and place the figures in the soil. As you cover the figures with soil, in unison say: "Our love has no beginning, our love has no end. And, like the Earth is round, the Sun is round, the Moon is round, together forever we are bound."

James Kambos

Notes:

June 15
Sunday

Father's Day

 2nd ♏

Color of the day: Gold
Incense of the day: Almond

Celebrating Fathers

Let's hear it for Dads everywhere! Today, let's celebrate our men and all their wonderful compassionate qualities with a Pagan blessing for the fathers in your life, or to celebrate your own fatherhood. Keep up the good work, for you hold the future in your strong and caring arms.

> Fatherhood is a sacred
> And joyous path,
> My child/ren and I will enjoy
> A bond that lasts.
>
> May the gods grant me
> Wisdom, strength,
> Humor, and love.
>
> Illuminate my family's days
> Like the Sun up above.

Ellen Dugan

Notes:

June 16
Monday

 2nd ♏
☽ → ♐ 5:19 am

Color of the day: White
Incense of the day: Neroli

Negativity Shield

People don't like to have negative energy nibbling at them. Plants don't like to be nibbled by herbivores, either. They have devised many defensive strategies to protect themselves, including bristly leaves, bitter taste, and thorns. Two plants with excellent protective qualities are thistle and hollyhock, both readily available during the summer. To make a protective charm, find a small metal box. Carefully gather a small piece of thorny thistle leaf and bristly hollyhock leaf. Press and dry them. Place the dried leaves in the box and seal it. Chant three times:

> Thistle and hollyhock,
> All harmful magic block.

Store the box in a safe place, and never open it. This will help against negative energy, psychic attacks, and other such unpleasantness.

Elizabeth Barrette

Notes:

June 17
Tuesday

2nd ♐

Color of the day: Black
Incense of the day: Geranium

happy Vacation Meditation

Disneyland opened in California on this day in 1955. Wear vacation clothes as you go into your sacred space. Begin by singing fun camp songs or travel songs to remind you of the fun you've had on vacation. Light myrrh-scented incense and light a candle in your favorite color. Breathe in the delightful, invigorating smell of the space and close your eyes. Find yourself in your vacation spot in the most perfect weather. See yourself in the center of all the action. Envision the delights of your vacation in happy detail. See your companions laughing, talking, praising you, and hugging you. Feel the perfect weather, and hear all the sights and sounds you anticipate. Notice the feelings that this anticipation awakens in you. Envision those feelings as a ball of wonderful light in your hands. Then take that ball of light and move it into your heart. Breathe in those feelings and let it infuse your whole being. When you are done, return to your sacred space. Let go of the expectations of your vacation and hold on to the feelings of pleasure.

Gail Wood

June 18
Wednesday

2nd ♐
Full Moon 1:30 pm
☽ → ♑ 5:51 pm

Color of the day: White
Incense of the day: Lavender

Prayer to the Moon

For those who live close to nature, the phases of the Moon are an invaluable guide for mundane and magical activities. Plants are not gathered during the waning Moon, for it is believed that their sap or essence moves into the root, making them dry or brittle. Therefore, plants were commonly gathered during the waxing Moon or at the Full Moon, when their power was at its highest. Here is a prayer to the bright face of the Moon:

> *Glory to you forever,*
> *Bright Moon, on this night.*
> *You are ever the glorious*
> *Lamp of the poor.*

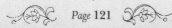

*May your luster be full to
every person in need, and
may mine be a good intent
toward all who look upon
her.*

Sharynne NicMhacha

Notes:

very real. Then blow the wish out
into the dandelion fuzz and watch as
it is carried off into the air.

Kristin Madden

Notes:

June 19
Thursday

 3rd ♑

Color of the day: Purple
Incense of the day: Mulberry

Dandelion Wishing

Summer is the time for those
happy little dandelions and
the wishes they bring to those that
believe. Take a walk and appreciate
all the dandelions you see. Allow
their brightness to fill you with joy
and ask what would make you really
happy. If you could have one wish,
what would it be? Decide on your
wish and find a dandelion in fuzz.
Ask permission, then pick it with a
prayer of thanks. Hold the dandelion
gently and state your wish out loud.
Use all your senses to make the wish

June 20
Friday
Summer Solstice ~ Litha

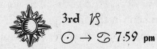 **3rd** ♑
☉ → ♋ 7:59 pm

Color of the day: Rose
Incense of the day: Frankincense

Solstice Celebration

Summer Solstice is the longest
day and the shortest night of
the year. Beginning tomorrow, the
turn of the wheel already decreases
daylight. This year, it falls on Friday,
the day of Venus. Take the day off.
Spend it with your loved ones. Enjoy
your extended family and friends. Tell
the people important to you that you
love them. It's a good day for a family
reunion. It's a good day to start planning a family reunion for next year—
on the Summer Solstice. Invite your
extended family to join you today in a

 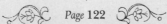

potluck. Reach beyond your extended family to those who may not have any family nearby. Include as many people as possible. Create an environment where everyone shares not only food but a bit of themselves.

Cerridwen Iris Shea

Notes:

earth] this mirror banishes negative images." Hold the mirror and the god/dess so that you see the deity's reflection. Say, "Lady/Lord, let your image banish negative images. Let me see the positive reflected." Look at yourself in the mirror, saying: "I banish the negative and see the positive. I see the Lady (or Lord)." Repeat "I see the Lady/Lord" over and over while sending power into the mirror. Say, "So mote it be." Look in the mirror every day for a month and say, "I see the Lady/Lord."

Deborah Lipp

Notes:

June 21
Saturday

 3rd ♑
☽ → ♒ 5:33 am

Color of the day: Blue
Incense of the day: Pine

Drive Away Self-Consciousness

When summer begins, we sometimes feel embarrassed about our appearance. This waning Moon spell banishes self-consciousness. On your altar, have a mirror, a representation of each element, and an image of a goddess or god. Ground and center. Pick up the mirror and say, "This reflects the positive and banishes the negative." Consecrate the mirror with the elements, saying, "By [air, fire, water,

June 22
Sunday

 3rd ♒

Color of the day: Amber
Incense of the day: Eucalyptus

Sun Stone Spell

This spell is to charge a stone with sunlight and whatever particular energy you desire. This is a good time to infuse a stone with energy for health and vitality or to lift your spirits and bring good cheer. First, select a stone that is associated with the Sun. This can be a metallic stone such as pyrite, or a piece of citrine, amber, or just clear quartz. In general, a clear or orange/yellow/gold stone will be the best choice. Place the stone in sunlight, either outside or in a sunny window. Visualize the sunlight infusing the stone with positive energy. To add your own personal touch, hold the stone in your palm and imagine the specific qualities you desire being absorbed by the stone through the Sun's rays. Allow the stone to sit in sunlight all day, then carry it with you or give it to someone who needs sunshine in her life.

Ember

Notes:

June 23
Monday

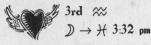

3rd ≈

☽ → ♓ 3:32 pm

Color of the day: Silver
Incense of the day: Narcissus

Love and Prosperity

This is the eve of St. John's Day, the Voodoo Midsummer celebration, and a day to perform spells for love, abundance, and protection. An old spell the British cast on this day is to walk around a church, clockwise, seven times at midnight. Sowing hemp seed as you walk, say:

> Hempseed I sow,
> Hempseed I sow,
> Let him that is my true love,
> Come after me and mow.

Look over your left shoulder and you should see an image of your lover. (Best to be mindful of the law if you try this old spell.) A voodoo charm for love and abundance is to make a string of pearls and little bells, visualizing a life rich with abundance and love. Now, make an offering of honey to Erzulie, goddess of love and abundance. Into the honey, put five cinnamon sticks, five cloves, and five pumpkin seeds. Light a vanilla candle and ask Erzulie for her blessing. Wear the string of pearls and bells as a talisman.

Lily Gardner

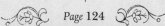

Notes:

Change things for the better,
Allow me to control.
My destiny, my destiny,
My destiny,
Three times spoke,
So mote it be.

Gather the items in the cloth, tie it, and keep it close for the next few days. Now, go out and seek your new fortune!

Nancy Bennett

Notes:

June 24
Tuesday

 3rd ♓

Color of the day: Gray
Incense of the day: Bayberry

Fortuna Luck Spell

Fortuna, goddess of fate and change, was honored today, and so if you are looking for a bit of luck or a change in your life, now is the time to take a chance with "she who brings." Gather together the following lucky items: a shamrock (or shamrock pin), a horseshoe (you can make one out of cardboard and tinfoil), and three coins. Place them on a green cloth. Imagine what you wish for: more money, a new job, etc. See yourself happy in that setting, smiling and enjoying the change. Then place your hand over the items and say:

Blessed Fortuna,
Smile upon me,
Guide me to my goals.

June 25
Wednesday

3rd ♓
☽ → ♈ 10:49 pm

Color of the day: Topaz
Incense of the day: Bay laurel

A Dreamer of Dreams

For today, become a dreamer about the life you could have, doing what you enjoy doing, and make plans to explore some aspect of the career path you wish to take. Look into taking a necessary class. Spend time exploring a business that does what you want to be doing. Even spending time at the library exploring books from different non-fiction sections might spark your passion to find out more. Use your favorite divination technique to question if this path might really be the one for you.

Laurel Reufner

Notes:

---

ship. Think about jealous fights, and how you'd prefer not to have them. In a circle, consecrate and name the finished doll: "You are jealousy, the green-eyed monster. You are my/our feelings of jealousy and pain." Greet the doll. Talk to it. Tell it about jealousy. Pour your deepest feelings of jealousy into the doll. Say: "I/we banish you. Leave here and return no more!" Throw the doll out of the circle. Close the circle. Take the doll to a dumpster or landfill. Repeat: "Leave and return no more!"

Deborah Lipp

Notes:

June 26
Thursday

 3rd ♈
4th quarter 8:10 am

Color of the day: White
Incense of the day: Nutmeg

Spell to Banish Jealousy

Jealousy plagues relationships. Working with your partner or by yourself, you'll create that green-eyed monster and then banish it. The energy you put into making a doll is part of your magic. You'll make a monster; however you imagine that. Just make sure it has green eyes! While making the doll, think about jealousy. Think how unpleasant it feels, and how it harms your relation-

---

June 27
Friday

 4th ♈

Color of the day: Purple
Incense of the day: Cypress

A Cleansing Rain Spell

Let the summer rain help you remove negativity from your life. When rain is forecast, gather these items you'll need for this spell: an earthenware dish or a terra cotta flowerpot saucer, and some soil. As the rain approaches, fill the saucer with soil and pack it firmly. While thinking of your problem write a word or two describing it in the soil using your finger. Or using a stick draw a simple outline in the soil depicting your issue. When the rain begins to fall, place the dish of soil outdoors. After the rain stops, the image you drew in the soil should be faded. Sprinkle the soil upon the ground as a sign of thanks and let Mother Earth aid you in solving your problem.

James Kambos

Notes:

deserve to be acknowledged in a sacred way. Why not create a butterfly garden to honor a significant event? The butterfly is a magical totem for inspiration in times of transformation. Their beautiful rainbow colors and lofty dance reflect our ability to transcend and fly free. Pick an open, sunny area and begin by planting a buddleia (a butterfly bush) at the back border of your garden plot. Trail a fragrant honeysuckle vine along the fence or a trellis. For an instant garden buy two-gallon perennials such as bee balm, lobelia, black-eyed Susans, and purple cone flower. Bright annuals like zinnias and cosmos will delight butterflies, and anything bright red will also attract hummingbirds, who are harbingers of joy.

Igraine

Notes:

June 28
Saturday

 4th ♈
☽ → ♉ 2:50 am

Color of the day: Indigo
Incense of the day: Magnolia

Butterfly Magic

A birth, a death, a parting of ways or a coming together—these are milestones in our lives that

June 29
Sunday

 4th ♉
Color of the day: Yellow
Incense of the day: Marigold

Pagan Grace

Many Pagans grew up "saying grace" over meals in a mainstream religion, and later abandoned the habit. Yet the idea of giving thanks for blessings received is profoundly Pagan, for we honor the spirits in all things, including plants and animals. Hunters in traditional Pagan cultures would say a prayer for the animals they killed; gatherers and farmers would address the plants they harvested. It is appropriate to practice thanksgiving in contemporary times as well, for all the bounty of our lives. So here is a Pagan prayer suitable for saying grace:

> Earth and sky
> And rain and sun,
>
> We give thanks
> For all you've done.
>
> Garden, pasture,
> Seed, and brood,
>
> Bless us with
> This gift of food.

Elizabeth Barrette

Notes:

June 30
Monday

 4th ♉
☽ → ♊ 4:03 am

Color of the day: Ivory
Incense of the day: Clary sage

Forgiveness Spell

Forgiving someone who has hurt you is not something you do for the person who did you wrong. Forgiveness is something you do for yourself, and for yourself alone. This is why forgiving someone who wronged you is so difficult. A spell that will help this process is to take a daisy on a windy day, and to pluck each petal while saying:

> While what you've done
> Is not forgot,
> I've let you go, I hate you not.
> Should your shadow
> Cross my door,
> Your presence won't
> Touch me anymore.
> I am free from all my anger,
> And I treat you as a stranger.
> In this time and in this hour,
> I forgive you, and now
> You have no power.

Watch the petals float away, taking your pain along with them.

Diana Rajchel

Notes:

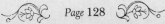

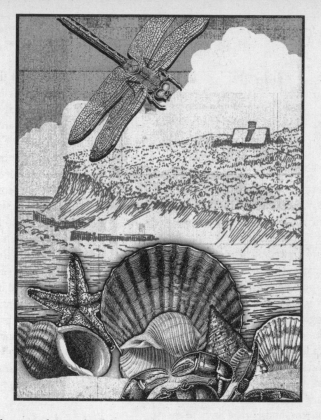

July is the seventh month of the year. Its astrological sign is Cancer, the crab (June 21–July 22), a cardinal water sign ruled by the Moon. An awesome majesty comes over the land now; tomatoes fatten, corn tassles out, and shaggy heads of monarda brighten the herb border. July is the high noon of summer, even though the Summer Solstice has passed. The Goddess is watching over the ripening fields and orchards. July's Full Moon was known as the Blessing Moon, and our forebears, who were close to nature, realized the importance of this time of year. They knew that if the crops were healthy in July, there was a good chance that they'd be blessed with a bountiful harvest. Independence Day on July 4 is the main holiday of the month. It's a time to be grateful for our personal freedom, and a time to count our blessings. Since July's astrological sign is associated with water, any magical activity using the element of water is very effective. Sea shells, sand, and seaweed can add power to spells this month. If you can take a trip to the shore this month, look for a seashell that attracts you. Bless it and keep it as a power object. By the end of July, apples begin to blush with color and Queen Anne's lace begins to appear along the roadsides. Dusk comes earlier now. Pause, and enjoy the glory of July.

July 1
Tuesday

 4th ♊

Color of the day: Scarlet
Incense of the day: Ginger

Thunderstorm Courage

The power of a July thunderstorm is one of the great spectacles of nature. A thunderstorm can be used to charge our strength and courage, and it's a wonderful time to work a spell for courage. In a small bowl, or with a mortar and pestle, crush together these courage-attracting herbs: one teaspoon each of dry black tea leaves, golden yarrow, and dried borage leaves. As you pulverize them, visualize yourself crushing your fears and obstacles, and say: "Tea, yarrow, and borage draw to me strength and courage." When it's safe to go outdoors, take your herb mixture. Facing south, say: "Let the thunder roll, let the lightning strike, let the sky turn black as night. Let all my fears take flight." After speaking this charm, hold the dry herbs in your hand and blow them toward the south. See your fears vanishing; you can do anything now.

James Kambos

Notes:

Holiday lore: Today is the first day of the season for climbing Mt. Fuji in Yamabiraki, Japan. Mt. Fuji is the highest peak in Japan and is revered in Japanese culture. Considered the foremother or grandmother of Japan, Fuji is an ancient fire goddess of the indigenous Ainu people. In modern times, the Ainu mostly resided on the northern island of Hokkaido. The name *Fuji* was derived from an Ainu word that means "fire" or "deity of fire." Each year since the Meiji era, a summer festival has been held to proclaim the beginning of the climbing season and to pray for the safety of local inhabitants and visitors or pilgrims to the sacred mountain. The two-month climbing season begins today, and ends on August 30.

July 2
Wednesday

 4th ♊
)) → ♋ 3:53 am
New Moon 10:18 pm

Color of the day: Yellow
Incense of the day: Lilac

Fresh Start Spell

Today is the New Moon, a time for beginnings and fresh starts. Now that summer is here, use this opportunity to boost your energy and passion, and to move forward in your life. For this spell you can burn a white candle for the New Moon and a green candle to represent all the boundless and growing energy of the summertime. Light the candles and repeat the charm.

> On this magic night of the
> July New Moon,
> Success in my new projects
> Will begin soon.
> A white candle for the Moon,
> And starts that are fresh,
> Green for luck and energy,
> May my spell be blessed.
> Now spin the magic around,
> Flow out and about,
> Prosperity in and
> Negativity out.

Ellen Dugan

Notes:

July 3
Thursday

 1st ♋

Color of the day: Turquoise
Incense of the day: Carnation

Festival of Cerridwen

Today is dedicated to Cerridwen, a Celtic goddess of fertility, magic, and shapeshifting. Her name means "White Sow," and that animal is her special symbol. Cerridwen also keeps the cauldron of rebirth, in which souls are rejuvenated before moving on to a new life. Honor Cerridwen with a feast involving her symbols. Serve a rich pork roast or barbecued ribs, along with foods that pigs adore, such as corn, nuts, and truffles. Decorate the table or altar with images of white pigs. Include a cast-iron cauldron if you have one. Invoke Cerridwen with words such as these:

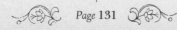

Cerridwen,
Crafty one,
Come and see
What we've done.

Cerridwen,
Great White Sow,
We call you—
Be here now!

Elizabeth Barrette

Notes:

July 4
Friday

Independence Day

 1st ♋

☽ → ♌ 4:15 am

Color of the day: Coral
Incense of the day: Violet

Spell for Freedom from Fear

Every Fourth of July there's lots of noise: explosions, firecrackers. This can be frightening. I often wonder how many people sit home, cringing, as the world outside explodes. This spell uses numerol-

ogy, aromatherapy, and affirmation to conquer fear. Begin your morning by grounding yourself in front of the mirror and saying, "I am safe. I am free." Modify the affirmation to your needs, but keep it positive—talk about courage rather than fear. Add numerology to your spell by using three sets of four (twelve) repetitions. In this way, your affirmation is both solid (four) and dynamic (three). Keep some tea (or a teabag) with you, and whenever you feel afraid, inhale the scent of the tea while repeating your affirmation. Courage herbs include black cohosh, tea, borage, thyme, and yarrow. To ease anxiety and bring peace, use lavender or vervain instead.

Deborah Lipp

Notes:

 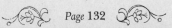

Holiday notes: On July 4, 1776, the Second Continental Congress adopted the Declaration of Independence. Philadelphians were first to mark the anniversary of American independence with a celebration, but Independence Day became commonplace only after the War of 1812. By the 1870s, the Fourth of July was the most important secular holiday in the country, celebrated even in far-flung communities on the western frontier of the country.

objects were often held in the possession of certain families, who kept them safe over many centuries. When someone needed the use of the stone, it was dipped into a silver vessel of sacred water, which the person was then given to drink. One of the last known instances of this type of charm was in the early 1800s, when a clan chief dipped the stone in a bowl of water gathered from a fairy spring. Here is a crystal spell for healing:

> Crystal gathered from
> Deep in the Earth,
> Bring me wellness,
> Luck and health.
>
> May your brilliant light
> Infuse my soul,
> Transform this water and
> Make me whole.

Sharynne NicMhacha

Notes:

July 5
Saturday

 1st ♌

Color of the day: Blue
Incense of the day: Rue

Crystal healing Spell

Quartz crystal has long been used in many cultures for healing a variety of illnesses, as well as for protection. In Scotland, round or oval-shaped amulets of rock crystal were used as protective charms and as healing agents. These rock-crystal

July 6
Sunday

 1st ♌
)) → ♍ 7:04 am

Color of the day: Orange
Incense of the day: Heliotrope

Pillow Charm

Get a good night's sleep with this simple dream pillow enspelled with the Earth's energy. In a small bowl, place one teaspoon each of vervain, lavender, and patchouli, and one quarter-cup of buckwheat. As you add each ingredient, pause a moment to imagine yourself waking up well-rested and eager to greet the day, then add the herb and mix it with the rest in the bowl. Hold a small piece of smooth obsidian in your hands for a moment, charging it to bring you pleasant dreams. Add the stone to the bowl of herbs for a moment, then stuff a small, tightly closing draw-string bag with the mixture. Tuck in a safe spot under your pillow.

Laurel Reufner

Notes:

July 7
Monday

 1st ♍

Color of the day: Gray
Incense of the day: Narcissus

A Merry Unbirthday

We've all had that one monumental bad day that we look back on with a feeling of hurt, frustration, or sorrow. Sometimes it's getting fired on your birthday, or your anniversary being forgotten. Sometimes it's tragedies coinciding with a major event. In life, there is no turning back time or re-doing. However, we can give ourselves special days that are special only because we declare them so. In Alice in Wonderland, Alice came upon an "unbirthday" party where it was not anyone's birthday at all, yet the day merited tea, cakes, and celebration. Take today, or a day when you have time to yourself, and declare it an "unbirthday." Dress nicely, and take yourself to dinner, a movie, a museum, or to some other place that interests you. Take someone with you, or not. Make it a point to try something new that you've been curious about for ages. Enjoy your day.

Diana Rajchel

Notes:

July 8
Tuesday

 1st ♏

☽ → ♎ 1:31 pm

Color of the day: White
Incense of the day: Ylang-ylang

Cutting Away the Fearsome Foe

In Tibet on this day, the monks performed an ancient ritual to eliminate negative forces and hindrances. Dressed in yellow robes, they used vocal and instrumental sounds to invoke creative awareness. Begin this ritual by allowing yourself to vocalize freely whatever sounds come forth, melodious or dissonant. Play music that inspires you to dance as you cast a circle, sprinkling flower petals or potpourri thrice around. Scent a basin of warm water with sandalwood oil and wash your feet. Dry them off well and rub them with a little olive oil. Using a henna paste, paint them artfully with spirals, circles, and other symbols. When you are ready, begin your ritual dance, improvising movement that you feel expresses the release of dark energy as you move counter-clockwise within your sacred circle. Then change direction and dance sunwise, pulling in toward your solar plexus feelings of joy and positivity as you chant a mantra of purification, "Om mani padme hum," and cut away the fearsome foe!

Igraine

Notes:

July 9
Wednesday

1st ♎

Color of the day: Brown
Incense of the day: Bay laurel

Day of Personal Mysteries

Wednesday is a day for psychic work and meditation. Nine is the number of mystery, power, and the nine muses. Explore your own personal mysteries. What inspires you? What desires, hopes, and dreams have you pushed away? What have you outgrown and can now release? What aspects of your personality do you wish to improve? Set up a small mirror. Light a candle and set it in front of the mirror. Write a loving letter to yourself about the issues you may ignore in your day-to-day life. As you write, glance up into the mirror once in a while. Catch your reflection and a glimpse of something beyond. This letter is for your eyes only—your communication with your deeper self. Feel free to hide it or even burn it when you're done. Today is a day to celebrate and explore your own personal mysteries.

                    Cerridwen Iris Shea

Notes:

achieve. Don't restrict yourself by any time limits. Then remove the Chariot card from your tarot deck. Study the card: see how determined and steady he appears. Visualize yourself being just as determined attaining your goals. Save your lists and study them from time to time.

                    James Kambos

Notes:

July 10
Thursday

 1st ♎
2nd quarter 12:35 am
☽ → ♏ 11:35 pm

Color of the day: Green
Incense of the day: Clove

Count Your Blessings Spell

Although we're past the Summer Solstice, July is a month of plenty as nature begins to mature. July is the seventh month; seven is the number of completion, so this would be a proper time to count your blessings. Write down seven things in your life for which you're grateful. Think about how you brought these things into your life and how you intend to keep them. Next, write a list of seven goals you still wish to

July 11
Friday

 2nd ♏
Color of the day: Pink
Incense of the day: Yarrow

Prosperity Charm

Select a coin or dollar bill and place it in a glass or clay bowl or jar. Cover it with earth and place a piece of aventurine or clear quartz on top. As you assemble the spell, imagine you are building a foundation for financial success. The fertile earth will increase your prosperity and the stone will further magnify it. Set the

 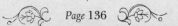

bowl in a northern corner of your home and repeat the following:

My prosperity will
Grow and flower,
Increasing my
Financial power.

Bills are paid
With funds to spare,
Money both
To save and share.

Keep the bowl or jar in place as long as you feel it is necessary.

Ember

Notes:

rant of your altar, make an offering to Yama of a dish of cooked rice and a pot of rainwater. Sit before the altar and think about those who have gone before you. Remember that your thoughts send vibrations throughout our interconnected universe, so wish your relatives well. Now focus on your breath. Inhale for five counts, holding the word "peace" in your mind as you inhale. Exhale for five counts, seeing yourself breathing peace out into the world. Meditate in this fashion for twenty minutes. At the end of your meditation, bow to Yama and say: "May the good of this practice benefit my ancestors, and all of us living in the world today."

Lily Gardner

Notes:

July 12
Saturday

2nd ♏

Color of the day: Black
Incense of the day: Sandalwood

Spell for Peace

Yama, the Hindu god of death, is honored today. Cover your altar with a black cloth. In the south quad-

July 13
Sunday

 2nd ♏

☽ → ♐ 11:50 am

Color of the day: Gold
Incense of the day: Hyacinth

Difficult People Spell

Office bullies are prevalent in corporate life. You are almost guaranteed to encounter a boss who thinks your job is easy, or the internal client who just doesn't like you and will do anything to get rid of you. In corporate life, these people are the tests you must face to achieve what you want from your work. Rather than admitting defeat and letting these people abuse and hurt you, anoint yourself with some olive oil that you've allowed to sit in the Sun for a day, and before going in to work every morning, say:

> I stand strong.
> I am strong.
> I stay strong.
> Strength is with me.
>
> By the power of the Sun,
> By the power of Jupiter,
> By the grace of commerce
> And by my honorable
>   actions.
> I do my work rightly.
> I am the one with
> The power to change.

Diana Rajchel

Notes:

July 14
Monday

 2nd ♐

Color of the day: Silver
Incense of the day: Lily

Honor the Ideals

Bastille Day commemorates the birth of the French republic and the fight for liberty, equality, and fraternity. Today is the ideal time to honor all those who work and fight for these rights. Take time to consider what these words mean to you and how you work for them in your life. Then make a list with two columns. In the first column, write down every way that you work toward these goals. In the second, write down ideas for how you might be more effective or take different actions in your fight. Then place three white candles around your list. As you light the first candle, honor all those who have worked for liberty, equality, and fraternity. With the second candle,

 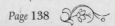

honor yourself for all that you have done in this fight. And with the last, choose to continue your work and try out your new ideas.

Kristin Madden

Notes:

debt. Put the pieces in the bowl and pour honey over it while chanting, "Money, money, sweet as honey, in my life please flow." Have fun with it and keep chanting and stirring until you are done, and end with, "As I will it, so mote it be." Bury the honey mixture in Mother Earth, asking her to bless this wish. Place the candle on your altar, and when it is burned down, replace with another green candle for continued prosperity.

Gail Wood

Notes:

July 15
Tuesday

 2nd ♐

Color of the day: Black
Incense of the day: Cedar

Bills and More Spell

Gather together a green votive candle in a glass holder, a paid bill, a jar of honey, a dime, and a small bowl. Do this in a happy, joyful frame of mind—do not do this spell when you're feeling upset about finances. Place the dime in the glass bowl and place the votive candle atop it. Light the candle with a deep breath, visualizing sufficient funds. Take your paid bill and rip it into tiny, tiny pieces, while cheering and applauding yourself for ending this

July 16
Wednesday

 2nd ♐
☽ → ♑ 12:20 am

Color of the day: White
Incense of the day: Lavender

Summertime Offering

Gather the sacred herbs of summer, and make an offering to the spirits of the Earth. The Celtic ancestors recognized the healing and magical properties of many plants, trees, and herbs, and utilized these in daily charms for many purposes. These included bog violet, bramble, chamomile, colt's foot, dandelion, elder, foxglove, ground ivy, heather, honeysuckle, mistletoe, mugwort, nettles, rue, sage, St. John's wort, and tansy. Hold a small amount of the herb you wish to work with in your left palm and cover it with your right hand. Ask the spirit of the plant to tell you the magical and healing powers that it has and learn how to develop an ongoing relationship with it.

> Herb of summer,
> Sun, and Earth,
> Tell me of
> Your spirit's work.

> Herb of thunder,
> Rain, and dew,
> Show me how
> To work with you.

> Herb of Moon
> And stars and wind,
> Our partnership
> Does now begin.

                    Sharynne NicMhacha

Notes:

July 17
Thursday

 2nd ♑

Color of the day: Purple
Incense of the day: Apricot

Leaving the Darkness Spell

Depression is never a good thing. Amaterasu retreated into a cave in despair and perhaps you have, too. Time for a change. You will need a dark colored candle, a white candle, and a lighter. Draw the drapes in your room. Stand before your altar and light the dark candle. Watch the flame and imagine it filled with all your suffering, doubts, and frustration. Breathe in deep. Say, "I extinguish this darkness from my life." Blow out the candle. As the smoke dissipates, imagine the dark things in your life fading away as well. Take a deep breath. Light the white candle. Say, "I welcome the light back into my life." Take the candle and, in a clockwise direction, open your curtains and windows. Move from room to room, expelling the darkness and letting the Sun shine in. When you have finished, extinguish the candle, but leave it on your altar for twenty-four hours. Break the dark candle into pieces and bury it.

                    Nancy Bennett

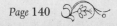

Notes:

By doing so, you have released blockage from clutter in your home and freed up the energy once more. Mix up an incense of equal parts dragon's blood resin, benzoin, and lavender blossoms; grind well in a mortar. Burn on a charcoal and waft the incense smoke through the house.

> Smoke of earth
> And fire and air,
> Clear my home
> And make it fair.
> Drive away
> All harm and fear,
> Only good
> May dwell in here.
>
> Lady Nephthys,
> Bless my house,
> Keep it free from
> Bug or mouse.
> Be welcome here,
> Creatures of light,
> While those unwelcome
> Will feel thy might.
> Protect me and mine
> As we dwell within,
> And keep us safe
> As we journey about.

Winter Wren

Notes:

July 18
Friday

 2nd ♍
☉ Full Moon 3:59 am
☽ → ♒ 11:40 am

Color of the day: Rose
Incense of the day: Thyme

home Energy Ritual

This Full Moon falls upon the birthday of the Egyptian goddess Nephthys, she who is mistress of the house, making this an excellent time for some magical housework. Spend time today focused on your home's energy. Slowly go through the rooms, seeing them with the eyes of a new visitor. Think about changes you would make to refresh the rooms and create a better flow of energy. As you go through the house, gather twenty-five items that have not been used for some time and are simply taking up space. Box up these items for donation to a charity, focusing on the idea of them bringing joy to someone else's life.

 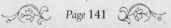

July 19
Saturday

 3rd ≈≈

Color of the day: Brown

Incense of the day: Ivy

Clear–seeing Spell

It's difficult to see things clearly. Often our own emotions get in the way of looking objectively at a problem or decision. Make your own charm to use when you need some objectivity. Take a quartz crystal and cleanse it in the smoke of some frankincense incense, then rub it with some mugwort. Hold it in your hands and impress upon it your desire to see things objectively, with a clear head and clear vision. Leave the crystal where it can catch the moonlight for the night and then the day's sunlight. Carry it with you. To use, simply hold it and focus on seeing things clearly.

Laurel Reufner

Notes:

July 20
Sunday

 3rd ≈≈

☽ → ♓ 9:07 pm

Color of the day: Yellow

Incense of the day: Frankincense

A Spell for Rain

Yemaya is a beautiful black mermaid and the goddess of the rain, the water, and the seven seas. Yemaya will answer your call for gentle life-giving rain so long as you are wise and word your spell carefully. Correspondences for Yemaya include coral beads, the colors blue and white, and seashells. Yemaya demands an offering, however, and a section of a fresh melon, sliced up and placed on a plate in the garden, works nicely. Be sure to leave the offering alone: allow nature and Yemaya to reclaim it as she sees fit.

> Yemaya,
> Lady of the seven seas,
>
> Send your life-giving rain
> Gently to me.
>
> Bless the Earth with a
> Mild shower that brings life.
>
> Let it fall softly, causing no
> Harm or strife.

Ellen Dugan

Notes:

Bury the cool candle wax outside in the yard, garden, or in a flower pot.

Ember

Notes:

July 21
Monday

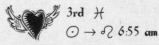

3rd ♓

Color of the day: Lavender
Incense of the day: Clary sage

Peaceful home Spell

Having a harmonious home often depends on the surroundings outside your home as well as within. To attract good neighbors, light a white or blue candle and recite the following:

> Let good neighbors
> Come our way,
> Keep the noisy ones at bay.
> Bring the quiet,
> Peaceful type,
> Ones that we are sure to like.
> Let us live here happily—
> For the good of all,
> So mote it be.

Visualize your ideal neighbors and allow the candle to burn completely.

July 22
Tuesday

3rd ♓
☉ → ♌ 6:55 am

Color of the day: Gray
Incense of the day: Cinnamon

Releasing Negativity Spell

In the course of life, anger can come between family and friends. Sometimes these hurts can be corrected by an apology. But sometimes we have lost contact with the other person and have no direct way to try to mend the issues. Even if apologies are made, it can be difficult to get past the ill feelings. Cast a circle of blue light, call in your guardians, and light lavender incense. Use a quill or athame to inscribe the word "forgiveness" on a blue candle three times, then dress the candle with honey-suckle oil and light it. Hold a chalice of water between your hands, and pour out all your negative feelings into the water. Let the water absorb the painful, hurtful thoughts and feelings. Say the word "forgiveness" nine times out loud, and meditate on forgiveness. Dismiss the guardians and the circle. Pour the water down the drain. Allow the candle to burn down naturally.

Winter Wren

Notes:

Water of the sacred clouds,
Water of the ancient swells,
Rain and mist upon us pour,
The land will blossom
evermore.

Place the water on one of your plants, infusing it with healthy bless-ings. In ancient Roman times this was the festival of Neptune, when shelters of leaves and branches were raised in fields to honor Neptune and ensure his help in bringing rain for the coming season. The locals would picnic under these cool structures. To further the spell, why not pack a fish lunch, think of Neptune, and eat al fresco?

Nancy Bennett

Notes:

July 23
Wednesday

 3rd ♓

☽ → ♈ 4:22 am

Color of the day: Topaz
Incense of the day: Marjoram

Neptune's Cooling Day

In the heat of the July summer, who wouldn't welcome a bit of rain? This spell is best done in the morning. Spread a silver or grey cloth on the ground, and place a bowl of water in the center. After calling directions, chant:

July 24
Thursday

 3rd ♈

Color of the day: White
Incense of the day: Nutmeg

Personal Cooling Spell

Late July can be uncomfortably hot. Here's a spell that will help you to keep cool. When feeling overheated, draw a cool bath. Add cooling ingredients like fresh mint, lemon balm, or a green tea infusion. Consecrate the bathwater with your athame, wand, or hand, saying: "Water, be blessed. Water, soothe me. May this water banish uncomfortable heat. Water, drive away the harsh heat of summer. So mote it be!" (Make sure you banish "uncomfortable heat," not "heat." You don't want hypothermia!) In the tub, ground and center. Now visualize the heat pouring off you into the water. Before you empty the bath, put some of the water into a sealed container. Drain the water, saying, "Water drains and I am cool. Uncomfortable heat is banished." Next time you're overheated, pour out a little water from the container, visualizing your heat draining away, saying, "Water drains and I am cool. Uncomfortable heat is banished."

Deborah Lipp

Notes:

July 25
Friday

 3rd ♈
☽ → ♉ 9:14 am
4th quarter 2:41 pm

Color of the day: Purple
Incense of the day: Vanilla

Protection from Crime

The goddess of robbers, Furina, (which is the name of a venomous snake), was honored on this day at the Roman festival of Furinalia. This reminds us to put up our guard against any criminal activity. This can easily be done while you are out in the world by a simple visualization. Imagine a golden helmet emanating from the crown of your head. See it very clearly in your mind's eye. One by one, draw four shields down across the front, back and sides of your body, closing around you like a suit of armor. Affirm your safety by declaring: "The shields of Athena protect me!" Protect your home by placing sardonyx, a stone of strength and protection against crime, around your house and garden to ward off any would-be robbers. Create a gem elixir with this crystal by placing it in water and charging it in the Sun for twelve hours. Keep it preserved with a good dose of alcohol. Before you leave the house, spray it over your body to cast a glamour of protection around you.

Igraine

Notes:

things you want to accomplish this year, along with anything you think may be limiting those goals. Fill your hand with salt over your sink and allow the energy of those limitations to fill the salt. Create a spiral in the sink with the salt, allowing that energy to be drawn from you by the salt.

Spiral of salt, purify me.

Pour a small amount of lemon juice into your hand and draw a spiral on top of the salt.

Spiral of lemon, cleanse me.

Turn on the water and watch it dissolve the spirals and take that energy down the drain.

Spiral of water, free me.

Turn off the water and feel that freedom to create.

Kristin Madden

Notes:

July 26
Saturday

 4ℏ ♉

Color of the day: Indigo
Incense of the day: Patchouli

halfway Spell

A bit more than halfway through the year is a good time to consider what might be holding you back from creating exactly the year you desire. Write down the top five

 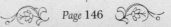

July 27
Sunday

 4th ♉
☽ → ♊ 11:55 am

Color of the day: Amber
Incense of the day: Juniper

Hatshepsut's Birthday

Hatshepsut was a female pharaoh
in Egypt. Attempts to erase
her from history by smashing the
temples and statues built during her
reign failed; in fact, she resides in
her own room in the Metropolitan
Museum of Art's Egyptian wing.
Hatshepsut was a patron of the arts.
Celebrate her birthday by performing an act of creation in her name.
Write, paint, dance, take photo-
graphs, cook, sew, create a collage—
perform any creative act and dedicate
it to her. Find a photograph of one
of her sphinxes and place it on your
desk. Do a bit of research and "discover" another artist history has forgotten. Honor that person's work in
Hatshepsut's name. She was a smart,
intelligent, determined woman, and
under her reign Egypt's intelligentsia
flourished. How can you continue
her legacy? By creating, yes, but also
by supporting and encouraging your
fellow artists.

Cerridwen Iris Shea

Notes:

July 28
Monday

 4th ♊

Color of the day: Ivory
Incense of the day: Rosemary

The Beauty Meditation

We are most beautiful when
we are happy. Light a pink
candle and burn lilac incense. Take
a deep breath and go into a meditative state. You are standing in your
favorite place in the world. You look
around and breathe in all that makes
you so happy. Breathe in the harmony and rhythm of that place. As
you come to feel the heartbeat of that
place, smile. And as you smile, you
notice a bright beautiful light close
by you. The light approaches you
and surrounds you. You feel stillness,
joy, and gladness there in the middle
of that light. As you breathe in, the
light moves inside you. Continue to

stay with that light until you feel it's time to leave. Whisper your thanks and allow the images to recede. Come back to your space and the here and now. Whenever you want to feel beautiful, visualize that bright light surrounding you and smile!

Gail Wood

Notes:

July 29
Tuesday

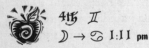

4th ♊
☽ → ♋ 1:11 pm

Color of the day: Red
Incense of the day: Basil

To Overcome Bad Habits

St. Martha, whose feast day is celebrated today, won fame for subduing a dragon that terrorized the villagers of Provence back in 48 CE. Ever since, people in need of strength have prayed to her. For this spell, you'll need a green candle, a small dragon figure, and a likeness of St. Martha. Arrange these items on your altar. Place the image of Martha in the south quadrant of your altar, the direction of will. Write down the bad habit you wish to rid yourself of on a slip of paper. Hold the paper in your dominant hand as you light the candle. Say: "St. Martha, I ask for your aid and protection. As you did overcome the dragon, I ask you to help me overcome my [name your habit]." Now visualize your day without the drag of your habit. Remember, it's important to replace your bad habit with a different, more healthy activity. Spend at least five minutes at the start of your day and five minutes at the end of the day doing this visualization. Carry the dragon as a reminder that you've overcome your addiction.

Lily Gardner

Notes:

 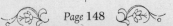

July 30
Wednesday

Color of the day: Yellow
Incense of the day: Honeysuckle

The Real Truth

The truth of a situation can get a tad . . . obfuscated, sometimes. Your date might not have had a family emergency, your co-worker might actually have received your email, and your landlord knew perfectly well you were planning on moving at the end of your lease. It's often your word or instinct against someone else's. In order to get around these periods of fuzzy information, try this spell for the truth to come to light. Gather a white candle, a pen, and some paper. Write the name of the dissimulating person on the paper. Surround this drawing with several little Suns or Sun glyphs. After nightfall, stand before a mirror and light the white candle. Hold the paper to the mirror while chanting:

> In the darkness,
> There is light,
> All things hidden
> In the night,
> Come, and be revealed.
> Secrets are unsealed.
> I will know the truth.
> I will have the proof.

Diana Rajchel

Notes:

July 31
Thursday

Color of the day: Crimson
Incense of the day: Jasmine

Thor's Day of Power

Thursday belongs to the Norse god Thor, and is ruled by the planet Jupiter. This is a good day for workings which relate to good health, physical strength, or prosperity. To increase your strength and vitality, wear the symbol of Thor: a hammer. You can find a Thor's Hammer pendant at most Pagan jewelry suppliers. String it on a purple, blue, or indigo cord. In the hour after sunrise, light two candles of matching color. Place the pendant between the candles and say:

> In your hour, on your day,
> Hear me as I stand and pray.

God of thunder,
God of might,
Lend your power
With this light.

In your symbol,
Store your strength,
Pour it out to me at length!

Wear the hammer pendant whenever
you need extra power.

Elizabeth Barrette

Notes:

August is the eighth month of the year and named for Augustus Caesar. Its astrological sign is Leo the lion (July 22–August 23), a fixed fire sign ruled by the Sun. The harvest begins, and on August 1 we observe the ancient harvest festival of Lammas. This is the first harvest festival of the year, and a time to honor the beginning of the grain harvests. Corn is ripening, and so are peaches and tomatoes. It is a month of rich color. Black-eyed Susans, sunflowers, goldenrod, and butterfly weed provide splashes of color along country lanes. In August, the Goddess blesses us with her bounty. Farmers' markets are overflowing with fresh produce, and county fairs showcase prize-winning vegetables and canned goods. Ancient Romans paid tribute to two of their greatest goddess figures in August: Diana and Venus. And for Christians, the feast day of the Virgin Mary is August 15. Native Americans honored their life-sustaining corn crop by referring to the August Full Moon as the Corn Moon. Magical activities for the month are as simple as preparing corn bread or making a corn or wheat doll to honor the harvest. August is summer at its most mature. It is a cicada's call in the afternoon heat, and the beauty of a tiger swallowtail butterfly lingering over the joe-pye weed. It is the pause before autumn's chill.

August 1
Friday
Lammas

 4th ♌
New Moon 6:12 am

Color of the day: Orchid
Incense of the day: Ginger

Lammas Corn Dolly

Lammas, the first of the harvest Sabbats, was traditionally celebrated with fresh bread and beer. At the heart of any harvest holiday is gratitude and generosity. We give thanks for the bounty in our lives and we share our bounty with others. The Lammas practice of making corn dollies dates back to ancient times when the Romans first introduced cultivation to the tribes of northern Europe. Made from the last sheaf of grain, the dolly was paraded through the village and treated with reverence or derision, depending on the tribe. Eventually the corn dolly became the good luck talisman for every farm. To make your corn dolly, gather together long stems of wheat, corn husks, dried alfalfa, or, if you're a city dweller, raffia. Fashion either an abstract figure or a more doll-shaped figure depending on your sensibilities. Likewise, the corn dolly can be left simple or dressed in cloth, feathers, and beads. Pass the dolly through the smoke of your ritual fire to bless her. Ask her to protect your household from theft, poverty, illness, and disaster. Your last year's corn dolly, if you have one, should be tossed in the fire with prayers of gratitude for a year's worth of good fortune. Blessed Be.

Lily Gardner

Notes:

Holiday lore: Lammas is a bittersweet holiday, mingling joy at the current high season's harvest with the knowledge that summer is soon at an end. Many cultures have "first fruit" rituals on this day—the Celt's version is called Lughnasadh; the Anglo-Saxon version called Hlafmasse. In the Middle Ages, the holiday settled on August 1, taking its current form for the most part, with sheaves of wheat and corn blessed on this day.

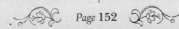

August 2
Saturday

 1st ♌
☽ → ♍ 4:59 pm

Color of the day: Brown
Incense of the day: Pine

Recharging

Recharge your energies today with some play time. If you're lucky and it's raining, take a walk in the rain and remember what it was like to be a kid splashing in the puddles. If it isn't raining where you are—it is August, after all—play in the sprinklers. Risk looking silly and goofy. You'll feel much better afterward.

Laurel Reufner

Notes:

August 3
Sunday

 1st ♍

Color of the day: Gold
Incense of the day: Marigold

Spell for Friendship

Today is Friendship Day! Lemons are associated with friendship; to sweeten them, how about lemon candy? Take six lemons. Visualize them as shining Suns that brighten friendship. Send energy into them, saying, "Friendship is here. Warmth and kindness are here. Blessed be." While you cook, visualize glowing friendship coming from the lemons. Peel the lemons and cut peels into strips. In a saucepan, cover peels with water and boil for twenty minutes. Drain, rinse, and set aside. Bring one cup each of water and sugar to a boil, stir, and reduce heat. Cook until you have a syrup. Add peel to syrup and cook five minutes over medium heat. Drain. Roll peels in one-third cup of sugar, coating both sides. Let stand on a drying rack for a few hours. Make gift packages labeled "For Friendship Day" and give to each of your friends or potential friends.

Deborah Lipp

Notes:

  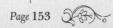

August 4
Monday

 1st ♏

☽ → ♎ 10:28 pm

Color of the day: Silver
Incense of the day: Lily

What A Wonderful World Meditation

Today is Louis Armstrong's birthday, who sang a well-known version of the song "What a Wonderful World." Find a quiet natural spot outdoors. Take three deep breaths and connect with Mother Earth. Breathe deeply and look around until your attention is focused on one object—perhaps a leaf, a tree, or blade of grass. Focus on it for three breaths and then close your eyes. As you breathe deeply, extend your consciousness toward it, feeling its spirit emerge. Ask permission to move closer and ask it to share its wonder with you. Meld with its spirit, seeking its wisdom. Feel, hear and see the marvels you're shown. When it is time, thank the spirit and move back to your body and own sense of individuality. Leave an offering of cornmeal and give thanks to the being and the wonderful world all around.

Gail Wood

Notes:

August 5
Tuesday

 1st ♎

Color of the day: White
Incense of the day: Geranium

Peach Wood Prayer Stick

Peach wood has many magical uses. It has been valued in Asia for its ability to repel negativity and to make magic wands. This spell uses peach wood to create a prayer or spell stick. August, when peaches are in season, would be a perfect time to do this. Obtain a slender branch from a peach tree (this may be deadfall or removed in a respectful manner). When the Moon is in a waxing phase, pray over it and carve your initials into it. Think of your magical purpose, then hide the stick until the Full Moon. At this time, cleanse the stick in the smoke of a protective herbal incense such as sage. Your peach spell stick is ready to use. Include your peach stick in any spell by holding it as you speak a charm, or use it to direct power to a specific location. Peach wood is especially good for love, fertility, or good luck spells.

James Kambos

Notes:

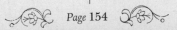

August 6
Wednesday

 1st ♎

Color of the day: Yellow
Incense of the day: Marjoram

Water healing

The sea has many magical and healing properties. In ancient Scotland, people treated certain ailments by using the water taken from the crests of nine waves and boiling nine stones in this water. Another option was to take water from nine springs or streams in which cresses grow, and boil the stones in that. At the time of the great harvest festivals (which could last for a week or more), people led their horses down to the edge of the water and had them swim through the waves for healing and protection in the year to come. Here is a water charm which you can use at the sea or any other body of water:

> By the power
> Of the ninth wave,
> With the magic
> Of the nine stones,
> I wash away
> What does not serve.
> Blessings of water
> I now invoke.
>
> May the Gods of the river,
> and the spirits of the sea,

> Bless me with your healing,
> As your power
> Flows through me.

Sharynne NicMhacha

Notes:

August 7
Thursday

 1st ♎
☽ → ♏ 7:26 am

Color of the day: Green
Incense of the day: Apricot

Spell to Find a Lost Item

Cast a circle as you desire and sit in the center. Visualize yourself sitting in the middle of a great map and, like a compass needle, your vision spins in all directions. But this compass needle will not automatically settle on north. Your compass is seeking a lost item. Close your eyes and imagine you are that spinning needle. Clearly visualize what you have lost and where you last saw the item. Allow your imaginary compass needle to stop when it feels right and see where your needle has come to rest. Look for your missing item in that direction. Use this chant as you visualize:

> North and south,
> East and west,
> Find the source of my unrest.
> Help me find
> What I have lost,
> A value that defies its cost.
> Return to me
> That which I need,
> As I will so mote it be.

                                            Ember

Notes:

August 8
Friday

1st ♏
2nd quarter 4:20 pm

Color of the day: White
Incense of the day: Alder

Attracting the Fairy Folk

Whether you dwell in the country or the city, you can make your residence more appealing to the fairy folk with a few thoughtful steps that can be done in your yard or in outdoor planters on your deck or balcony. Cultivate a few attractive plants—bluebells, lily of the valley, ferns, cowslips, or rosemary. Within these plantings, embed a small, attractive bowl as a place for the fairies to bathe and frolic. Tie a few tiny silver bells onto the plantings. Add a couple of dried milkweed pods, complete with milkweed down, for the fairies to use as beds. A simple but lovely fairy house can be made from a birdhouse and added into the fairy garden. Remember to leave gifts of shiny glass beads, sequins, silver charms, or the like. The fairies love sparkly gifts just as much as we do. Above all else, remember to speak words of welcome and invitation to them whenever you are near the fairy garden.

                                            Winter Wren

Notes:

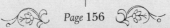

August 9
Saturday

 2nd ♏

☽ → ♐ 7:10 pm

Color of the day: Gray
Incense of the day: Magnolia

Dreams and Reality

Every night we visit a realm of infinite possibility. This is the land of dreams, ruled by symbol and populated by the subconscious. Here magic is a prominent natural law. What happens here may seem ephemeral, but it can have profound effects on our waking lives. When you need to build a bridge between dream and reality, use this spell. Place an amethyst crystal on or near your bed. As you fall asleep, say these words:

> Dreams of shadow,
> Dreams of light,
> Hear and heed
> My will this night.
>
> Dreams of truth
> And dreams of lies,
> Let me walk
> Through sleeping skies.
>
> Dreams of water,
> Dreams of mead,
> Bring me to
> The things I need.

> Dreams of silk
> And dreams of steel,
> Manifest my will
> Made real.

Images, answers, and ideas may come during sleep; you may recognize dream-bits in waking space. Follow these clues to your goal.

Elizabeth Barrette

Notes:

August 10
Sunday

 2nd ♐

Color of the day: Yellow
Incense of the day: Eucalyptus

An Offering to the Sea

August is vacation month, and many of us spend time by the sea reflecting on her great mystery. The sea celebrates the union of Earth and sky. Her magical moondance of ebb and flow in step with wax and wane, inhale and exhale, is the very breath of spirit. We can sit by her side and witness the wheel turning, our own cyclic nature, and the power to transform our lives. To honor her mystery, rise when the Sun rises. Have an abalone shell to use as your altar. As you walk to the beach, gather small objects such as a seed pod, a bird's feather, a perfectly round stone that looks like the Full Moon, a twig in the shape of a rune, wild sweet peas, or sparkling sea glass. Give each object a purpose or symbolic meaning as you place it in your abalone shell. When you have reached the beach find a perfect spot that feels right to you. Cast a circle with driftwood. Sit down and place your sea altar before you. Raise your face to the warm Sun and greet the gods and goddesses of the sea. Ask them to accept your offering for their blessing of positive change and transformation.

Igraine

Notes:

August 11
Monday

 2nd ♐

Color of the day: White
Incense of the day: Neroli

Shh, I'm Reading

Remember those long, lazy summer days as a kid? Where there was nothing to do but sit under a tree and read the latest Nancy Drew, Beverly Cleary, or, in more recent years, J. K. Rowling's newest Harry Potter? Recreate that sense of wonder, endless time, and a portal to a magical world today. Call in "well." Play hooky from your life for a day. Get one of your favorite childhood tomes or that book you "haven't had time to read." Go to a park or a beach or a museum or a coffee shop or even just a favorite chair at home. And read for as long as you like.

Cerridwen Iris Shea

Notes:

August 12
Tuesday

2nd ♐
☽ → ♑ 7:42 am

Color of the day: Black
Incense of the day: Bayberry

Give Me Strength

Summer brings out hot tempers and hotter heads. Here is a good spell to get you through those moments when all those around you are acting stupid. Find yourself a quiet space, away from the crowd. You can do this in your car, in the restroom, or even inwardly. Breathe in three times. Fashion your thumbs in a chain, interlocking with each other. Chant:

> Mighty Hercules,
> Break this chain
> Of little wit
> And feeble brain.
>
> Rude tongues waggle,
> Cause me pain,
> Challenge sane minds
> To remain.
>
> Hot heads cool,
> Peace regain,
> Give me strength
> To break this chain.

Chant until you feel that the spell is working, and then release your thumbs, smile and breathe. You have made it through! As soon as possible,

go outside and raise your hands to the sky and hail the mighty Hercules.

Nancy Bennett

Notes:

August 13
Wednesday

2nd ♑

Color of the day: Brown
Incense of the day: Bay laurel

Power of Hermes Charm

For blessings in travel and communication today, place one celery seed in each shoe. Visualize the god Mercury or Hermes before you in golden light with winged helmet and shoes. Say, "Hermes, thrice blessed, I thank you for your presence in my life. Grant me ease of travel and communication. Help me to be quick and clear of mind and speech. Allow me to wing my way through challenges with grace." See him reach out and touch your shoes, filling you from the feet upward with his golden light. Feel that you are

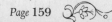

now filled with the blessing of the winged messenger. Any time you feel frustrated or at a loss for the right thing to say, take a deep breath and recall this feeling. Allow his blessings to flow through you.

Kristin Madden

Notes:

into fourths and squeeze the juice into the bowl. Sprinkle some drops of lemon juice around you or in the space you wish to freshen, breathing deeply of the scent. Hold the bowl up while fanning the cleaning power of lemon juice around you, and envision everything taking on a fresh, clear glow. Chant, "Clear awareness everywhere, sparkle and freshness in the air." Afterward, make the remaining juice into lemonade, drinking mindfully, imbibing the sweetness of a new vision.

Gail Wood

Notes:

August 14
Thursday

2nd ♑
☽ → ♒ 6:56 pm

Color of the day: Turquoise
Incense of the day: Carnation

A Breath of Fresh Air Spell

To cleanse yourself or a space and to bring a fresh perspective, perform this spell to bring relief from the "same old, same old." You will need a fresh lemon, a knife, a shallow bowl, and a fan. This will work to clear your brain and aura, or you can do it to clear the energy in your living and working space. Burn incense with mint in it and light a white candle. Cut the lemon

August 15
Friday

2nd ♒
Color of the day: Pink
Incense of the day: Cypress

In honor of Women

In Christian Catholic tradition, today is the Assumption of the Virgin Mary. This day the mother of

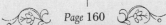

Jesus took her seat in heaven. Some tales say that this marked her death, while others say that she was taken, body and all, into the heavens. This is a day to commemorate all mothers and the sacrifices women make for the continued health and survival of their families, and is even a public holiday in France, Spain, Cameroon, and Guatemala. A fitting way to commemorate the day is to light a blue candle or a blue novena candle with Mary on it (you can purchase them from a grocery store). Rub a little olive oil on the candle before burning it (olive oil was used to anoint royalty) and speak your own prayer to the divine mother. This is a day to pray for women activists to find peace and success in their efforts.

Diana Rajchel

Notes:

August 16
Saturday

2nd ≈≈
Full Moon 5:16 pm

Color of the day: Blue
Incense of the day: Sandalwood

Spell for healing

The season of harvest has begun, and tonight's Full Corn Moon promises to be a time of plenty and abundance. Pull a little of that first harvest energy into your Full Moon celebration tonight and rejoice in the fertility and bounty of the Earth. This quick Full Moon ritual would be appropriate for either closing up a group ritual or working by yourself. Consider setting up your altar with green and gold candles, ears of corn, and fresh sunflowers (these blossoms promote wealth and fame). Green herbs from the garden would add a touch of herbal magic, too. Try spearmint to promote prosperity, basil for love, lavender for protection, and arrange some pretty and fragrant yellow roses for friendship. When your ritual is done, send everyone home with a rose as a token or if you worked solitary, just enjoy the bouquet. Happy August Esbat!

Tonight we/I celebrate the Full Corn Moon,

May the Lord and Lady Grant us/me a boon.

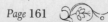

In this season of plenty
Grant us/me prosperity,

By the magic of nature and
Bound with three times three.

Ellen Dugan

Notes:

"Sowelu," (⚡) the rune for wholeness. This rune symbolizes self-realization. Carve this rune on an orange candle. Light the candle, close your eyes, and visualize a deep well, the Well of Possibility. Try to keep your mind focused on the well. What messages occur to you? You may wish to throw the runes for clarification.

Lily Gardner

Notes:

August 17
Sunday

 3rd ♒
☽ → ♓ 3:46 am

Color of the day: Amber
Incense of the day: Almond

Runic Spell for Wisdom

August 17 marks the day Odin, the Norse god of war and magic, hung himself from the World Tree in his search for wisdom. After nine days without food or drink, he peered "down to the deepest depths," the Well of Possibility, and discovered the runes. The runes served as an ancient alphabet for Odin's people to use in their spell work and as a divination tool. For this spell, use

August 18
Monday

 3rd ♓
Color of the day: Black
Incense of the day: Hyssop

Psychic Sweeping Ritual

Energy patterns in our homes tend to get gunked up, making them uncomfortable places to live. Practicing feng shui and clearing out clutter can go a long way toward alleviating that; however, a little psychic sweeping is just the thing to quickly remove that gunky buildup and make you more at ease in your own home. To begin, place a lit white candle on either your altar or the center of your table. Next, mindfully sweep your home. Remember to get in all the corners where energy can pool and to get behind the furniture. Pick stuff up off the floor and tuck it away. Sweep toward a doorway and immediately remove anything you sweep up to a location outside the home.

Laurel Reufner

Notes:

Sometimes disputes resolve gracefully; other times, you must assert yourself in ways that other people just won't like. Use this charm to store power for when you need to say no and make it stick. You will need a square of red cloth, red thread, and a red stone such as a garnet. You'll also need at least one Mars herb such as garlic, thistle, or pepper, and an essential oil like dragon's blood, galangal, or ginger. Bundle the herb and stone into the cloth, add one drop of essential oil, and tie with thread. Focus on absorbing the Mars energy of the day. When you need the stored power, apply one drop of essential oil to the bundle and one to your wrist, and carry the bundle with you.

Elizabeth Barrette

Notes:

August 19
Tuesday

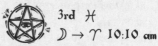

3rd ♓

☽ → ♈ 10:10 am

Color of the day: Gray
Incense of the day: Basil

Mars Day Charm

Today is Tuesday, ruled by Mars. Sacred to the god of war, this is a good time to prepare for conflict.

August 20
Wednesday

 3rd ♈
Color of the day: Topaz
Incense of the day: Lilac

Spell for Temperance

If you are concerned about substance abuse or drinking, but don't believe you are an addict or alcoholic, a spell for temperance (balance, moderation) can be a good choice, and is wise to perform during a waning Moon. On your altar, have representations of the four elements, a piece of amethyst, a symbol of substance use, and a symbol of sobriety (for example, a shot of whiskey and a shot glass full of water). Optional: the Temperance tarot card and a drum or rattle. Ground and center. Pick up each elemental symbol one at a time, saying "I am balanced by [air, fire, water, earth]." Repeat "I am balanced, I am temperate" over and over while drumming, rattling, or clapping your hands. Send power into the amethyst. Drink the water, saying, "I choose this." Carry the amethyst with you as a temperance charm. Pour out the whiskey near your front door.

Deborah Lipp

Notes:

August 21
Thursday

 3rd ♈
☽ → ♉ 2:38 pm

Color of the day: Green
Incense of the day: Balsam

Thor's Hammer Spell

Today is the Feast of Thor. Well, this worked out nicely. This date falls on a Thursday, the day of the week that is named after Thor. Thor is a popular Norse god, whom the people call on for protection and to be blessed with fertility and abundance. Today you have a perfect opportunity to work magic for prosperity with Thor. However, since this festival day falls on a waning Moon, this spell calls for the removal of worry and monetary problems. This spell will hammer out any problems for you quite nicely.

> Under this steamy August
> evening's waning Moon,
> Thor, remove all blocks to my
> prosperity soon.
> I call instead for prosperity
> true,
> Thor, please guard and
> protect all that I do.

Ellen Dugan

Notes:

August 22
Friday

3rd ☿

☉ → ♏ 2:02 pm

Color of the day: Purple
Incense of the day: Rose

Organizational Change

Being disorganized is nothing to be proud of, but if messy is the only pattern you've known, getting your act together requires the challenging process of changing how you think. This may take repetition until it all sinks in. Take three cards out of a tarot deck: the Strength card, the High Priestess card, and the Star card. Strength represents your power to change. The High Priestess represents your will to change. The Star represents the change achieved. Clear a space in your messiest area and set these cards out. Every day for two weeks, take a moment and visualize yourself inside each of these cards. As each day goes by, the influence of the symbols in the card will affect the way you think, until pulling yourself and your clutter together will be a small matter to you. Aid the spell by seeking out new methods of time management.

Diana Rajchel

Notes:

August 23
Saturday

3rd ☿

☽ → ♊ 5:48 pm

4th quarter 7:49 pm

Color of the day: Black
Incense of the day: Sage

Feast of the Furies

The Greek furies (or Erinyes) hounded transgressors in order to gain retribution for those wronged. They chased Orestes after he murdered his mother and her husband in the House of Atreus cycle, and it took Athena's intervention to save him. I don't find the furies frightening; I find them helpful. The furies give no quarter and take no prisoners. If you invoke them to do harm because it suits your ego, they will turn on you and there is no escape. But their energy can also be harnessed as a positive catalyst in your life, especially if your life is in danger. Even if you do not need their help right now, honor the positive side of anger. Go to the furies with an open heart and a clear conscience. Because sometimes, you need anger in order to survive.

Cerridwen Iris Shea

Notes:

August 24
Sunday

 4th ♊

Color of the day: Orange

Incense of the day: Hyacinth

Wellness Massage Oil

Massage is good for both body and soul, and certain aromas can change your whole outlook on life. This special oil relaxes you as it gets your energy flowing and can be used both as a perfume and massage oil. Blend six teaspoons of extra-virgin or cold-pressed olive oil with nine drops of the essential oils of cedar and chamomile. As you pour the blended oils into a brown or cobalt glass bottle, visualize yourself filled with light, revitalized by the Sun and these sacred herbs. You are purified and strengthened by this oil. Placing your hands around the bottle, fill it with this energy. Keep in a dark, cool place and warm slightly before using.

Kristin Madden

Notes:

August 25
Monday

 4th ♊

☽ → ♋ 8:18 pm

Color of the day: Lavender

Incense of the day: Narcissus

Sacred Space Ritual

In late August, a silvery early morning mist settles over the hills and along the river of my Appalachian valley. It's a cool, cleansing mist that signals that the season is turning towards autumn. It reminds me that this is a good time to also cleanse any space where we live or do magical work. To do this, obtain a sage and cedar ceremonial smudge stick. Burn the stick according to the instructions. Facing east, begin walking around the room or your home in a clockwise direction. After you return to your starting position, raise the stick to thank the sky, then lower it toward the floor to thank the Earth. Remain in the east-facing position and, using the smudge stick, make the shape of a pentagram or cross in the air to seal your sacred space. End by saying: "North, east, west and south. Good energy in, bad energy out."

James Kambos

Notes:

August 26
Tuesday

 4th ♋
Color of the day: Scarlet
Incense of the day: Ginger

Vehicle Protection Amulet

At noon, face south and place a red or white candle in a glass dish. Place a garnet in the dish and sprinkle the stone and candle with a pinch of salt, dried dill, and dried basil. Add some ground dragon's blood if you have it. Light the candle. Visualize the energy from the candle infusing the stone and herbs and repeat the following:

> Fire, flame infuse this stone
> To shield, protect and guard
> From vandals, thieves,
> Or any threat—
> Keep away all harm.

After the candle burns out and cools, collect the stone and any loose herbs and place them in a red drawstring bag. Keep this bag in your vehicle or carry it with you.

                    Ember
Notes:

August 27
Wednesday

 4th ♋
☽ → ♌ 10:51 pm
Color of the day: Yellow
Incense of the day: Lavender

Crystal Clearing

Crystals are another precious gift of Mother Earth. It is not necessary to have a new crystal for every purpose or working. Crystals can be reprogrammed to new uses with just a bit of forethought and planning. When a particular working for which you have charged a crystal is completed, under a waning Moon, collect up the crystals no longer in use and thank them for their energy in your working. Clear them by first smudging them with sage and cedar smoke and then cleansing them in a salt water bath followed by a good rinsing in clear, running water. Place the cleared crystals in a windowsill where they can receive light from the Moon as she passes through her cycle. After a full Moon cycle, the crystals are once more ready to be charged with a new purpose and a new working.

                    Winter Wren
Notes:

August 28
Thursday

 4th ♌

Color of the day: Purple
Incense of the day: Clove

A Spell for Standing Strong

There are times we need to stand our ground—even though all we really want to do is run away from a situation that we find difficult to confront. We feel we are being threatened and thrown off balance. This spell is for reestablishing your power and equilibrium and overcoming fear. Find a tall staff in the woods and spray paint it a glittering gold to represent strength and courage (in a pinch an old broomstick will do). Wrap it in ivy vine to promote overcoming obstacles and to break down self imposed barriers. As the Sun reaches its zenith, place your golden staff before you, firmly planted in the ground, and state:

> By my will and by my right,
> I will stand strong,
> Prepared to fight
> Against my fear
> And not take flight.
> I'll shift from shadow
> Into light.

Raise your staff to the sky.

Igraine

Notes:

August 29
Friday

 4th ♌

Color of the day: Coral
Incense of the day: Mint

Rushes Ritual

In Britain, during July and August, the very first harvest was the harvest of rushes, which were gathered and used to carpet the floors of houses and churches. A procession known as a "rush-bearing" took place to the accompaniment of pipes, drums, and bells. Groups of young women carried bundles of rushes decorated with ribbons and flowers, or sometimes woven into the shape of triangles or spirals. Gather rushes from the water's edge to carpet your sacred space, and place rush-weavings on your altar to honor and connect with the spirits of Earth and water in the waxing powers of the summer season:

> Offerings from
> The flowery Earth,
> Gifts from the watery places
> Where my footsteps
> Tread the path of old,
> These fragrant rushes
> Strewn about
> From where the Earth
> And waters meet.
> Their powers grow,
> And thus grow mine.

Sharynne NicMhacha

Notes:

and get out of the rut! Keep your clean slate at hand and use it when needed. This spell is best made during the waxing Moon.

Nancy Bennett

Notes:

August 30
Saturday

4th ♌
☽ → ♍ 2:18 am
New Moon 3:58 pm

Color of the day: Indigo
Incense of the day: Rue

Motivational Spell

When you are stuck in a rut, think of one thing you want to change or attain. This could be a bad habit or a new skill. First thing every morning for seven days, write it down on a child's blackboard and place the blackboard somewhere you will see it. At the end of seven days (you should have seven lines) chant:

> Seven times my goal is set,
> By my strength it will be met.
> Once erased, like dust to
>   wind,
> In action raised, it will begin.

Now it's time to wipe the slate clean

August 31
Sunday

1st ♍

Color of the day: Gold
Incense of the day: Frankincense

Dream Magic

There are steps you can take to encourage your dream work. The first of these is a dream pillow. It is simple enough for you to make your own small one to tuck inside your pillowcase with your sleeping pillow. Combine two tablespoons each rose petals and lemon balm with one tablespoon each costmary, catnip, lavender buds, and cloves. Insert the mixture into a fabric envelope, then stitch the envelope closed with silver thread and place it inside your pillowcase. For a bedtime dream bath, combine three tablespoons lemongrass, two tablespoons each orange peel and thyme, and one tablespoon each cloves, cinnamon, and lavender. Grind well. Tie the mixture into a piece of cheesecloth or a washcloth and place it in your bath. While soaking in the tub, relax and meditate on what you wish to accomplish in your dream journey this night. Finish your bath and go directly to bed, allowing yourself to relax and sleep.

Winter Wren

Notes:

September is the ninth month of the year. Its name is derived from the Latin word *septum*, which means "seventh," as it was the seventh month of the Roman calendar. Its astrological sign is Virgo, the maiden (August 23–September 23), a mutable earth sign ruled by Mercury. Cool misty mornings and an occasional splash of autumn color in the woodland tells us September is here. The afternoons are still warm, and the last of the garden's produce is harvested. The cidery tang of windfall apples coming in from the orchard is on the air now. Chipmunks and squirrels are busy readying their nests for winter. In the old days, September was the month that the "blizzard" pantry was stocked in preparation for bad weather. Mabon, or the Fall Equinox, is the main holiday of September. It is the second harvest sabbat and the first dark sabbat. The Great Son Mabon returns to the womb of Mother Earth for rest and renewal, just as nature does at this time of year. In September we contemplate the dual nature of life and death. Although we are surrounded by the abundant harvest of pumpkins, apples, and grapes, at the same time nature prepares to enter the dark season. One of the most glorious sights of September is its Full Moon, the Harvest Moon. It glows with a pale golden color, and is the crown jewel of the September night.

September 1
Monday
Labor Day

 1st ♍
☽ → ♎ 7:44 am

Color of the day: Silver
Incense of the day: Rosemary

Barbecue Magic

First celebrated in 1882, Labor Day is a national tribute to the contributions of workers in the strength and prosperity of the United States. Most American workers have the day off today and are enjoying the day with friends and family. And this is a great day for barbecue magic. Before laying your coals, have everyone present write down all that they are thankful for about their work. For some it may take some thought, but just having a job can be a blessing. Encourage them to jot down ways that they might be more productive or happier in their work and any goals for future work they would like to do. Crunch up these papers and lay them beneath the coals. Light the papers first with everyone watching. As they burn, visualize those thanks and wishes transforming and being released to the universe.

Kristin Madden

Notes:

Holiday lore: Many Greeks consider this their New Year's Day. This day marks the beginning of the sowing season, a time of promise and hope. On this day, people fashion wreaths of pomegranates, quinces, grapes, and garlic bulbs—all traditional symbols of abundance. Just before dawn on September 1, children submerge the wreaths in the ocean waters for luck. They carry seawater and pebbles home with them in small jars to serve as protection in the coming year. Tradition calls for exactly forty pebbles and water from exactly forty waves.

September 2
Tuesday
Ramadan begins

 1st ♎

Color of the day: Gray
Incense of the day: Ylang-ylang

harvest Mare Spell

The harvest was a time of many ancient folk customs in Wales. These were often connected with the *Gwrach* ("Hag") or the *Caseg Fedi* ("Harvest Mare"), an ornament made from the last tuft of grain to be harvested. Reaping hooks were skillfully cast toward the last sheaf, and whoever touched the sheaf cried out that they had gotten *"Gwrach, gwrach, gwrach!"* (A hag, a hag, a hag!), or else *"Pen medi bach mi ces!"* (I got a little harvest-mare!). Weave a small horse from straw and set it on your harvest altar. Make offerings of cakes, ale, and the first fruits of the harvest:

> O spirit of the corn,
> Hag of the harvest,
> Divine harvest mare,
> I honor you!
>
> She who transforms
> And nourishes,
> Goddess of the Earth,
> The fields, and the grain.
>
> I welcome you,
> And bid you farewell

> As you cycle through the year
> And bless us again!

> Sharynne NicMhacha

Notes:

September 3
Wednesday

 1st ♎
☽ → ♏ 4:02 pm

Color of the day: Brown
Incense of the day: Honeysuckle

Courage to Seek help Spell

We all suffer from feeling sad, and while we can boost ourselves through short down-periods, persistent depression needs medical treatment and emotional support. When you're so sad you know you're going to need help, give yourself the boost you need to ask. Take a bath scented with mints, and have a cinnamon incense or cinnamon-scented candle burning while you take the bath. Inhale it, and allow yourself to feel its energizing quality. After you've gotten out and dried off, don some red clothing; a red shirt will do just fine. It's important you be comfortable and feel you look good. Add a fresh energizing cologne. Look at yourself in the mirror, and see yourself as healthy, and a normal person reaching out with a normal need. Then pick up the phone and call a friend or a medical facility and ask for help.

Diana Rajchel

Notes:

and place them in a bowl in the center of your altar. Light two white candles. Run your fingers through the herb and say: "Lavender, lavender, bring us contentment." Repeat this until you feel your energy transfer to the herb. Pour one cup of boiling water over the enchanted sprigs, then cover the bowl as the herb steeps. When it has cooled, strain it and sprinkle drops of the infusion over those areas you've cleaned out. Visualize your life this autumn as a peaceful, happy time. Sprinkle the infusion over your discarded items. Visualize your possessions bringing happiness and use to their new owners.

Lily Gardner

Notes:

September 4
Thursday

1st ♏

Color of the day: Turquoise
Incense of the day: Nutmeg

Lavender Clearing Spell

This is a good time of year to go through your house, cleaning closets and ridding yourself of possessions that have outgrown their usefulness. Bag all those items that can be recycled or given away. Now, take several sprigs of lavender for purification

September 5
Friday

 1st ♏

Color of the day: Pink
Incense of the day: Thyme

Freya's Love Spell

Tonight you can combine the energies of the waxing Moon phase and the loving energies of a Friday (which is Freya's day and connected to Venus) in your spell work. This is the perfect opportunity to work a spell that draws romance and attraction into your life. It also boosts your own confidence as well. To begin, light a pink candle and repeat the charm:

> Rosy pink candle
> Burning warm and bright,
> Lend your magic to mine
> On Freya's night.

> May I walk in beauty
> Each and every day,
> Bring romance into my life
> In the best possible way.

Ellen Dugan

Notes:

September 6
Saturday

 1st ♏

☽ → ♐ 3:11 am

Color of the day: Blue
Incense of the day: Sage

A Day for Plaid

September always puts me in a "plaid" mood. Perhaps it is because, in all my elementary school years, I always wore plaid on the first day of school. The pattern of plaid also gives me comfort—the weave reminds me of interconnectedness. Why not celebrate with a picnic, indoors or outdoors, on a plaid blanket? Wear plaid. Lie on a plaid couch to read a book (maybe it has a plaid cover). Celebrate your plaid curtains. Do a bit of research and see if you have a clan tartan in your lineage—and learn the meaning behind it. Celebrate the pattern of the fabric as a symbol of the patterns in your life.

Cerridwen Iris Shea

Notes:

September 7
Sunday

 1st ♐
2nd quarter 10:04 am

Color of the day: Amber
Incense of the day: Eucalyptus

Altar of Light

The Sun is our ultimate source of light, and nothing captures this light quite as beautifully as crystals. To create an altar of sunlight, set up your items outside or near a sunny window. Use a table or even a box or bookshelf and arrange various crystals and stones that sparkle. Sit and meditate while gazing on the shimmering stones. For an evening altar, use candlelight. Arrange various candles so their light shines on crystals and makes them glow. Find candle holders carved from crystals or use colored glass as well. Meditate on the light and consider how we take light for granted and the power that the element of Fire has in our lives. Remember that light contains all colors and harness this ultimate healing light for your individual needs.

Ember

Notes:

September 8
Monday

 2nd ♐
☽ → ♑ 3:45 pm

Color of the day: Ivory
Incense of the day: Clary sage

Cider and Spice Protection Spell

In a small saucepan combine one cup of cider, one stick of cinnamon, and nine whole cloves. Heat until the mixture is warm and fragrant. Remove from the heat, let cool slightly, and stir clockwise while saying: "Cider strengthen me, cinnamon protect me, clove cleanse me." Pour the potion into an earthenware bowl. After dark, pour the mixture around the garden or home. Speak this charm:

> I have brewed this potion
> With my hand,
> To protect my home
> And my land.
> No dark spirits
> Shall dwell in this place,
> For I have blessed
> Every crevice and space.
>
> Any friend who comes,
> Night or day,
> Shall be welcomed
> To sit and stay.
> But no foe
> Shall darken my door,
> Today, tomorrow,
> Or forever more.

When you've finished, press the cinnamon stick and cloves into the earth.

James Kambos

Notes:

September 9
Tuesday

 2nd ♑

Color of the day: Maroon
Incense of the day: Cinnamon

Moving On Spell

Gather together things that represented you in the past. These could be old photos, favorite outdated clothes, etc. In an old trunk, place the items in one by one. Thank them for being part of you when needed, thank the person in the photo for being strong for the time. But now it is time for new beginnings. Close the trunk and say,

For the past is behind me
And the new way
In front of me.

Time to evolve,
Time to move on.

I thank the person I was
And I welcome the person
I am yet to be.

Store the trunk, but do not open it for at least one year. Then open it and have a remembrance evening, going through your old things. At this point you may wish to discard some, or add other things to the trunk. Remember that this trunk represents you, and respect it as you respect yourself.

Nancy Bennett

Notes:

September 10
Wednesday

2nd ♑

Color of the day: Topaz
Incense of the day: Bay laurel

Turquoise Wealth Charm

Many cultures have valued turquoise for its beauty and its properties of protection and attracting wealth. It can be used in several ways to draw prosperity into your life. Perform this rite a few days after the New Moon, when the crescent is visible in the sky. Avoid looking at the Moon until the proper time. Hold a piece of turquoise in your hand. Visualize your magical need—money—manifesting in your life. Move outside and gaze upon the Moon. Then directly shift your gaze to the turquoise. With that action, the spell has begun. Carry the stone with you until the money arrives.

Winter Wren

Notes:

thousands more forever changed. While the attacks struck terror into our hearts, it also brought us together as a country and a world as thousands poured time, efforts, and healing thoughts into New York, Pennsylvania, and Washington. Today should be a day of remembrance for the tragedies, heroics, and miracles of 9/11. On your altar or other safe place, light a pair of white candles. Then sit quietly, watching them burn, as you contemplate the positive changes brought about by such great tragedy. Visualize and focus on the world becoming a better place of tolerance for one another.

Laurel Reufner

Notes:

September 11
Thursday

 2nd ♑
☽ → ♒ 3:19 am

Color of the day: White
Incense of the day: Apricot

Remembrance Ritual

Today marks the seventh anniversary of the terrorist attacks on the United States, leaving more than three thousand people dead and

 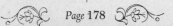

September 12
Friday

 2nd ♒

Color of the day: Rose
Incense of the day: Vanilla

Metal Elemental Spell

Chinese magical tradition recognizes five elements: earth, metal, wood, fire, and water. Metal relates to the colors gold and silver, the west, meticulous behavior, sense of smell, and spicy flavors or fragrances. Working with metal improves your relation with the elemental spirits of machinery. To commune with metal elementals, you'll need a fan and a stick of spicy incense such as cinnamon, clove, or sandalwood. You can work this in your car, near your computer, or near other important equipment, etc. Light the incense and waft the smoke around. Then say:

Little bright spirits,
Meticulous and steady,
Masters of metal,
Come hear my praises.

Without you,
Nothing would work.
You are essential.
You are everywhere.

Gears, springs,
Bearings, motherboards,
For this I give thanks.

Whenever you need to deal with machines, remember to treat them nicely; the metal elementals will remember you fondly and help everything go well.

Elizabeth Barrette

Notes:

September 13
Saturday

 2nd ♒
☽ → ♓ 12:04 pm

Color of the day: Gray
Incense of the day: Ivy

The Sweet Things in Life Spell

Today is Roald Dahl's birthday, author of *Charlie and the Chocolate Factory* and many other children's books. Sit down and get comfortable in your favorite chair or couch in your home. Cuddle up in a warm comforter or blanket; surround yourself with happy things. Have a warm mug of hot chocolate and a plate of chocolate cookies in your lap. Close your eyes and think of all

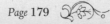

the sweet things in your life and send out wishes for your life to be filled with even more sweetness. Focus this warm, happy feeling and direct it into the mug of chocolate and the cookies. Slowly and deliberately, sip and savor the drink and eat the cookies.

> From the spirits
> I ask this favor,
> My sweet life
> I will savor.
>
> Bring me sweetness
> And delight
> As I eat chocolate
> Dark and light!
>
> As within, so without,
> So I will without doubt.

Be happy, and as you drink and eat, feel the energy infuse throughout your body and your life.

Gail Wood

Notes:

September 14
Sunday

2nd ♓

Color of the day: Orange
Incense of the day: Juniper

Spell for Wisdom from the Moon

Did you know that Full Moons last three days? All the documented effects of the Full Moon (from changes in the crime rate to changes in fish behavior) last from the day before Full until the day after Full. So today you can use Full Moon energy even though tomorrow is when the Moon is Full. Sit in a circle of white candles and light them in clockwise sequence. Hold up a mirror so that it catches candlelight and your face. If you are outdoors, catch moonlight in the mirror as well as (or instead of) candlelight. Feel moonlight rushing into the mirror, into your face. Ask the goddess to tell you your path for the next month. Receive her wisdom through the Moon. Meditate on what you receive. When ready, thank the goddess and let the candles burn down on their own.

Deborah Lipp

Notes:

 Page 180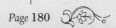

September 15
Monday

2nd ♓
Full **M**oon 5:13 am
) → ♈ 5:39 pm

Color of the day: Lavender
Incense of the day: Narcissus

Untangling Deception Spell

Today is mystery writer Agatha Christie's birthday (1890–1976). The Full Moon is a perfect time to seek clarity and untangle deception, either from others or from ourselves. Gather together a clear glass bowl or a silver metal bowl and ten yards or more of yarn in the color of your choice. Under the Full Moon, preferably outdoors, cast a circle and create sacred space in your preferred manner. Tangle—but don't knot—the yarn, while chanting, "In my life I perceive deception, tangled up and clouding perception." When the yarn is tangled but not knotted, place it in the bowl. With a deep breath, hold the bowl up to the Full Moon and ask, "O Mother Goddess, bright one. Illuminate my perception and bring me clarity." When you feel she's filled your bowl with her clear wisdom, lower it. Slowly remove the yarn by pulling one end and ensuring that it is removed as a single strand. Open your heart and mind to hear the wisdom that will come as you unwind the yarn. Thank the Moon goddess and close your circle as you are accustomed. Place the yarn on your altar for one Moon cycle and then burn it or bury it.

Gail Wood

Notes:

Holiday Lore: Keirou no Hi, or "Respect for the Aged Day," has been a national holiday in Japan since 1966. On this day, the Japanese show respect to elderly citizens, celebrate their longevity, and pray for their health. Although there are no traditional customs specifically associated with this day, cultural programs are usually held in various communities. School children draw pictures or make handicraft gifts for their grandparents and elderly family friends or neighbors. Some groups visit retirement or nursing homes to present gifts to residents.

September 16
Tuesday

 3rd ♈

Color of the day: Black
Incense of the day: Cedar

Misty Protection Charm

Celtic myths and folktales are full of stories about the power of mist. Those who are about to undergo an otherworld encounter often find themselves in an open landscape, suddenly surrounded by a magical mist. When the mist parts, they are in an unknown land, and frequently have interactions with gods or the spirits of the Sidhe (or fairy folk). Interestingly, the Gaelic word for mist, ceò, also means "amazement." If you find yourself in a misty landscape, use this charm to encourage and intensify a positive spiritual experience with the spirits who dwell in the mist:

> Spirits of mist, spirits of dew,
> I open my heart
> And soul to you.
>
> Gods of mist, gods of rain,
> I walk along
> This path again.
>
> Those who dwell
> Within this place
> I honor you
> And ask for peace.

> Gods and spirits of the mist,
> May this encounter
> Be truly blessed.

Sharynne NicMhacha

Notes:

September 17
Wednesday

3rd ♈
☽ → ♉ 8:56 pm

Color of the day: Yellow
Incense of the day: Lavender

Hildegard of Bingen

Hildegard of Bingen was an extraordinary woman of the twelfth century. She was a nun in Germany, a visionary, mystic, composer, poet, healer, and an herbalist. She was well-traveled and highly regarded by those in power during her time. Consider her words and meditate on them.

> I, the fiery life of divine wisdom, I ignite the beauty of the plains.
>
> I sparkle the waters, I burn in the Sun, and the Moon, and the stars.

*I am the breeze that nurtures
all things green.*

*I encourage blossoms to
flourish with ripening fruits.*

*I am led by the spirit to feed
the purest stream.*

*I am the rain coming from
the dew that causes the
grasses to laugh with the joy
of life.*

Ellen Dugan

Notes:

September 18
Thursday

 3rd ♉

Color of the day: Purple
Incense of the day: Carnation

Ritual Writing

The Autumn Equinox is a few days away. It's time to be thinking about putting together a ritual of celebration for Mabon. The first part of creating a ritual is to write a statement of purpose. This is to voice the intention of your rite and perhaps what you hope to accomplish. It can

be a dedication of sorts, or it can be an introduction that is as simple as a general welcome. You may choose to use astrological correspondences or simply describe the energy that is present at this time. Here is an example of what you might say as a possible statement of purpose for Mabon:

*The wheel turns once again.
It is Mabon, the Autumn
Equinox, and we stand in
reflection of our fruitfulness
this past year. What do we
have to be grateful for? As
the Earth moves into perfect
balance with the Sun and
the dark shadows light, we
ask our Lord who prepares
to leave the yellowing wood
and spiral into the caves
of Samhain, and our Lady
who's love is timeless, tho'
she prepares for the sleep of
winter, to let us embrace this
night with our understanding of beauty, grace, and
love. Allow these qualities of
Libra's equilibrium to infuse
each one of us so that we
may find our way as we move
quietly inward, toward the
twilight of Autumn's song.*

Igraine

Notes:

 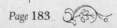

September 19
Friday

3rd ♉

☽ → ♊ 11:17 pm

Color of the day: White
Incense of the day: Yarrow

Banishing Old Memories Spell

Get a white cord or ribbon, a green fluorite bead, a cup of water, and an empty bowl. Pour the water into the bowl, saying "River of forgetfulness, wash me clean and bless me. Take away [name the specific memory] and leave my mind strong and clear." Dip the cord into the water, saying, "White of purity and innocence, renew me." Dip the bead into the water, saying, "Stone of perspective, clear my mind." Now concentrate on the memory, pouring it into the cord. The memory is gone from your mind and is now in the cord. Pour the water out on the ground. Put the bead on the cord. Wear the cord around your ankle or wrist until it falls off on its own. When the cord falls away, the memory will be completely gone.

Deborah Lipp

Notes:

September 20
Saturday

3rd ♊

Color of the day: Indigo
Incense of the day: Rue

Breaking Bonds

This is a spell for release. You may desire freedom from a particular attachment, a broken heart or bad relationship, financial burdens, a job, or even a bad habit. You will need a piece of twine or string, scissors, and a black or purple candle. Tie the ends of the cord together. As you tie the knot, visualize this bond as the controlling force from which you wish to break free. Name the bond aloud. Next, pick up the scissors. Imagine them as a sword you carry into battle. Pass them through the candle flame, envisioning the fire as your passion to be free, empowering the blades. Then, say the following:

> As the Moon wanes,
> Release this bond.
>
> As the candle expires,
> Release this bond.
>
> As I cut the cord,
> Release this bond.
>
> I am free.

Cut the cord, then bury it. Allow the candle to burn out.

Ember

Notes:

nion with all that is. Music and dancing make a traditional conclusion to the festivities.

Elizabeth Barrette

Notes:

September 21
Sunday

 3rd ♊

Color of the day: Yellow
Incense of the day: Heliotrope

Feast of the Divine Trinity

The ancient Greeks observed the rites of Eleusis, whose inner mysteries are lost to the mists of time. Yet fragments remain that can be used to reconstruct new rituals. This day was the feast of the divine trinity, honoring Demeter, Kore, and Iacchos. For this ritual, it's best to have three celebrants: an older woman for Demeter, a younger woman for Kore, and a man for Iacchos. Together they represent life, death, and rebirth. Bedeck the altar with flowers, golden apples, cider, and barley cakes. Iacchos the torchbearer should light golden candles, while Demeter and Koré share the bounty of food and cider in commu-

September 22
Monday

Mabon – Fall Equinox

3rd ♊
4th quarter 1:04 am
☽ → ♋ 1:48 am
☉ → ♎ 11:44 am

Color of the day: Gray
Incense of the day: Neroli

Preserving Our Resources

Mabon is the second harvest festival in the wheel of the year, an opportunity to say thanks once more for the bountiful harvest. The resources of our Earth are precious and finite. In this spirit, this date has been declared Car Free Day in many places in the world. Car Free Day events highlight the many problems caused by our dependence on the private automobile, including air pollution, global warming, stress, and safety issues. In honor of the harvest of the blessings of Mother Earth that sustain us in the year ahead, plan today to go about your life without the use of your vehicle. Consider taking public transportation, riding your bike, or walking as you tend to your day's schedule. Encourage the promotion of this as a community-wide event in your city as others have done around the world. Celebrate the Earth by giving back to her.

Winter Wren

Notes:

in a world of creation, and many of us are actively creative ourselves. We all have inherent creativity, whether we acknowledge it or not. Create an altar to Atum, giving thanks for all that is good in your world and your life. Create a song, a dance, a story, a painting, a poem. If you and your partner want to have a child, this is a good day to conceive one. Celebrate the creation around you by performing an act of creation yourself. Consider how to live your life as a constant act of positive creation.

Cerridwen Iris Shea

Notes:

September 23
Tuesday

 4th ☽

Color of the day: White
Incense of the day: Geranium

honor to Atum

Atum is the creator god in the Egyptian pantheon. He was conceived in Ptah's heart and is considered to be "perfection." We live

September 24
Wednesday

 4th ☽
☽ → ♌ 5:13 am

Color of the day: Brown
Incense of the day: Lilac

Spell for a Safe Journey

When Mercury turns retrograde, travel plans will often be changed or delayed. Smooth sailing is not to be expected. Petty aggra-

vations may be the worst of it, but be prepared to take a deep breath and go with the flow. Whether you are going on a short trip or a long journey, it is especially important at this time to protect yourself as everything goes awry. The magic of this simple rune spell will guide you safely to your destination. Create a runic talisman by cutting a circle out of red felt or construction paper. On one side, draw a six-pointed star or hexefus. This is an occult symbol of power, also known as a "Witch's foot." On the other side draw a capital R, the symbol for Rad. This is the rune of travelers, both in the astral and mundane worlds. Before you leave on your journey, tuck your talisman in a pocket and say:

> Hexefus protect me,
> By this rune direct me,
> As I roam o'er land and sea,
> Trusting you'll deliver me
> Safely to my destiny.
> So mote it be!

Igraine

Notes:

September 25
Thursday

 4th ♌

Color of the day: Green
Incense of the day: Mulberry

Time to Send a Message Spell

If you have a secret message you wish to send to someone, tonight is the night. First, light several candles or hurricane lamps in the room. Call upon the directions to aid you. Then write upon a piece of paper the secret you wish to pass on. Say:

> May you hear my words,
> Though unspoken.
> May this secret pass to you,
> Unbroken.
> Through dark of night,
> This secret shall be
> Revealed only between
> You and me."

Now fold the note and place it in a piece of dough or bread and roll it in tight. Leave it on your altar for the night and wait for the phone to ring. It will be someone who wishes to know your secret. Once this knowledge is passed safely, bury the message in your dough outside in your garden.

Nancy Bennett

Notes:

September 26
Friday

 4th ♌
☽ → ♍ 9:52 am

Color of the day: Purple
Incense of the day: Violet

Spell for Abundance

September 26 falls in the middle of the greater Eleusinian mysteries, a time honoring Demeter and Persephone. On this day, the holy basket of Demeter was paraded through the streets. On seeing the basket, people shouted, "Hail Demeter." The holy basket of Demeter contained sesame (for riches), carded wool (one's finished work), grains of salt (kinship), a serpent (resurrection), pomegranates (Persephone's fruit), reeds (a plant both fragile and flexible), ivy (healing and protection), and cake (prosperity). Build your own Demeter basket. You may want to substitute certain items in your basket, but try to have your substitutes correspond with the same attributes. Center your Demeter basket on your altar. Light a yellow-gold candle and pray to Demeter for good health and abundance throughout the year.

Lily Gardner

Notes:

September 27
Saturday

4th ♍

Color of the day: Blue
Incense of the day: Patchouli

Birdfeeder Blessing

With autumn comes harvest, especially of grains and seeds. Autumn is also the time when people start putting out birdfeeders to help wildlife get through the cold, hungry time to come. By leaving food for other creatures, we create an exchange of energy that strengthens the web of life and magic. Here is a blessing to say as you fill your feeder for the first time this season:

Autumn comes calling,
The winds of the fall
Stir up a hunger
In one and in all.

Fill up the feeder
With every good seed,
Those who are hungry
May find what they need.

Millet and sunflower,
Thistle and wheat,
Lay out a feast
For the winged ones to eat.

As I have given,
So let me receive,
Bounty in balance
For all that I leave.

Elizabeth Barrette

Notes:

Do you hear insects? Leaves blowing in the wind? Animals? Do you hear traffic rushing by, or sirens? See this all as a big circle, radiating out from where you live. What is your place in all of this movement?

Diana Rajchel

Notes:

September 28
Sunday

 4th ♏
☽ → ♎ 4:05 pm

Color of the day: Gold
Incense of the day: Marigold

Inner Divinity Spell

Some sense of the spiritual, and of our connection to the spiritual, adds meaning and purpose to our daily lives. You don't have to be a theist to wonder how we and everything we share Earth-space with got here. Taking that wonder into your daily life can give you a sense of creativity, awe, and responsibility. This spell is to help you connect to the mystery that is life. Go outside after dark, to a place where you are safe and where your neighbors won't be watching. Your own backyard, or an apartment courtyard or poolside, is fine. Close your eyes and listen closely to what's going on around you.

September 29
Monday

 4th ♎
New Moon 4:12 am

Color of the day: Silver
Incense of the day: Hyssop

Home and Hearth Spell

At this time of year our activities turn inward. And since this is a New Moon, it would be appropriate to renew our spirit and ready the home for the quiet months ahead. With the Sun in Libra, work to create a safe, cozy haven for you and your family. Seasonal decorations are a good place to start. Mums, pumpkins, squash, and Indian corn aren't just for looks—they'll charge your environment with fertility and prosperity. Scent the home with fragrant candles—apple, pumpkin pie spice, and cider scents are good choices. Bittersweet should be hung outside or inside, and it's an excellent addition to an autumn love spell. For some New Moon magic, try writing a wish on a red or orange maple leaf and then releasing it on the autumn wind. During this New Moon, don't forget to ready your property for the wild creatures you share your space with. Bird feeders should be cleaned and filled. Leave some corn for the squirrels. Doing these things now will keep our animal friends coming back. For a New Moon exercise, bless an orange candle. Light it and think of something you'd like to change in your home, or environment. Scry into the flame and your answer shall be found.

James Kambos

Notes:

September 30
Tuesday
Rosh hashanah

 1st ♎

Color of the day: Red
Incense of the day: Cinnamon

Atonement Spell

This is the time of Rosh Hashanah, the days of judgment and remembrance. It is a time of prayer in hopes that one is not found lacking on Yom Kippur, when they are judged on their actions of the past year. Light a purple candle, set a bowl of water before it, and sit watching the flame's reflection dance in the water. Try to judge yourself honestly, and see where some atonement of your own might need to take place. Make a mental note of the more pressing transgressions, vowing to abolish bad habits from your life and to make amends for the wrongs that have been committed. Take steps to forgive those who have made transgressions against you as well, lightening your karmic debt.

Laurel Reufner

Notes:

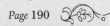

October is the tenth month of the year. Its name is derived from the Latin word meaning "eight," as it was the eighth month of the Roman calendar. Its astrological sign is Libra, the scales (September 23–October 23), a cardinal air sign ruled by Venus. The color comes quietly. Scarlet. Orange. Gold. Suddenly, every hill, neighborhood, and roadside is ablaze with color. Every color in the rainbow spills across the October landscape. It is pure magic. October skies are the bluest of the year, and in the distance the haunting cry of wild geese can be heard as they fly in V-formation, following an instinct as old as time. Every doorstep is decorated with signs of the season—pumpkins, mums, and friendly ghosts can be found in most neighborhoods. Soon the pumpkins are carved with fanciful faces and turned into jack-o'-lanterns. And we're reminded the Wiccan observance of Samhain, or Halloween, is at hand. Samhain is the last harvest festival of the year and a time to remember the spirits of the dead. Seasonal magic can include simply lighting a jack-o'-lantern to guide the way for visiting spirits. October's Full Moon, the Blood Moon, bathes the harvested fields with an amber light. The Blood Moon encourages us to honor our ancestors. It illuminates the gateway between the physical and spiritual worlds.

October 1
Wednesday

1st ♎
☽ → ♏ 12:26 am

Color of the day: Brown
Incense of the day: Marjoram

Faithful Lover Spell

Today traditionally celebrates Fides, the Roman goddess of faithfulness. Ask her help to strengthen a relationship. Take a picture of you, one of your beloved, and some red yarn. Place the pictures facing each other and say: "In our eyes we see the love that can be between each other." Wrap the red yarn round the pictures three times and say: "Tied to each other, our hearts are linked in faithful thoughts and actions." Place these in a white envelope and seal it. Draw a picture of an eye on the front. Say:

> Great Fides,
> Encourage the love inside,
> Faithfully it will grow.
> If not to be,
> Soon reveal to me,
> Through this all-seeing eye
> So that I will know.

Nancy Bennett

Notes:

Holiday lore: According to Shinto belief, during the month of October the gods gather to hold their annual convention. All of the *kami* converge on the great temple of Isumo in western Honshu, and there they relax, compare notes on crucial god business, and make decisions about humankind. At the end of this month, all over Japan, people make visits to their local Shinto shrines to welcome the regular resident gods back home. But until then, all through the month, the gods are missing—as a Japanese poet once wrote:

> The god is absent;
> the dead leaves are
> piling up,
> and all is deserted.

October 2
Thursday

Ramadan ends

1st ♏

Color of the day: Green
Incense of the day: Jasmine

Practical Giving

Today is Eid-al-Fitr, a holiday celebrated by Muslims at the end of Ramadan. This day is marked by a feast and gifts made to the poor. The nature of these gifts is highly practical, such as clothing, money, and food. To honor this day, choose an organization that assists the impoverished and give them a small but useful-to-them gift that you have endowed with the energy to bring about positive change in the world. If you are unable to sacrifice money, then light a white candle and kneel before it, seeing your own neighborhood or your own city becoming healthier, stronger, and safer. Once the candle is finished burning down, bury the wax in a park or other area near the part of the city you feel needs the most help.

Diana Rajchel

Notes:

October 3
Friday

 1st ♏
☽ → ♐ 11:14 am

Color of the day: Purple
Incense of the day: Mint

Tree Magic

Autumn is a perfect time to explore the beauty of the forest. Use this season of transformation and introspection to connect with the wisdom and power of the tree spirits, who display their inner fire at this time of the turning wheel. Once you have found a tree you feel deeply connected with, sit at the base of the tree and connect with your center of power. Envision yourself seated at the base of Ygdrassil, the world tree of the Norse, and repeat this charm to work with its power:

> Tree whose branches
> Reach Heaven and Earth,
> Tree of three roots,
> Supporting the ash.
> Beneath the third root
> In the land of frost
> The spring of wisdom
> And understanding.
>
> May my roots extend
> Into the Earth,
> May my branches reach
> Toward the skies,
> May the power of three
> Bless all I do,
> As I drink from the well,
> As I drink from the well.

Sharynne NicMhacha

Notes:

October 4
Saturday

1st ♐

Color of the day: Gray
Incense of the day: Magnolia

St. Francis' Day

St. Francis of Assisi wrote about praising the creator through "Brother Sun," "Sister Moon," and "Mother Earth," and about honoring the four sacred elements and the joy of rebirth. Use this day to pay homage to your deity through nature. Spend some time outdoors, feed the birds, go hiking, or simply meditate on the sacred qualities of the natural world and how each part is vital to our survival. Make an offering by setting out birdseed or planting a tree. Use this chant for meditation if you desire:

> Earth, air, fire, water,
> All unite to make a whole.
>
> Body, mind, heart, blood,
> Build the world and the soul.

Ember

Notes:

October 5
Sunday

1st ♐
☽ → ♑ 11:48 pm

Color of the day: Gold
Incense of the day: Almond

Gone Fishing Spell

Attach a comb to a piece of fishing line. Cast it onto the waters where you wish to fish and say:

> Sedna bring for me
> Gifts from the cold old Sea
>
> Make my line true
> To bring me good fish
>
> I comb your tangles
> And make this wish.

Run the comb attached to the line over the waters thrice. Sedna, an Arctic goddess of the Inuit, lives under the arctic waters. In early days shaman would make the dangerous journey into the cold waters to comb her hair and ensure a good harvest.

Nancy Bennett

Notes:

October 6
Monday

 1st ♑

Color of the day: Lavender
Incense of the day: Lily

Spell for Balance

Today celebrates Vishnu, the Hindu protector of creation and preserver of the cosmic order. It is said that Vishnu sleeps on the coils of the serpent-headed god, the universe unfolding from Vishnu's dream. When there's disorder in the universe, Vishnu awakens and battles the forces of chaos. Light a blue candle for Vishnu on your altar. Think about what is out of balance in your life. Perhaps you have too little time for creative pursuits or perhaps you need more money. Write your need on a slip of paper, then hollow out an unripe pumpkin and put your wish inside. This is the traditional means of asking a boon of Vishnu. When the pumpkin turns soft, thank the god and bury the pumpkin in the ground.

Lily Gardner

Notes:

October 7
Tuesday

 1st ♑
2nd quarter 5:04 am

Color of the day: Maroon
Incense of the day: Basil

A Magic Broom Spell

The Witches' broom is as much a part of the Craft as the pointed hat or cauldron. Once charged with magical intent, the Witches' broom, or besom, can serve many purposes. It can direct energy like a wand or athame. You can even cast a circle with it. And as we'll see here, it is perfect for protecting the home. First pluck three straws from your broom and light them like a candle. Carry them through your home like a smudge stick to clear out any negativity. For protection, sprinkle some salt near your front door, then sweep the salt away from your home. To bless a new home, anoint the tips of the bristles with a bit of honey and sweep your front porch. And if a grouch has just left your home, sprinkle some ground cloves at your front door, grab your trusty broom, and sweep his energy away.

James Kambos

Notes:

October 8
Wednesday

 2nd ♑

☽ → ♒ 12:03 pm

Color of the day: White
Incense of the day: Lavender

Your Tarot Avatar

Obtain your tarot avatar by doing the numerology on your birth date. Add together your month, date, and year of birth until you arrive at a number less than twenty-two (for example: 11/23/1977 = 1+1+2+3+1+9+7+7=31 = 3+1=4). Go through your favorite tarot deck and pull out the Major Arcana card that corresponds to the number you obtained. Study this card until you can picture it clearly with your eyes closed. Picture the card in your mind's eye and then blow up that image as though you were viewing it life-sized through a patio door. See yourself opening the door and walking out into the landscape of the card. Take your time. Explore this setting as completely as you wish. When you are ready, approach the main figure in the card respectfully and ask that he or she share with you messages about your life journey. Thank the figure for his or her assistance and return to your own world. Return to the card whenever you wish for further insight.

Winter Wren

Notes:

October 9
Thursday
Yom Kippur

 2nd ♒

Color of the day: Purple
Incense of the day: Balsam

Making Amends Spell

There are times when we know we've hurt another person and need to make it right, but for some reason, we cannot do it in person. Before doing this spell, make sure that there is no possible way to heal the hurt directly with an in-person conversation. Find a yard of colored ribbon appropriate to the person or the issue, and a bowl in which you can burn something safely. In a meditative state, focus your energy and thoughts on the issue and the person. Say what you would if you could be together with that person. When you are finished, place the ribbon on your altar along with the burning bowl. Cast a circle and call in the deities and spirits as you are accustomed. Hold the ribbon in your projective hand and say, "I acknowledge that harm has been done" and, starting with air, cleanse the ribbon with each element.

> By the power of air,
> Clear hurt away,
>
> By the power of fire,
> Burn hurt away,
>
> By the power of water,
> Wash hurt away,
>
> By the power of earth,
> Cleanse hurt away.

Place the ribbon in the bowl and burn it until it is ashes. Close your circle, thanking the spirits present. Put the ashes in running water so that the energy is dispersed.

Gail Wood

Notes:

October 10
Friday

 2nd ≈
) → ⟩⟨ 9:31 pm

Color of the day: Pink
Incense of the day: Cypress

Magical Mirror Confidence

If you have a mirror, you have a magical doorway into romance and confidence. But first, imagine that you are looking into a dirty old mirror with a rusty frame. You are dull and difficult to see. Imagine that you wash away all the dirt from the mirror and its frame. See that your reflection has cleared too. You look light and shining, beautiful and confident. Visualize yourself exactly as you have always dreamed of being. Now open your eyes and pick up your mirror. Anoint it with lavender or clove oil and say, "Mirror, mirror, I see me. I am god/dess, light and free." Keep the mirror covered with a pink or red cloth whenever you are not using it. Periodically, look in the mirror, calling to mind your clear and beautiful reflection. Repeat to yourself, "Mirror, mirror, I see me, I am god/dess, light and free."

Kristin Madden

Notes:

October 11
Saturday

 2nd ♓

Color of the day: Brown
Incense of the day: Pine

Thesmophoria

At this time, ancient Greeks celebrated the holiday of Thesmophoria. They honored women and women's rights, and performed rites at the temples of various goddesses, chiefly Demeter and Artemis. Holy women would dress in gowns of royal purple and red, then read aloud from sacred liturgies. Offerings of piglets were made at the shrine of Demeter, symbolically returning to her some of the bounty she bestowed on her people. Today is an ideal opportunity to work magic for women's rights. You might send energy to a woman who is running for office, or donate money to a women's organization. Hold a prayer circle for victims of domestic violence. Honor the Goddess as manifest in the women you know. Wear red and purple, and decorate your altar with flowers in those colors.

Elizabeth Barrette

Notes:

October 12
Sunday

2nd ♓

Color of the day: Amber
Incense of the day: Frankincense

Returning Object Spell

This spell will bring back something that is gone from your home, whether it was stolen, borrowed and not returned, or lost while you were out of the house. Make a drawing or model of your house out of paper, clay, balsa wood, or whatever you like. Create a floor plan in the model, and make sure the door in the model is open. Now make an image of the lost item in the same material. At your altar, ground and center. Sprinkle the images with vetivert. Consecrate the home model, saying, "This is my home." Consecrate the object, saying "This is _____."
Have "home" on one end of the altar, and the object on the other. Chant, "Coming home, coming home, coming home" with force and focus while walking the object toward home. Walk it right into the door and place it inside. Shout, "It is home! It is home! So mote it be!" The item will come back to you.

Deborah Lipp

Notes:

October 13
Monday
Columbus Day (observed)

 2nd ♓
$\mathcal{D} \rightarrow$ ♈ 3:07 am

Color of the day: Ivory
Incense of the day: Hyssop

Fresh Air Spell

This spell is to create a room-cleansing mist to cleanse a space of negative energy and create a positive atmosphere. Make a "tea bag" by adding equal parts of rosemary and sage to a piece of cheesecloth. Tie the bag and toss it into water that is just at the brink of boiling. Allow this infusion to steep until it's partially cooled. Remove the cheesecloth bag and pour the mixture into a clean spray bottle. Sprinkle in a few drops of peppermint and orange essential oil and add a sprig of dill and a pinch of sea salt. Place the bottle on your altar or a table and allow it to cool completely. If you wish, make a circle of quartz crystals around it and focus your intent on specific issues you wish to manifest. Spray the mixture into the air of any room you would like to freshen with positive energy.

Ember

Notes:

October 14
Tuesday
Sukkot begins

 2nd ♈
Full Moon 4:02 pm

Color of the day: Black
Incense of the day: Ylang-ylang

Hunter's Talisman

With the crops cleared, the deer, rabbits, pheasants, quail, and other animals are easy to see as they roam through the fields looking for food. Thus, the Full Moon after the Harvest Moon is called the Hunter's Moon. Other names include Blood Moon, Travel Moon, and Dying Grass Moon. Hunting for food is an ancient and honorable tradition, pitting the hunter's wits and skill against the prey's cunning and speed. Magic to aid hunting ranks among the oldest of human activities. This charm attracts prey within range. You need some cracked corn, and a talisman of leather, bone, antler, feather, etc. from the type of animal you wish to hunt. For the three nights of the full Hunter's Moon, go into the woods or fields and pour out a handful of corn. Hold the talisman in your dominant hand and say:

> As it was, it remains today:
> Death feeds life,
> And life honors death.

Come to me, my prey!
I will give you a good death,
And praise you
With my breath.

When you hunt, carry the talisman. If you don't hunt yourself, you may cast this spell for a friend.

Elizabeth Barrette

Notes:

Place the bag on your altar before a white candle. Light the candle and repeat three times:

As these words are spoken,
Bad luck is broken.

Bad luck will now flee;
From its influence I am free.

Bad luck goes out the door
And troubles me no more.

Leave the bag on the altar until the candle burns out naturally, then carry the bag near your heart for seven days.

Winter Wren

Notes:

October 15
Wednesday

 3rd ♈
☽ → ♉ 5:31 am

Color of the day: Topaz
Incense of the day: Bay laurel

Bad Luck Banishing

Sometimes, it seems that in spite of our best intentions and efforts, things just are not running in a positive manner. Often we attribute this to a run of bad luck—but the cycle can be broken. In a small draw-string pouch, place a couple of pinches of each of the following: angelica root, African ginger, fennel seed, holy thistle, clove, and basil. Add a small piece of citrine and secure the bag.

October 16
Thursday

 3rd ♉

Color of the day: White
Incense of the day: Mulberry

Feed the World Prayer

World Food Day was established in 1945 by the United Nations to create awareness of all the people worldwide who suffer from hunger each day. All over the globe, nations come together by hosting week-long events in observation of this special day. Our world has the means to feed us all, and yet hundreds of millions of people are chronically malnourished. Take a moment today to reflect and pray for abundance for all. Annapurna is the Hindu goddess of food. She is empowered with the ability to feed everyone who hungers. She also symbolizes the divine aspect of nourishing care. She carries a jeweled vessel containing food and a spoon to distribute it to those who are impoverished. Call her light into being today by saying this prayer:

> Annapurna,
> For those in need,
> Use your vessel
> To nourish and feed
> All who hunger
> In body and soul.
> Food for the world
> Is our ultimate goal.
> Blessed be!

Make your offering by committing a day this week to feed someone in need.

Igraine

Notes:

October 17
Friday

 3rd ♉
☽ → ♊ 6:25 am

Color of the day: Rose
Incense of the day: Alder

Feast of Sekhmet

Sekhmet is a ferocious, lion-headed goddess—part of a triad, along with Bast and Hathor. In one of her furies, she killed men who displeased her and drank their blood until the gods mixed it with enough wine to put her to sleep. When she awakened, she couldn't remember why she was so angry. In honor of Sekhmet, honor the positive aspects of controlled anger. Ask Sekhmet to guide you in channeling your anger for use in positive change, rather than lashing out at anyone causing harm. Drink a glass of red wine or a red non-alcoholic beverage in her honor.

Cerridwen Iris Shea

Notes:

October 18
Saturday

3rd ♊

Color of the day: Black
Incense of the day: Sandalwood

honoring Persephone

As the year turns to the darkest nights, we honor Persephone as she returns to her underworld kingdom. Forget images of a shy maiden tripping among the flowers: Persephone is both a strong and beautiful queen and a goddess. This is a woman in her sexual prime. Picture a young woman with long brown hair, who holds up a torch to help light your path in the darkest of times. Persephone can help you learn to mature with grace, to move forward, and to walk your own unique path in life.

> Persephone,
> Bringer of the seasons of life,
>
> Help me to move onward
> Without pain or strife.
>
> Hold up your torch,
> Help illuminate my path,
>
> Bring me courage
> And wisdom that lasts.

Ellen Dugan

Notes:

October 19
Sunday

3rd ♊
☽ → ♋ 7:40 am

Color of the day: Orange
Incense of the day: Hyacinth

Spell to Lose Weight

Do you have cravings for a particular food or drink that you know puts on the pounds? Using the repelling properties of garlic (I'm speaking magically here), this sure-fire spell works best during a waning Moon. Take a potato chip or a piece of cookie, or whatever the food is that causes your weight to soar, and bury it in your garden or at the bottom of a planter. Add soil. Say:

> Let garlic's magic radiate
> Repel, repel, don't hesitate
> I give it up
> And lose the weight!

Plant three cloves of garlic on top. Water as you would any plant. As the garlic grows, your cravings will lessen.

Lily Gardner

Notes:

 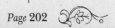

October 20
Monday
Sukkot ends

3rd ♋

Color of the day: Silver
Incense of the day: Rosemary

Safe Travel Spell

This is the last day commemorating Sukkot, a Jewish holiday in which many families honor their ancestors who came across the desert by constructing and staying in temporary dwellings. If it is not too cold, throw up a tent outside. Alternatively, construct an altar in a room you would not normally use, such as a garage. In either space, bring in things you would normally use to travel: a walking stick, a backpack, or even a set of car keys. Place them in the ritual space and say:

> In my future travels
> Let me be blessed
> By the strength of those
> Who have traveled before me.
>
> Allow me to be guided
> To a safe haven
> No matter
> How distant I am.
>
> Let the ancestors
> Infuse these tools
> So that I may always
> Return to my promised land.

This is a good day to plan trips, or organize your pictures of other adventures. Spend as much time as you can in this space today, and then take it down at night.

Nancy Bennett

Notes:

October 21
Tuesday

3rd ♋
4th quarter 7:54 am
☽ → ♌ 10:35 am

Color of the day: White
Incense of the day: Ginger

Protective Smoothie

For protection with an added antioxidant boost, make yourself a berry smoothie today. In a blender, mix half a cup of milk and four ounces of vanilla yogurt with one cup of frozen blackberries, blueberries, and raspberries. Throw in a small handful of ice and blend until smooth. As it blends, imagine a protective shield surrounding you, and try this chant to raise some extra energy.

Fruit of blue and
Red and black,
I ask you please
To watch my back.

Berries of the
Earth and Sun,
Bless me until
This day is done.

Drink deeply and feel the blessings of the sacred smoothie filling you, body, mind, and soul.

Kristin Madden

Notes:

senting an element, the fifth element being spirit or akasha. If you want to ensure that bad luck from this year does not follow you into next year, slice an apple cross-wise and see all of your bad luck going into the fruit. Take the fruit and throw it in a compost heap or bury it at the corner points of your property. As it rots, your bad luck rots away and is recycled into the ground. You may also take the seeds and plant them, each seed representing a wish you have for the coming year.

Diana Rajchel

Notes:

October 22
Wednesday

4th ♌
☉ → ♏ 9:08 pm

Color of the day: Yellow
Incense of the day: Honeysuckle

Bad Luck Banishing Spell

In the French Republic calendar, today is Pomme or Apple Day. This is a day to appreciate the harvest. The apple in particular is a magically useful fruit: when sliced cross-wise, the seed pattern forms a natural pentacle, each point repre-

October 23
Thursday

4th ♌
☽ → ♏ 3:40 pm

Color of the day: Crimson
Incense of the day: Clove

The Magic Cup

The chalice or cauldron is a powerful symbol of abundance, healing, and wisdom. The liquid within these sacred vessels possesses many magical attributes. The Welsh

poet-seer Taliesin received his gift of poetic inspiration from the cauldron of Cerridwen. The Irish hero Finn mac Cumhaill encountered some fairy women, and drops from their chalice fell into his mouth, giving him the gift of prophecy. This metaphor extends into the land, where hollowed stones gather rain or dew. At the source of the River Clyde in Scotland was a hollow stone filled with water, which was considered to be a magic cup:

> On Tintoch tap
>> there is a mist,
> And in that mist
>> there is a kist,
> And in that kist
>> there is a caup,
> And in that caup
>> there is a drap.
> Tak up that caup,
>> drink off the drap,
> And set the caup
>> on Tintoch tap.

Sharynne NicMhacha

Notes:

October 24
Friday

 4th ♏

Color of the day: White
Incense of the day: Rose

heal Your Cat Spell

This Friday night, tap into the loving energies of a Venus day and the tides of the waning Moon and work this spell for healing your beloved enchanted cat. Burn a green candle for Bast and a pink candle to invoke warm, fuzzy feelings and to represent the affection you feel for your kitty. Add a picture of your cat to rest between the candles, or just a few loose strands of cat hair (you know there are a few of those lying around—probably on your clothes). Once the candles are lit, hold your cat gently in your lap or arms, and repeat the charm.

> Cat-headed goddess Bast,
> Please hear my call,
>
> Send healing to my cat
> As the night falls.
>
> With the energies of
> Tonight's waning Moon,
>
> Banish sickness and injury,
> Bring health soon.

Ellen Dugan

Notes:

October 25
Saturday

 4th ♍
☽ → ♎ 10:47 pm

Color of the day: Blue
Incense of the day: Ivy

Conjuring the Muse

A muse can be a tricky thing to conjure when you need one. Try to summon some inspiration from yours with a few simple actions. First, clean your altar or sacred space. It's hard to be inspired when there is dust and excess clutter all over. Light your altar candles and a golden (or yellow) candle for inspiration. Invite your muse to visit you and sit in reflection for a few minutes, watching the flames flicker and dance. Then, go do something relaxing. Trust that your subconscious is working, and that when you return to your work you'll be newly energized and inspired.

Laurel Reufner

Notes:

October 26
Sunday

 4th ♎

Color of the day: Yellow
Incense of the day: Juniper

Spells for Protection

As we near the cold, dark days of winter, this is a good time to protect your household from theft, fire, and the demons of depression. Be sure you've cleared your house of disorder and unneeded possessions before you begin these spells. Make a garland of sprigs of marjoram and juniper boughs and hang it on your front door to protect you and yours from hostile spirits. A bunch of hazel twigs tied with a woman's hair will protect the house from fire. Keep this charm on your mantle if you have a fireplace, or in a cupboard by the stove if you don't. Prayers for safe-keeping can be written on bay leaves and thrown in the fire for further protection.

Lily Gardner

Notes:

October 27
Monday

 4th ♎
Color of the day: Gray
Incense of the day: Clary sage

Substitution Charm

Yarrow is an all-purpose blooming herb. It is an easy perennial to grow in direct Sun and a wonderful addition to any Witch's garden. I often think of yarrow as the herbal equivalent to the white, all-purpose spell candle. Yarrow may be used in an emergency to substitute for any other magical herbs in your spell work. Just use the dried yarrow blooms instead, and then repeat the following herbal spell substitution charm. Please note: this information is for herbal charms and spells only. This information is not intended to treat any medical issues.

> *Yarrow is the magical*
> *All-purpose herb,*
>
> *Elements four gather 'round*
> *And hear my words.*
>
> *Switch one herb for another,*
> *It will work out fine,*
>
> *I seal this magic up*
> *With the sound of a rhyme.*

Ellen Dugan

Notes:

October 28
Tuesday

4th ♎
☽ → ♏ 7:47 am
New Moon 7:14 pm

Color of the day: Red
Incense of the day: Cedar

Diwali

Diwali is the Hindu "Festival of Lights," and India's most important holiday. Because it is calculated by the lunar Hindu calendar, it falls on different days each year. Gifts are exchanged on Diwali—often sweets or candles or candleholders. The home is decorated and oil lamps are lit. Fireworks are common. It is a joyous celebration focused on family, good fortune, and hope for the future. The first day of this five-day celebration, the home is lined with oil lamps and marigolds, and prayers and sweets are offered for long life and to ward off early death. The offering should be made near a sacred tree. In Bengal, Diwali is the festival of Kali Puja, when Ma Kali, the fierce mother goddess of death and rebirth, is worshipped. Kali worship is sometimes reserved for the second day of Diwali. In other parts of India, the focus of Diwali is Lakshmi or Krishna. The fourth day of Diwali is the Hindu New Year. Regional variations let us know, as Westerners, that it's okay to celebrate light and deity in whatever form we choose during this sacred time, as long as we enjoy ourselves. May our lights shine brightly!

Deborah Lipp

Notes:

October 29
Wednesday

1st ♏

Color of the day: Brown
Incense of the day: Lilac

The Call of Wild Hunt

On windy moonlit autumn nights, when clouds scud across the sky, the Wild Hunt can be heard. The Wild Hunt is a ghostly cavalcade of spirits, led by the lord of the shadows as they ride from the otherworld to carry back the souls of the newly departed. As recently as the mid-twentieth century this phenomenon was reported in England. If you should be alone on such a night, light a candle and intone the following words:

> Riding on the night wind,
> Free and unreined

The riders of the Wild Hunt
Ride untamed.

The hunting horn
Sounds its blast,
A hundred stallions
Thunder past,
Stars gather
In their flowing manes.

As the door to the
Otherworld opens again,
Carrying spirits
Of those who've come before,
And those whispered about
In secret lore,
The huntsmen rush
Through the shadow of trees,
Leaving their message
On the autumn breeze.

They turn the cosmic
Wheel of fate,
For they are the keepers
Of the gate.

James Kambos

Notes:

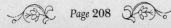

Holiday lore: Many villages in the English countryside share the tradition of "lost-in-the-dark bells." Legend tells of a person lost in the dark or fog, heading for disaster, who at the last moment was guided to safety by the sound of church bells. The lucky and grateful survivor always leaves money in his or her will for the preservation of the bells. This day commemorates one particular such case, a man named Pecket in the village of Kidderminster, in Worcestershire, who was saved from plummeting over a ravine by the bells of the local church of St. Mary's. In honor of this event, the bells still ring every October 29.

to destruction. In older times the mischief was harmless, and merry-making was in celebration of the harvest and anticipation of winter. To reclaim the harmless merry-making, sense of mischief, and good cheer, go into a meditative state. You find yourself in a clearing at the edge of a forest at night-time. There is a big bonfire and people are dancing all around it, laughing and having a good time. You can hear drums, fiddle music, and singing. The rhythm catches you and you feel a song well up inside you. You begin to sing along, and one of the dancers reaches out and pulls you into the dance. You enter wholeheartedly into the frenzy. Finally the music slows and you walk slowly up the path, singing your song. Breathe deep and return to the here and now.

Gail Wood

Notes:

October 30
Thursday

 1st ♏

☽ → ♐ 6:41 pm

Color of the day: Turquoise
Incense of the day: Myrrh

Merry Mischief Meditation

Today is known as Devil's Night or Mischief Night. In many cities in recent times, harmless mischief has unfortunately escalated

October 31
Friday
halloween ~ Samhain

 1st ♐

Color of the day: Coral
Incense of the day: Orchid

Samhain Dedication

Golden leaves curl and crackle, falling, baring skeleton trees. We can hear the geese call like the horns of Herne, beckoning us back home. We feel our bones, raw and fragile. The chill night air reminds us of where we have been before. We return to death's door, remembering where we came from, reentering Gaia's womb. The ancient ones call to us. They tell us the Earth is magic. Our bodies are rooted here, entwined in time yet reaching skyward, seeking the one sacred source that radiates from the invisible world, a world of whispers. Words, images, symbols come softly, freely, and awaken our senses. They beckon us. We are of the old craft and we know where our magic lies—between space and time, connecting both worlds, seeing, unseeing. Tonight we celebrate Samhain. Illusion fades as we enter the gateway into the Witches' world. As above, so below; as within, so without; as the universe, so the soul. We see the one power in the phases of the Moon. We see the one power in the heat of the Sun. Together they represent our heavenly parents; the Goddess and the God; Queen of the darkness and Father of the light. In many names and guises they reveal themselves to us. Tonight we will don the mask of a chosen one and align ourselves with that deity in perfect love and perfect trust.

State the god or goddess that you wish to dedicate yourself to for this coming year. Place a white, black, or red mask on your face as you say the name and light a votive in his or her honor. Playing trance music, journey with your chosen deity. Journal the messages you receive.

Igraine

Notes:

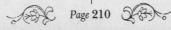

November is the eleventh month of the year. Its name is derived from the Latin word for "nine," as it was the ninth month of the Roman calendar. Its astrological sign is Scorpio, the scorpion (October 23–November 23), a fixed water sign ruled by Pluto. November is a month of quiet beauty. The colors of autumn have faded and fallen leaves crunch underfoot. The wild grasses have been bleached a tawny color and rustle in the breeze. But beneath the bareness there is promise: if you look closely at the bare branches, they are covered with next year's buds. November teaches us there is a tomorrow. The season's first fires glow on the hearth and firewood is stacked by the door. A good magical activity for a November night is to write a request on a piece of paper using soot from a previous fire, then burn it. Meditate on your wish as the paper burns. At Thanksgiving we gather family and friends and celebrate what we have to be grateful for. To appreciate the magic of a November night, one should walk beneath November's Full Moon, the Frost Moon. The sky, no longer obscured by a canopy of leaves, is open. Stars glitter. These are the same stars our most ancient ancestors gazed at in wonder. November nights are a time to contemplate the great mysteries—the Earth, stars, wind, and our place in the cosmos.

November 1
Saturday

Day of the Dead – All Saints' Day

 1st ♐

Color of the day: Indigo
Incense of the day: Sage

Contact Your Ancestors

This All Saints' Day ritual will allow you to contact a departed ancestor. Upon your altar spread a plain black cloth and set a magic mirror. Behind the mirror light three candles—one white, one yellow, and one silver. Begin by saying, "Let me see a face from the past, as I gaze into this looking glass." Softly call the name of the person you are looking for. You may see or feel a presence. Ask questions if you wish. If the contact should fade or you want to end it, purify the mirror by anointing your finger with salt water, then making the shape of a pentagram before the mirror. Thank the spirit and, taking your white candle, lead the spirit's presence into your kitchen where you've set a bit of their favorite food. Bid them farewell by saying, "In peace you came, in peace be gone. So mote it be." Snuff out the candles.

James Kambos

Notes:

Holiday lore: The time between sundown on Samhain to sundown today, the Day of the Dead, was considered a transition time, or "thin place," in Celtic lore. It was a time between the worlds when deep insights could pass more easily to those open to them. Through the portals could also pass beings of wisdom, of play, and of fun. And while in time these beings took on a feeling of otherness and evil, as our modern relationship between the realms has been muddled, today can be a day to tap into the magic and wonder of other worlds.

November 2
Sunday

Daylight Saving Time ends 2 am

 1st ♐
☽ → ♑ 6:13 am

Color of the day: Yellow
Incense of the day: Hyacinth

Sun Shining Spell

Today is Sunday, which of course is ruled by the Sun. This is an auspicious time for matters of fame

and success—an ideal day to ask for a promotion, submit a manuscript for publication, or volunteer for a public ritual. Here is a little spell to help you shine. You will need two gold or yellow candles and a ring symbolizing the Sun. Amber, sunstone, an Eye of Ra, or a Sun-face ring would be ideal. Light the candles and hold the ring between them, saying:

> Sun in glory,
> Star of day,
> Fill me with your
> Golden ray.
> Fame-bright god of
> Light divine,
> Bless me now
> And make me shine!

Visualize yourself glowing with energy. Let the candles burn down on their own, if practical. Wear the ring, and people will be drawn to bask in your glory.

Elizabeth Barrette

Notes:

November 3
Monday

 1st ♑

Color of the day: Silver
Incense of the day: Neroli

A Ritual for Success

These are the early days of the Witches' New Year, which was celebrated at Samhain. If you missed an opportunity to consider your plans and resolutions for this coming year, you still have time. Let this be a Moon of claiming three goals that you want to achieve before year's end. Begin by stating: "In the cauldron of Cerridwen, I will work in preparation and manifestation toward the successful outcome of my present aspirations. Tonight I ask the goddess Cerridwen to bless this rite and join me in reflection."

> Old one, sage crone, keeper
> of the cauldron, I ask to stir
> your magic brew tonight
> for inspiration! The les-
> sons I have learned through
> the shift of time and space
> change the shape of things
> to come with each turning of
> the season. The wisdom of
> the universe can be mine for
> the claiming. I need only mix
> the magic for the potion to
> find sight.

Three drops of grace shall
pass my lips. Require me to
name them, enlightened by
this moonlit night and your
dark prophecy.

Sit in silence and meditate briefly.
Then ask yourself, what are the
three most important tasks that you
need to accomplish successfully this
year? When you have the answers,
state them clearly aloud and then
write them down in your journal
or book of shadows. Then say:
"Cerridwen, in the naming of these
three aspirations at this waxing Moon
in Capricorn, I pledge a year and a day
to keep my focus alive in order that I
may achieve my goals. My affirmation
will be 'Success comes easily to me.'"

Igraine

Notes:

November 4
Tuesday
Election Day

 1st ♑
☽ → ♒ 7:01 pm

Color of the day: Maroon
Incense of the day: Cinnamon

Hearth and Home Blessing

A spell to bless your hearth and
home. As the colder days begin,
we turn our focus on the inside of
our homes. Try this cozy spell to
protect and bless your home. This
spell calls on Vesta, the Greco-
Roman goddess of the hearth flame.
For this spell you will need one red
cinnamon-scented candle in a coordi-
nating holder. The color red is sacred
to Vesta, and the cinnamon will promote protection and prosperity. Light
the candle and say:

I call on Vesta,
Goddess of the hearth flame,

You bring hope and peace
To those who call your name.

With your loving presence
This house surround,

Only good luck, joy,
And wealth will be found.

Ellen Dugan

Notes:

November 5
Wednesday

 1st ≈

2nd quarter 11:03 pm

Color of the day: Topaz
Incense of the day: Lilac

Travel Talisman

Gather all or any combination of the following dried herbs and flowers: rose petal, lilac, foxglove, devil's shoestring, wormwood, orris root, and witch hazel. In the morning if possible, facing east, place a moonstone or piece of turquoise in a white pouch and add the herbs. Visualize a safe and pleasant journey and a joyful return home as you tie the pouch closed with a ribbon or string, making three knots. Repeat the following each time you tie the string: "Safe journey, safe return, so mote it be." Carry this talisman when you travel.

Ember

Notes:

November 6
Thursday

 2nd ≈

Color of the day: Green
Incense of the day: Carnation

Prosperity Spell

Draw money your way using Luna's light. You'll need a way of burning incense over a bowl of water (the bowl doesn't need to be very big). Add some spring water and drop in a few silver coins. Sit the bowl in a spot where it can catch the moonlight. Arrange your burner and light a stick of your favorite spicy incense. As the incense burns, think of Luna's light charging the water and coins with increased prosperity. Leave it all sit overnight. Afterward, carry the coins with you.

Laurel Reufner

Notes:

November 7
Friday

2nd ≈

☽ → ♓ 5:43 am

Color of the day: White
Incense of the day: Vanilla

Kitchen Witchery

Call upon the fairies to assist you with this Kitchen Witch spell. Ask them to spark your imagination and help you to divine what's in store for you in the coming weeks. Wee Witches will enjoy conjuring up this spell with you too! Dream up twelve possible fortunes that you would like to befall you in the very near future. These can be as diverse as "fall desperately in love" to "get a raise at work" to maybe "find hidden treasure." On thin strips of parchment paper, write these twelve fortunes with a non-toxic silver marker. Stir up a batch of brownies, muffins or cookies and slip a fortune into each square or piece. As you put your pastries in the oven, chant this incantation:

> In the realm of elf and fairy,
> Aid me on my way.
> Tell me if I am to marry.
> Will I win today?
>
> Promise me
> The Sun and Moon,
> Show me what's in store,

> Let good fortune
> Find me soon,
> Divine what I ask for.

When your brownies are ready to eat, pick just one. Open the parchment. Your fortune is told!

Igraine

Notes:

November 8
Saturday

2nd ♓

Color of the day: Brown
Incense of the day: Rue

In Memory of Kings

Just after Samhain, the time is ripe for spooky incidents. While a few may look forward to an encounter, our forebears did not. To spy the Wild Hunt, or angry Sidhe, or even departed loved ones in the new season was viewed as a bad omen for the coming year. To protect themselves after having such encounters, some people would request a special Christian mass, sprinkle salt on their doorways, and recite incantations. While such incidents aren't heard of much these days, in the event that you see a wild ride thundering

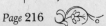

through the woods some night, get yourself home as quickly as you can. With chalk, draw a five-pointed star, point upwards, on the doors and windows, saying:

> I do not ride with the
>   horse and scythe,
> I do not ride in the woods.
> I stay behind, by the fireside,
> And tend my business inside.

Diana Rajchel

Notes:

thin hair, add three tablespoons of warm honey. Put a picture of someone with great hair near the sink. Plunge your athame or wand into the hair recipe, visualizing beauty and good health. Say, "Healthy, growing, strong!" Using your hands, coat your hair with the consecrated mixture, repeating "Healthy, growing, strong!" over and over as you do so. Keep visualizing! Wrap your hair in a warm towel or plastic wrap for fifteen minutes. Continue to visualize and repeat your hair mantra, gazing at a candle or the picture you selected. Then wash your hair as usual.

Deborah Lipp

Notes:

November 9
Sunday

 2nd ♓
☽ → ♈ 12:26 pm

Color of the day: Orange
Incense of the day: Heliotrope

Spell for healthy hair

Bad hair days are a minor problem, but they can be an embarrassment and a cause for low-level stress that adds up. Set up at your bathroom sink. Warm half a cup of sweet almond oil. For normal hair, add half a cup of warm rose water. For dry hair, make a tea of dried rosemary leaves and add half a cup. For

November 10
Monday

 2nd ♈

Color of the day: Ivory
Incense of the day: Lily

Animal Invocation

In Celtic tradition, animals associated with the underworld were thought to have special magical or healing attributes. This was true for animals who dwelt under the Earth and in bodies of water that originated underground. Holy wells in Ireland sometimes contained a salmon, trout, or eel that was considered extremely sacred and gave the well its power. In Scotland, serpents were associated with healing, transformation, and wisdom because of their ability to shed their skin, and their connection with the underworld. Fill a cauldron with spring water and repeat this spell to connect with the power of these magical creatures:

> I dip my spirit into the well,
> The well of wisdom and
>   transformation,
> The transformation of soil
>   and water,
> The waters that flow beneath
>   the Earth,
> The Earth that holds the
>   mysteries,
> The mysteries of serpent and
>   salmon.
> Salmon of wisdom I call
>   to you
> As I dip my soul into
>   the well.

Sharynne NicMhacha

Notes:

November 11
Tuesday
Veterans Day

 2nd ♈
☽ → ♉ 3:05 pm

Color of the day: White
Incense of the day: Bayberry

Veterans Day Reverence

No one in his right mind wants or likes war. As Pagans, even Warrior Pagans, many of us are actively against the needless wars driven by greed. Those with ideology are sacrificed so others can profit. However, we must still respect and honor those who have gone to fight, deeply believing and caring about the freedoms and lives of so many people they've never met. Take the time to go to your town's honoring ceremony today. Even if you disagree with your city, state, and federal officials, Veterans Day ceremonies are moving and reverential. Light a candle for all those veterans, all over the world, who gave of themselves, physically and emotionally.

Cerridwen Iris Shea

Notes:

Historical lore: Veterans Day commemorates the armistice that ended the Great War in 1918. Oddly, this war ended on this day, November 11, at 11 am (the 11th hour of the 11th day of the 11th month). Though Congress changed Veterans Day to another date in October at one point during this century, in 1968 they returned the holiday to November 11, where it stands today. The number 11 is significant. In numerology, it is one of the master numbers that cannot be reduced. The number 11 life path has the connotation of illumination and is associated with spiritual awareness and idealism—particularly regarding humanity. It makes sense then that this collection of 11s commemorates the end of an event that was hoped to be the War to End All Wars. Unfortunately, it wasn't the last such great war, but we can at least set aside this day to ruminate on notions of peace to humankind.

November 12
Wednesday

 2nd ♉

Color of the day: Yellow
Incense of the day: Lavender

Bathroom Break

Travel can be so stressful. Even a simple commute to work can leave you tight and angry. Rather than reaching for a cup of coffee to make you feel better, head for the bathroom. Take a seat in a private stall and lock the door. Then breathe. Notice how you are breathing and then allow it to slow down until you are inhaling to a count of four and exhaling to a count of four. Feel your body relax. Tense and relax your scalp, your lips, your shoulders, and move down through your body until you no longer feel any stress anywhere. And then if you decide to have that coffee, make it a café mocha and fully appreciate the blessings of chocolate.

Kristin Madden

Notes:

November 13
Thursday

 2nd ♉
Full Moon 1:17 am
☽ → ♊ 3:11 pm

Color of the day: Crimson
Incense of the day: Apricot

A Frost Moon Spell

November's Full Moon, the Frost Moon, beckons us to look deep within. Occurring during the month when the Sun is in Scorpio, the Frost Moon is a potent time to look beyond the obvious. Nature seems to be dying. Dry leaves click as they skitter along country lanes and suburban streets. And during the chilly nights, the ebony darkness is pierced by the eerie sound of a hooting owl. But take a closer look and you'll see nature is only resting. Tree branches are covered with buds containing next year's flower and leaf. In the following spell take advantage of this transitional period to set your goals for the future in motion. Cut three bud-covered tree branches and tie them together with green ribbon. After dark, stand outdoors beneath the Frost Moon. Carry with you the bundle of branches and a silver coin: they symbolize growth and success. Looking at the Moon, speak your most secret wish. With deep reverence raise the coin and branches and speak this charm:

*All nature is still,
But as the world retreats into darkness
My wish will be nurtured,
And eventually fulfilled.*

Keep your coin and branches until the spell does its work.

James Kambos

Notes:

November 14
Friday

 3rd ♊
Color of the day: Rose
Incense of the day: Rose

Spell for Learning

Sometimes we find that it is difficult to take new knowledge into our minds. The Greek goddess of wisdom, Athena, may provide aid in this task. Place a piece of polished tiger's-eye to the right of a yellow candle on your altar. Light the yellow candle. Write this chant on a piece of parchment as you read it aloud:

*Hail, Athena! Come forth
to fill my mind with your
wisdom bright. Help me to
keep my mind alert and clear,*

knowing that learning is nothing to fear. With your wisdom, I ask, make my mind keen, and make my studies stay with and enlighten me for years to come.

Fold the paper seven times and set it aflame in your burning dish. Gather the ashes and scatter them outdoors. Let the candle burn and charge the stone while you study. Keep the stone with you when you need to write papers, take exams, or study.

Winter Wren

Notes:

November 15
Saturday

 3rd ♊

☽ → ♋ 2:52 pm

Color of the day: Blue
Incense of the day: Patchouli

Sweep It Away Spell

Let's clean house! This is the perfect time to banish negativity, clean up any stray vibes from old spells, and to remove junk and clutter that has accumulated. We have the energies of a waning Moon and the daily planetary energies of Saturn to work with here, so let's get to it. To begin, burn your favorite cleansing incense while you physically dust, sweep, vacuum, and pick up. Then light a white candle and place it in the center of your home. Now repeat the spell verse:

> By the power of Saturn's day
> And the closing week,
>
> All negative energy and
> Bad vibes now must leave.
>
> Depart old spells
> And stray worn-out charms,
>
> Now dissolve benignly
> And cause no harm.
>
> By all the power
> Of hearth and home,
>
> This house is cleared
> As my charm is sung!

Move the candle to a safe place and let it burn out.

Ellen Dugan

Notes:

 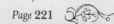

November 16
Sunday

3rd ♋

Color of the day: Amber
Incense of the day: Marigold

Sunday Spell for Success

Gather together stones that represent the Sun or the element of fire. Find pieces of clear quartz, shimmering pyrite, citrine and amber, even copper or gold jewelry. Arrange your combination of stones and gems around a cluster of yellow and white candles on a glass plate. Draw on the power of the Sun for success in any endeavor you are pursuing. This could be related to a job, school, sporting event, or even a relationship. As you light the candles, recite these words:

> May this journey I'm on
> Be blessed,
> With pleasure, goodwill,
> And success.
>
> May good fortune
> Look upon my work,
> And guide my efforts
> Without hurt.
>
> Let achievements
> Come to me,
> For the good of all,
> So mote it be.

Ember

Notes:

November 17
Monday

3rd ♋
☽ → ♌ 4:07 pm

Color of the day: Lavender
Incense of the day: Narcissus

Spell for Religious Tolerance

Queen Elizabeth I gained the throne on this day in 1558. As power shifted from the Catholic Mary to the Protestant Elizabeth, a new wave of religious persecution began. Sound familiar? Begin your spell by lighting one white and two blue candles. These candles symbolize the three monotheistic religions, the Christian, Muslim, and Jewish faiths. Include on your altar pictures of religious and political leaders you feel need more tolerance. Hold each picture, one at a time, and visualize that person at peace. Visualize that person tolerant of other peoples' beliefs. The Buddha said:

> All we experience is preceded
> by mind, led by mind, made

*by mind. Speak or act with a
peaceful mind and happiness
follows like a shadow that
never leaves.*

Lily Gardner

Notes:

one item that someone else has put
down. Here is a chant to sing while
loading and unloading the blanket:

*Give meaning to
The life you live.
We are all
Just passing through,
Giving what we have to give,
You to me and me to you.*

Elizabeth Barrette

Notes:

November 18
Tuesday

3rd ♌

Color of the day: Red
Incense of the day: Geranium

Grateful Giving

Autumn is a time of being grateful for what we have. But it's
easy to get too caught up in having
and forget about the magic of giving—especially in a culture that
encourages consumerism instead of
consciousness. Gift-giving is a beautiful way to strengthen the bonds
of friendship and family, weaving a
community together. For this bit
of magic, you'll need a blanket and
several other people. People should
bring one or more items they no
longer need, but that are still appealing. For every item you put on the
blanket to give away, you may take

November 19
Wednesday

3rd ♌
4th quarter 4:31 pm
☽ → ♍ 8:12 pm

Color of the day: White
Incense of the day: Marjoram

Magical Cleaning

It stands to reason that our magical
tools should be cleansed periodically, and the waning Moon is the
best time for that task. Gather up
your tools and place them on a clean
cloth away from your altar. Assemble
a bowl of salt water, a burning
smudge incense blend, a smudging

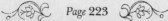

feather or fan, some clean cloths and a white candle. Light the white candle and invoke your guardians. Begin a methodic cleaning of your tools, wiping down with salt water those that can be exposed to water without harm, and then passing them through the smoke from the smudge while focusing on clearing and cleansing them from unnecessary influences. For items that cannot get wet, pass them three times through the smoke from the smudge or hold them near to the smoke while directing it with the feather or the fan. Thank your guardians and return your tools to their proper places.

Winter Wren

Notes:

is a great spell inspired by the north. Before you leave, find a quiet spot near the house. Using several flat stones, construct an Inukshuk—a human form made from rocks in Inuit tradition. (Don't be afraid to use glue if you're concerned about it toppling.) Walking in front of it, touch your third eye and then touch the headlike part of the statue. Chant:

> Ever watching am I.
> Ever in your hearts, am I.
> Till my return, stone
>   Inukshuk,
> Stand strong like my love.

A smaller version of this statue can be constructed for inside an apartment or given as a gift to a child who will miss you. It can even be given as a going-away present.

Nancy Bennett

Notes:

November 20
Thursday

  4th ♏

Color of the day: Turquoise
Incense of the day: Nutmeg

Remember Me Spell

If you are planning a move or a vacation and want to be remembered by those you leave behind, here

November 21
Friday

 4th ♏
☉ → ♐ 5:44 pm

Color of the day: Pink
Incense of the day: Yarrow

healthy Skin Magic

Both men and women can look their best every day with some healthy skin care. Throw in a little magic and you are ready for anything! To keep your skin healthy and glowing, mix half a cup of oatmeal and half a cup of water to form a paste. Add three teaspoons of milk and one tablespoon of honey. Apply to your face. As it dries, feel the cleansing and tightening of the paste. Visualize yourself healthy and radiant. Then wash it off with warm water. After this deep cleaning, tone your skin with a rosewater splash: blend three cups witch hazel, two tablespoons rose oil (for dry skin) or half a cup dried rose petals (for oily skin), and one teaspoon of rosemary or lavender. As you mix, visualize yourself refreshed and youthful. Strain out the herbs and splash it on your face.

Kristin Madden

Notes:

November 22
Saturday

4th ♏
☽ → ♎ 3:20 am

Color of the day: Black
Incense of the day: Ivy

Be here Now Spell

On this day in 1963, President John F. Kennedy was assassinated in Dallas, Texas. Most Americans alive at the time can say where they were when they heard the announcement. When it is important to pay attention and be fully present in your life every moment, place sandalwood incense, patchouli oil, a brown or white candle, and a small bowl of soil from a garden or natural outdoor space on your altar. Call in your deities and light the incense while grounding your energies with Mother Earth. Light the candle and focus your attention on the flame, asking for focus. Take the bowl of soil and lift it up to the universe and chant:

> By the wisdom
> Of this dark soil,
> When distracted
> By my life of toil,
> Freedom from distraction
> Is my vow.
>
> I will be here now!
> I will be here now!

Anoint your body in a star shape, saying "be here now" with each step: left foot, right hand, left hand, right foot and forehead. Extinguish the candle and thank spirit. Later, when you feel yourself distracted, whisper "I will be here now" to yourself.

Gail Wood

Notes:

stores. Allow it to steep until the tea glows with a rich honey-gold. Inhale the jasmine-scented steam, and allow the scent to fill you while you concentrate on breathing the jasmine into the areas of your body that carry the most tension. Once you feel your body releasing that tension, drink the tea, savoring each sip. Then go out and face the crazy situation at hand, carrying the calm of the jasmine tea with you.

Diana Rajchel

Notes:

November 23
Sunday

 4th ♎

Color of the day: Gold
Incense of the day: Eucalyptus

Stress Banishing

It's only normal to look at the coming Yule season with a sense of dread and an intense desire for aspirin. The holidays consistently poll as the most stressful time of year. Rather than letting family squabbles and work rushes make you crazy, take the bite out of stress with this small spell. Boil yourself some jasmine tea; you can buy a box at local grocery stores, or better yet at privately owned Asian grocery

November 24
Monday

 4th ♎
☽ → ♏ 12:54 pm

Color of the day: White
Incense of the day: Hyssop

Protection Charm

Every culture has its beliefs about the use of amulets, which are objects placed in the home or worn or carried on the person for protection. In Scotland, bracelets of leather, copper, braided hair, or red coral were often worn for protection. Necklaces of lucky stones or pebbles protected against drowning, lightning, or robbery. Silver coins, iron objects, and the berries and twigs of the rowan tree were also commonly used, as well as herbs like rue. Here is a protective charm to recite whenever you want to intensify your protective field:

> Power of silver,
> Power of stone,
> Protect me fully,
> And my home.
>
> Power of rowan,
> Power of rue,
> Bless and shield
> All that I do.
>
> Power of thread,
> Power of bone,
> My power intact,
> And left alone.

Sharynne NicMhacha

Notes:

November 25
Tuesday

 4th ♏

Color of the day: Gray
Incense of the day: Basil

Shield of Gold

The beliefs of soldiers in times past have imbued the golden coin with protective powers. Prepare this safety charm for the warrior in your life, whether he or she is a cop on the streets or a soldier overseas. You will need to get your hands on a Sacagawea dollar coin or one of the new presidential coins. A picture of the person you wish to protect would help as well, but a firm mental image will do. Hold the coin in your hands and go into a meditative state. Visualize strong currents of protective white light moving about your warrior. Build her up and make her truly strong before sending all of that energy into the coin. Ask her to carry the coin on her person.

Laurel Reufner

Notes:

November 26
Wednesday

4th ♏

Color of the day: Yellow
Incense of the day: Honeysuckle

Banishing Spell

The Tibetans celebrate a festival on this day dedicated to Agni Tara, the Hindu goddess of fire. Use the energies of fire and the waning Moon to banish negative energies in your life. This spell uses highly flammable spirits, so please be careful. Place your cauldron on a fireproof surface. Pour an eighth of a cup of 151 proof rum into the cauldron. Hold your dominant hand over the spirits and push the causes of your problem into the cauldron. Think about the thoughts you've been feeding the problem and push them into the cauldron as well. When you feel emptied of the negative energy, stand clear and light the rum. Say:

> Blazing force of Agni Tara,
> Transform me with your
>   light.
> Hearken for my need is dire,
> Consume it with this rite.

Thank the goddess. Act as if the problem is truly gone.

Lily Gardner

Notes:

November 27
Thursday
Thanksgiving

4th ♏
☽ → ♐ 12:14 am
New Moon 11:54 am

Color of the day: Green
Incense of the day: Balsam

Liar's Tarot

The New Moon is a traditional time for divination. Try this divination game I call Liar's Tarot. It is a great activity in or out of ritual for a group meeting on a New Moon. You'll be surprised by the wisdom it imparts. Ground, center, and merge as a group. Do an invocation asking for wisdom. Shuffle the cards. Now each person takes a card and does not look at it. Hold the card up to your forehead facing out. Everyone sees your card except you. Now, starting with the person at your left and going around clockwise, each person reads your card for you. It might be that some people in the group know tarot and others do not, but everyone should read. Tarot lends itself to this sort of spontaneous, I-don't-know-what-I'm-talking-about divination, which is often effective and meaningful. Each person will receive multiple readings, all the way around the circle. After all readings are done, look at your card. Meditate on the card tonight. You might want to take notes on the reading before you go to bed. This is your card and your reading for the next two weeks, until the Full Moon. Walk with it, think on it, and let it seep into your being.

Deborah Lipp

Notes:

take steps to make it right. Forgive yourself and then take action to make amends. Do this in honor of Ma'at, not in fear of her.

Cerridwen Iris Shea

Notes:

November 28
Friday

1st ♐

Color of the day: Purple
Incense of the day: Mint

Salute to Ma'at

In the Egyptian calendar, this is one of Ma'at's days. Ma'at is the underworld goddess who judges the dead by weighing the heart of the deceased against an ostrich feather. If the heart is heavier than the feather, the deceased is doomed. Instead of waiting until death, use today to lighten your heart. Is there anything for which you feel you need to atone? Has anything happened since you swept your emotional hearth on Palm Sunday for which you need to ask forgiveness? Today is the day to

November 29
Saturday

1st ♐

☽ → ♑ 12:48 pm

Color of the day: Blue
Incense of the day: Sandalwood

Let It Snow Spell

Cold and crisp outside? Or is your skiing weekend in danger of being canceled due to lack of the white stuff? A spell to make it snow may be in order. This spell is best done in the evening. Put shaved ice in a blue bowl. Light a blue candle and place it in the bowl, adding more ice if needed to stabilize it. Then say:

*Goddess of the northern
cold,
Goddess of the snowy fields,*

*Bring me snow
From your clouds on high,*

Upon the Earth,
May it be revealed.

Let it snow and let it stay,
So in your honor,
We can play!

Leave the candle to burn out, then place the water outside on the ground. Go to bed and dream of soft white snow.

Nancy Bennett

Notes:

November 30
Sunday

 1st ♍

Color of the day: Yellow
Incense of the day: Juniper

Multiplying Spell

Today marks the Feast of St. Andrew, the patron saint of fishermen and mariners. Andrew was a fisherman from Galilee who became one of Jesus' first disciples. He is well remembered for the Bible story where he participated in creating a feast for a crowd out of only five loaves of bread and a couple of fish.

He reminds us of the miracles in our own lives whereby positive intention causes good things to multiply. Think of something you need more of in your life, be it love, money, faith, or compassion. Thoughtfully prepare a stew of fish and vegetables as you welcome the goodness and magic of St. Andrew into your home. Toast him with a glass of red wine. Then stir in the magic of multiples by reciting:

A loaf of bread,
This fine fish stew,
A glass of wine
To toast Andrew
And bid him come,
Sit by my side
And dine with me
As I confide
A wish that
At the very least
Will grow from fallow
Into feast.

State your wish.

Igraine

Notes:

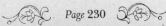

December is the twelfth month of the year. Its name is derived from the Latin for "ten," as it was the tenth month of the Roman calendar. Its astrological sign is Sagittarius, the archer (November 23–December 22), a mutable fire sign ruled by Jupiter. Just as the fox has glided silently through the frozen December woodland, Winter has crept quietly across the land. The silence comes and snow frosts the pines. The nights are long, but there is still reason to rejoice. In December, at Yule (the Winter Solstice), the return of the Sun God is celebrated, and the Yule log is burned to represent the strengthening Sun. Hanukkah, Kwanzaa, and Christmas are celebrated around the world, each with their own special message. The month is known for the preparation of special foods and pastries; kitchens everywhere are filled with the scents of spices and herbs. Holiday lights twinkle and seasonal decorations, rich with Pagan magical symbolism, adorn many homes. Pine and the Yule tree represent eternity. Holly and mistletoe are used to draw love and protection. Nuts symbolize fertility. Candles and stars are symbols of divinity. December's Full Moon is the Cold Moon. It is a moon of ice and frost, distant but beautiful. New Year's Eve brings us to the threshold of another year. One year ends, one begins. And the enduring pattern of the seasons continues.

December 1
Monday

1st ♑

Color of the day: Lavender
Incense of the day: Lily

Peace Invocation

One of the greatest accomplishments of the magical path is a deep connection with a sense of peace. Peace brings us increased awareness and vision, harmony and understanding, wisdom and ability. When you seek a deep connection with this inner place, create a spiral on your third eye with hallowed water, and hold a sacred stone over your heart. Breathe in and out deeply nine times, intoning this modern adaptation of a traditional Scottish prayer:

> The peace of the gods,
> The peace of all humans,
> Be upon each thing
> Which my eyes take in,
>
> Upon my body,
> Which is of the Earth,
> Upon my spirit,
> Which came from the old ones.
>
> Peace between neighbors,
> Peace between kindred,
> Peace between lovers,
> The deep peace of joy,
> The peace of the old gods,

> The peace of the fairy bowers,
> The stillness of peace,
> The breath of peace everlasting.

Sharynne NicMhacha

Notes:

December 2
Tuesday

1st ♑
☽ → ♒ 1:44 am

Color of the day: Gray
Incense of the day: Cedar

A New Chance at Freedom Spell

Bona Dea was a Roman goddess exclusive to women. She was prayed to by slaves seeking freedom and by women who needed aid in health matters. Make a paper chain out of construction paper. Place it around an object you wish to be free of, such as a bad relationship or a job (a picture of where you work, or of the person you wish to be free of, will suffice). Around the chain of paper, fix an altar with a variety of food, and wine with two glasses. Take some deep breaths and center yourself and chant:

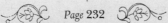

Bona Dea, free me,
From this [object],
Release me.

Bona Dea, free me
From these chains
That hold me.

Bona Dea, free me,
So that I can be me.

Take the chain in your hand and break it into pieces. Rip the picture into pieces as well. Now sweep these into the fire, sit down and eat. Pour the wine and invite the good goddess, making sure to toast her and your newfound freedom.

Nancy Bennett

Notes:

December 3
Wednesday

1st ♒

Color of the day: Brown
Incense of the day: Bay laurel

Wishing on a Star

The Moon is cresting in Aquarius. In the Major Arcana of the tarot, the Star card corresponds to this zodiacal sign. The Star can represent hope, faith, and the promise of a guiding light. Try this simple tarot spell if you need a wish granted and there's a cloud cover in the night sky. Perch the Star card upon your altar. Light a lavender candle as the crescent Moon rises. Quieting your mind and softening your gaze, allow the vision of the eight-pointed star to become a beacon of sparkling light, glimmering in the twilight. Point your wand or right index finger directly at the star. Feel its warm magic and begin to chant:

Star of wishes
That come true,
Light my way
And guide me to
A vision of
My future prize.
Illumine where
My fortune lies.

State your wish and wait for the answer by closing your eyes, breathing into total relaxation, and engaging your intuitive voice. Hear it whisper to you.

Igraine

Notes:

December 4
Thursday

 1st ≈
☽ → ♓ 1:23 pm

Color of the day: Green
Incense of the day: Jasmine

Budget Talisman

By now, spending for the holidays has kicked into high gear. Try this to help you curb your spending and help yourself stay on a reasonable budget. Light an orange candle on your altar (for control) and ring it with white shells. Dress the candle with the scent of mulberries to help you focus and maintain your will to avoid spending more than you can afford. When you go out to do your holiday shopping, take a shell along to remind you of your goals. If you need extra strength, anoint the shell with mulberry oil before leaving your home.

Laurel Reufner

Notes:

December 5
Friday

 1st ♓
2nd quarter 4:25 pm

Color of the day: White
Incense of the day: Violet

Yuletide Romance Spell

Friday is ruled by the planet Venus, and concerns such things as romance, love, fertility, and birth. The day's name comes from the Norse goddess of love, Freya. She is ideal to invoke for winter romances. The holiday season provides opportunities to meet new people at parties and other social occasions. Use this spell to draw attention to yourself. You will need a necklace of gold or amber, two candles of pink or gold, and amber essential oil. Light the candles and hold the necklace between them, saying:

> Golden Freya,
> Lady of grace,
> Shine your beauty
> Upon my face.
>
> Sun of fire,
> Necklace of gold,
> Send me someone
> Whom I can hold.
>
> Gentle goddess,
> Daring and free,

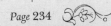

Let all their eyes
Be drawn to me.

Accept invitations to all promising events. When you go, wear the necklace and a dab of amber oil. Freya's grace will attract good attention.

Elizabeth Barrette

Notes:

completely and the right herbs. Then put the bag under your pillow and leave it there while you sleep. For gentle dreams, place lavender, rose, and chamomile in your bag. For visionary dreams, use lavender, passionflower, and nutmeg. If you want happy dreams, try mullein, lemon balm, and elderflower. And if you are looking for passion in your dreaming, add rose petals and jasmine flowers with a few drops of sandalwood pure essential oil.

Kristin Madden

Notes:

December 6
Saturday

2nd ♓
☽ → ♈ 9:44 pm

Color of the day: Indigo
Incense of the day: Pine

Dream Pillow

All things are possible during dreaming. It has been called the gateway to power and has been used to gain insight and foreknowledge for thousands of years. Dream pillows are a wonderful way to jumpstart the kinds of dreams you want to have. All you need is a small cloth bag that can be closed (or stitched)

December 7
Sunday

2nd ♈

Color of the day: Amber
Incense of the day: Frankincense

Defense Against Surprise Attack

To be ready so that gossip and verbal attacks aren't a surprise, try this spell. Gather together patchouli incense for its protection and grounding powers, a tincture with nettle for its bodily cleansing ability and prickly defensive nature, a small glass of water, and a small black candle in a glass holder. After performing your regular devotions and asking the elements and your deities to be present, light the black candle and, holding up to spirit, chant, "Fire and black hold them back, glass so clear keep protection near." Put a couple of drops of the nettle tincture in the glass of water and, holding up to spirit, chant, "By the power of nettle, keep me on my mettle. With water so smooth, my feelings please soothe." Drink the water, envisioning your resistance to attack being strengthened. Thank the spirits. Allow the candle to burn down completely and bury the remaining wax in the ground. Repeat as necessary.

Gail Wood

Notes:

Holiday lore: Cultures around the world have shared a penchant for the ritual burning of scapegoats, enemies, and devils. There is something primal about the roar of a large bonfire and its ability to bring purging light to a community. Today is such a day in the highland towns of Guatemala. Men dress in devil costumes during the season leading up to Christmas, and children chase the men through the streets. On December 7, people light bonfires in front of their homes, and into the fires they toss garbage and other debris to purify their lives. At night, fireworks fill the air.

December 8
Monday

2nd ♈

Color of the day: White
Incense of the day: Rosemary

Bodhi Day

Today is the Buddhist Bodhi Day, the day of awakening. "Bodhi" is often translated as "enlightenment." In 596 BCE, Prince Siddhartha Gautama sat under a

 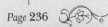

Bo tree for seven days, meditating. On the eighth morning he awoke enlightened, and knowing the Four Noble Truths. He became the Buddha, the Enlightened One. Bodhi Day celebrates this awakening. Bodhi Day is an excellent day to meditate, especially under a tree. It is also celebrated by drinking tea, eating cake, and doing readings (divination). Today would also be a good day to try the I Ching.

Deborah Lipp

Notes:

in Mexico, 2004. The intent is to send the message that combating corruption is the responsibility of all governments. There are traditions of Witches who have a history of combining magic with activism, and today is the day to tap into that activist spirit. What is your cause? Whether you care about the rights of women in oppressive regimes or about reducing the smog index in your own city, today is a day to take action and put some magic behind it. Write a letter to your editor, or to your representative. Make a phone call. Then light a candle and speak to Lady Liberty. Ask her to tip her scales towards justice. Place the candle in a window, where other people can see the light you're sending out in the world.

Diana Rajchel

Notes:

December 9
Tuesday

 2nd ♈

☽ → ♉ 1:52 am

Color of the day: Maroon
Incense of the day: Ginger

Pagan Activism

Today marks International Anti-Corruption Day, the anniversary of a conference against corruption held by the United Nations

December 10
Wednesday

2nd ♉

Color of the day: Yellow
Incense of the day: Honeysuckle

A Yule Tree Blessing

Did you remember to bless your Yule tree? Here is a quick and easy waxing Moon blessing that even children could do. To bless the Yule tree, purchase or make a gold Sun-shaped ornament. It could be rustic and handmade by the children or store-bought and fancy. Hang this ornament last upon the tree and repeat the following lines.

> The evergreen is a tree
> Full of magical lore,
>
> It brings prosperity and
> Charm as in days of yore.
>
> Now bless our home,
> Bringing us good cheer and
> Solstice fun,
>
> While we celebrate the return
> Of the newly born Sun.

Ellen Dugan

Notes:

December 11
Thursday

2nd ♉
☽ → ♊ 2:33 am

Color of the day: Turquoise
Incense of the day: Myrrh

Spell to Impress

This spell is designed to get on the good side of a boss (or teacher). It uses a powerful tool often not discussed in the occult: metaphor. "Apple polishing" is a metaphor for currying favor with a superior. In this spell, we'll use the metaphor to create the reality. Buy the most beautiful apple you can find. Get a bright yellow cloth. Burn cinnamon incense. Repetitive motion is very effective in spells. Rhythmic activities such as drumming, weaving, or reciting verse, all help induce a trance state and aid concentration. You're going to polish the apple rhythmically. You might choose one word to repeat while polishing, such as "approval" or "success" or "impress." Ground and center. Visualize how successful you are, and how much the boss approves of your work. Polish the apple while continuing this visualization. When you finish, say "So mote it be!" Give your polished apple to the boss as soon as possible.

Deborah Lipp

Notes:

December 12
Friday

 2nd ♊
Full Moon 11:37 am

Color of the day: Pink
Incense of the day: Cypress

Full Moon Messages

The winter Moons are a wonderful time for divination and spiritual self-study. December's Full Moon is known as the "Cold Moon," or "The Moon of Long Nights." As the light of the Sun becomes weaker, night magic and the power of the Moon becomes more potent. This water spell combined with the energies of the Full Moon will enable you to scry with better success. First set up your scrying altar in a private space where you'll be undisturbed. Cover the altar with black cloth and fill your cauldron half full of spring water. You may decide to place a quartz crystal or a piece of obsidian in the bottom of the cauldron. Place a silver candle next to the cauldron.

Next draw a warm bath. Light a few candles and add three drops of lemongrass, three drops of mimosa, and three drops of magnolia to your bath water. These oils are powerful aids for psychic ability. Swirl the oils around with your receptive hand. Lean back in the tub and soften your gaze. As you breathe in the essences, feel the watery parts of you being drawn to the Moon. Imagine the tides, the sea creatures, yearning toward the Moon. You are yearning toward the Moon. You, too, are a creature of the Moon. The Moon has a message for you. When you feel you must leave the bath and discover the message, approach the scrying table. Turn the lights off and light the silver candle. Cast a magic circle around your space, then seat yourself at the table. Keep a soft, unfocused gaze. Empty your mind of doubt and worry. Just breathe and watch. You will see images. The Moon has spoken.

Lily Gardner

Notes:

December 13
Saturday

 3rd ♊
☽ → ♋ 1:39 am

Color of the day: Blue
Incense of the day: Magnolia

Votive Candle Offering

St. Lucy is depicted in a white gown, crowned with glowing candles and bearing sweets and coffee or mulled wine. Treat yourself to something sweet and make a votive offering. The simple act of lighting a candle can be a profound spiritual expression when accompanied with sincere intent. Most of us light candles so often that it has become routine. But this time, be mindful of what light gives us, what your candle stands for. Recall how it must have felt to discover fire. Imagine how awe-inspiring it must have been to behold something so powerful and mysterious long ago. Candles have been part of spiritual traditions for centuries; votive actually means "offering." Tonight, light a candle for something meaningful to you. If you make candles, pour a special one for today.

Ember

Notes:

December 14
Sunday

 3rd ♋

Color of the day: Orange
Incense of the day: Almond

Fairy Invitation

Don't forget the fairies of winter. During the darkest days of the year, why not work a little charm and invite the benevolent fairies of winter to stay in your house through the Winter Solstice festivities? They can hide out in the greenery and take refuge in the Yule tree and enjoy the holidays with you. According to tradition, a family who kindly invited the fairy folk out of the cold was rewarded with prosperity in the coming year. Stand at the threshold at sunset—a classic between time—and invite them in. You will notice this spell is worded carefully to avoid fairy mischief. Happy holidays!

Gentle fairies of the winter
Hear my call,

I invite your caring presence
To my hall.

You are welcome within,
So long as you stay
Mischief free!

You may rest here with us
And enjoy the revelry!

Ellen Dugan

 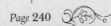

Notes:

Daughter of Thiazi,
In eagle form,
Mother of children
To Odin born,
She who is powerful
In her own right,
I honor your powers
On this night.

Sharynne NicMhacha

Notes:

December 15
Monday

3rd ♋

☽ → ♌ 1:22 am

Color of the day: Gray
Incense of the day: Clary sage

Skadi Independence Spell

One of the most interesting goddesses in Norse tradition is Skadi, a powerful and independent deity. She came down from the mountains to marry Njord, the sea god. Their marriage was not successful, because neither was willing to live away from home. Skadi returned to the hills, where she went about on skis and hunted with a bow. Here is a poem to honour and invoke Skadi:

Goddess of the wintry hills,
Divine huntress,
A goddess alone,
Consort of the ocean god,
Returned at last
To your mountain home.

December 16
Tuesday

3rd ♌

Color of the day: Red
Incense of the day: Ylang-ylang

Steady Spending Spell

This is the holy day of Sapientia, a Roman goddess from whom knowledge abounds. During these busy, cold days leading up to Yule, one can sometimes lose one's head with all the fuss, bother, and buying. Here is a spell to steady oneself before impulsive acts lead to bad purchases. Before going shopping, gather your thoughts, breathing deep. Hold your wallet/purse in your hand and chant:

> From my hand to your hand
> But not without thought,
> Sapientia, I seek thy wisdom
> Before my gifts are bought.
> Guide me to good choices
> And from bad ones, away,
> Sapientia, goddess of wisdom,
> Guide me on this day.

Lists can also be blessed with this spell, especially if you are looking for a hard-to-find item. Simply request it at the end of the spell, saying the item three times and visualizing yourself getting a good bargain.

Nancy Bennett

Notes:

December 17
Wednesday

 3rd ♌
☽ → ♍ 3:35 am

Color of the day: Topaz
Incense of the day: Marjoram

Pleasant No Matter What Day

Today is officially Be Pleasant No Matter What Day. Why? Because I said so. You haven't even recovered from Thanksgiving and Samhain yet, and Yule fast approaches. Everyone is overtired, overstretched, overwhelmed, over-cranky. Therefore, today is the day for *you* to make the effort. Be pleasant to everyone in every situation, no matter what. Don't be a doormat. Kill 'em with kindness if you have to. Smile. Say "hello," "please," and "thank you." No matter what. You'll be pleasantly surprised at how many "pleasantries" are returned. And at how much stress, all the way around, is alleviated.

Cerridwen Iris Shea

Notes:

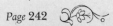

Holiday lore: Saturnalia was the Roman midwinter celebration of the solstice, and the greatest of the Roman festivals. It was traditional to decorate halls with laurels, green trees, lamps, and candles. These symbols of life and light were intended to dispel the darkness of the season of cold. The festival began with the cry of "Io Saturnalia!" Young pigs were sacrificed at the temple of Saturn and then were served the next day. Masters gave slaves the day off and waited on them for dinner. Merrymaking followed as wine flowed and horseplay commenced. Dice were used to select one diner as the honorary "Saturnalian King." Merrymakers obeyed absurd commands to dance, sing, and perform ridiculous feats. It was also a tradition to carry gifts of clay dolls and symbolic candles on one's person to give to friends met on the streets.

December 18
Thursday

3rd ♏

Color of the day: Crimson
Incense of the day: Clove

Candlelight Divination

Candles are an important part of the holiday season. They add warmth and beauty to any holiday décor, they symbolize divinity, and magical tradition tells us that a candle flame can "speak" to us and answer our questions. Take a break from the holiday rush and work this spell. You'll need a new white, red, or green taper. Sit quietly and think of your question, then light the candle. Carefully watch the flame. If the flame burns steady, the answer to your question is yes. If the flame cracks and sputters, but then burns with a steady flame, you'll face an obstacle; then your wish will come to you. If the flame sputters out completely, your wish won't come to you at this time. Wait about a week and try again.

James Kambos

Notes:

 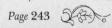

December 19
Friday

3rd ♏
4th quarter 5:29 am
☽ → ♎ 9:23 am

Color of the day: Purple
Incense of the day: Orchid

Opalia

This day was the celebration of the goddess Ops during the Roman observance of Saturnalia (in addition to the celebration held in her honor in August). They asked her for blessings of abundance and gave their friends year-end gifts for good fortune, such as holly sprigs, and they decorated temples with green boughs—an early form of "decking the halls." Ops is an Earth Mother, and her name means "plenty." Use this friendship bough to bestow blessings of abundance on your friends. Use a hot-glue gun to decorate a real pine bough or an artificial piece of sturdy pine garland with red and gold ribbons and symbols of abundance, such as fruits and nuts (dried or artificial). Complete it with this blessing:

> May the home
> That displays this wreath
> Be blessed with
> Abundance and peace,
> Wealth, health,
> And good fortune,

Now and always.
Blessed be.

Ember

Notes:

December 20
Saturday

4th ♎

Color of the day: Black
Incense of the day: Sandalwood

A Prayer for Peace and Tolerance

This day was recently established as All Faiths Day. Pagans, Christians, and Jews joined hands to celebrate in unity the winter holy days of Yule, Christmas, and Hanukah. In honor of this newfound day of interfaith sharing and communion, we offer a prayer for peace and tolerance.

> To all guardians of the light
> And of the purest love,
> Send us your radiant wings
> That we may ascend
> And rise above intolerance,
> Bias, and disgrace.

 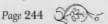

Open our hearts to all life
Regardless of god
or scripture.
Let us discover our
Splendor and spark,
Igniting the flame of
divine love
Within us all.
Peace, peace, peace.
So mote it be!

Send forth the smoke of incense as a subliminal force invoking peace, harmony, and co-creative ways of living.

Igraine

Notes:

December 21
Sunday
Yule – Winter Solstice

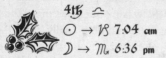

4th ♎
☉ → ♑ 7:04 am
☽ → ♏ 6:36 pm

Color of the day: Gold
Incense of the day: Hyacinth

Yule Meditation

Yule is the ancient holiday celebrating the Winter Solstice, a time when the Sun is at its weakest

and the calendar is coming to a close. Although most customs, beginning with Saturnalia, have to do with light, prosperity, and luck for the New Year, many of us find ourselves at odds with the manic party energy surrounding the holidays. Why not celebrate this Sabbat, the longest night of the year, by aligning ourselves with the dormant energies of winter? Begin this spell after dinner. Turn the radio, television, and all your electric lights off. Dress yourself in a fresh pair of pajamas. If you have a fireplace, by all means build a fire. If not, burn a stout red candle. As you gaze into the flames, try to empty your mind of worldly concerns. Breathe and look into the flames with a soft focus. Images will begin to suggest themselves to you. Give yourself the gift of at least an hour of this quiet time.

Lily Gardner

Notes:

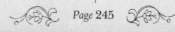

December 22
Monday

hanukkah begins

 4t5 ℳ

Color of the day: Silver

Incense of the day: Neroli

Rededication Ritual

Originally a ceremony of rededication, the Jewish festival of lights, Hanukkah, begins today. As the old year winds down, this is a beautiful time to re-examine your life and rededicate yourself to your gods and your chosen path. Imagine that you are walking along a trail that reflects the life you have been leading up to now. Be aware of the type of trail, anything you pass along the way, and how all this makes you feel. How would you change your path? What would you eliminate or add? Choosing one candle to represent each change, write that new goal on the candle. Then light the candles one at a time, taking the time to imagine how that goal attained would look and feel to you. Then rededicate yourself to your gods, your self, and your chosen path.

Kristin Madden

Notes:

Holiday lore: The Yule season is a festival of lights, and a solar festival, and is celebrated by fire in the form of the Yule log—a log decorated with fir needles, yew needles, birch branches, holly sprigs, and trailing vines of ivy. Back porches are stacked with firewood for burning, and the air is scented with pine and wood smoke. When the Yule log has burned out, save a piece for use as a powerful amulet of protection through the new year. Now is a good time to light your oven for baking bread and confections to serve around a decorated table; sweets have an ancient history. They are made and eaten to ensure that one would have "sweetness" in the coming year. Along these lines, mistletoe hangs over doorways to ensure a year of love. Kissing under the mistletoe is a tradition that comes down from the Druids, who considered the plant sacred. They gathered mistletoe from the high branches of sacred oak with golden sickles. It is no coincidence that Christians chose this month to celebrate the birth of their savior Jesus. Now is the time when the waxing Sun overcomes the waning Sun, and days finally begin to grow longer again. In some Pagan traditions, this struggle is symbolized by the Oak King overcoming the Holly King—that is, rebirth once again triumphing over death. And so the holly tree has come to be seen as a symbol of the season. It is used

in many Yuletide decorations. For instance, wreaths are made of holly, the circle of which symbolized the wheel of the year—and the completed cycle. (*Yule* means "wheel" in old Anglo-Saxon.)

December 23
Tuesday

  4th ♏

Color of the day: Black
Incense of the day: Bayberry

Larentalia

This date marks the ancient Roman festival of Larentalia to honor the Lares, who were the esteemed guardians and protectors of families. With this in mind, it is a good time to renew the protections upon your residence. Choose four quartz crystals. Dedicate one to each of the directional/elemental guardians. Place each crystal in a window or over a doorway facing its dedicated direction. As you place the crystal, chant:

> *Keepers of the [direction] gate, I invoke you to keep watch over my home. Grant me and mine your protections, keep out negative*

influences and unwanted energies. Hail and welcome.

Once all four crystals are in place, return to the center point of your home and see clearly a ring of white light going from one crystal to the next, protecting your dwelling within.

> *By the powers of the guardians, my home is safe, my family secure. So mote it be.*

Winter Wren

Notes:

December 24
Wednesday
Christmas Eve

4th ♏
☽ → ♐ 6:13 am

Color of the day: White
Incense of the day: Lilac

A Christmas Chant

Christmas chants were once common throughout Scotland, and on Christmas Eve groups of men or boys went about from house to house chanting traditional songs.

These were known as *fir-duan* (song-men) or *Gillean Nollaig* (Christmas lads). When they had sung two or three songs at a house, sacred cakes or "bannocks" were handed out to them through the window. Here is a modern adaptation of one of their traditional chants, which can be used for either Solstice or Yuletide celebrations:

> Sun of the dawn,
> Sun of the clouds
> Sun of the Earth,
> Sun of the stars
>
> Sun of the rain,
> Sun of the dew
> Sun of the heavens,
> Sun of the Moon
>
> Sun of the flame,
> Sun of the sky
> Sun of the elements,
> Sun of the light.

Sharynne NicMhacha

Notes:

December 25
Thursday
Christmas

 4th ♐

Color of the day: Purple
Incense of the day: Mulberry

The Undefeated Sun

The festival of Dies Natalis Solis Invicti, the undefeated Sun god, was celebrated in ancient Rome when the duration of daylight began to increase after the Winter Solstice. Once again, a little at a time, the days begin to grow longer once more. It is an excellent time for quiet meditation on what you seek to accomplish in the seasons ahead. Choose a quiet time and place, away from the hustle and energy of the day. Focus on your inner energy, your own inner spark. What seeds do you want to plant and nurture as the Sun blesses the Earth with light and warmth once more? Ponder those things and then note them on a piece of parchment. Fold the parchment into quarters and cup it in your hands. Visualize a ball of warm sunlight filling your hands and surrounding the paper with its radient ambience. Hold it there for a few moments, and then place the paper in a secure place on your altar to gain energy in the days ahead.

Winter Wren

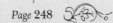

Notes:

You can't force someone to see your point of view if they truly have no interest in doing so. This spell only nudges or helps along an already willing person to see your perspective.

Laurel Reufner

Notes:

December 26
Friday
Kwanzaa begins

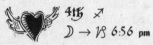 4th ♐
☽ → ♑ 6:56 pm

Color of the day: Coral
Incense of the day: Thyme

Empathy Ritual

Do you sometimes wish a loved one understood you better? A little empathy is in order. You'll need three candles (two pink and one white) and a picture of each of you. Place your image under the pink candle on the left and the other under the pink candle on the right. Light all of the candles. Centering yourself, look into the central (white) candle's flame, saying the following: "May you walk in my shoes. See things from my perspective and understand." Switch the photos under the candles and allow them to burn down. Note:

December 27
Saturday

 4th ♑
New Moon 7:22 am

Color of the day: Indigo
Incense of the day: Sage

A Star Spell for the New Moon

Stars are among the most ancient of all spiritual and magical symbols, and they are revered by most major religions. They serve as symbols of hope, trust, beauty and fame. In December, stars take on special significance since they're linked to religious holidays and are a sign of the season. And naturally stars serve as our link to the heavens, as well as our loftiest ambitions. This New Moon begins as the year is about to end. Not only does combining New Moon energy with the star power create awesome possibilities, the stars will also illuminate our path as we enter a new year. For this spell, go all out when you decorate your altar. Cover the altar with a white or silver cloth. Use as many white and silver candles as you wish, and a few small mirrors. At the center of the altar place a clear bowl filled with plain spring water, and your wand or athame. This spell isn't meant for a specific wish; instead you should concentrate on bringing into your life as many new opportunities as possible. If you can, take your wand or athame and go outside. If the night is clear, gaze at the stars as if you see them for the first time. Point your athame or wand towards the sky and draw down the star energy. Return to your altar and gently dip the tip of your athame/wand into the bowl of water. Watch the ripples grow, envisioning your own power growing. When new opportunities begin coming to you, don't be afraid to reach for the stars.

James Kambos

Notes:

December 28
Sunday

 1st ♑

Color of the day: Yellow
Incense of the day: Marigold

Inside Out

December 28 is referred to, in various European sources, as "the unluckiest day of the year." No work should be done, nothing new started. It's time to turn this fear inside out. Today will be the Day of Replenishment. Meditate. Read. Spend time with family and friends. Clear up any clutter, both physical and mental, from the old year. Bless your new journal for the New Year, create the file folders for your monthly bills, tidy up your desk, throw out the old food from the refrigerator and the cupboards. A new year, with new challenges, is about to begin. Celebrate what is dearest to you about the old year, so you can approach the new one with a clear heart.

Cerridwen Iris Shea

Notes:

December 29
Monday

hanukkah ends – Islamic New Year

 1st ♑

☽ → ♒ 7:42 am

Color of the day: Ivory
Incense of the day: Narcissus

East vs. West

It was once said to me that all too often, Westerners focus on the "do" to our own detriment, while Easterners live simply to "be." Because "being" is framed in terms of "doing nothing" we often have difficulty finding the stillness required to simply meditate, be with ourselves, know ourselves, and just be. Challenge that frenetic Western sensibility. Take a timer and practice sitting still. It may take more than one day to sit still for a full five minutes. The only goal of this exercise is to stay in the same place for a set period of time. You may hear inner voices complain about the waste of time, and all the things you should be doing. They're not on your side. Focus on staying where you are, and when it's time to do again, you'll go about it at peace.

Diana Rajchel

Notes:

December 30
Tuesday

1st ♒

Color of the day: White
Incense of the day: Cinnamon

Midwinter Sleep Charm

Winter is a time of peace and rest. Unfortunately, the hectic hustle and bustle of the holiday season often make it difficult to get to sleep. One night as I lay awake in bed, the image came to me of a dragon sleeping peacefully in its lair of thick, impenetrable stone. Along with that came this little rhyme:

> These things I give
> To the waking world,
>
> Now let me sleep
> With my great wings furled.

One by one, I called up all the thoughts that were keeping me awake, and I piled them into a heap. I repeated the rhyme each time I added something to the heap. Everything would still be there in the morning, and I could deal with it then; but in the meantime, I could get some sleep. It worked.

Elizabeth Barrette

Notes:

December 31
Wednesday
New Year's Eve

 1st ♒

☽ → ♓ 7:27 pm

Color of the day: Topaz
Incense of the day: Lavender

Betwixt and Between Meditation

New Year's Eve is neither the current year nor the coming year, so it's time to find the magic of betwixt and between. Bring a party hat and noise-makers into your sacred place. Remove all calendars and clocks. Go into a meditative state and find yourself in a place surrounded completely by a swirling fog. Unafraid and with interest, you look around. Emerging from the fog are images and messages that you need to know right at this point in your life. Watch and listen. Appearing in your left hand is an item that symbolizes the year passing and will be a guide for what to do about your history. Appearing in your right hand is an item that symbolizes what the coming year will bring and will be a guide for what to do as the future unfolds. Take a deep breath and return to the here and now, in your own place and body.

Gail Wood

Notes:

A Guide to Witches' Spell–A–Day Icons

 New Moon Spells

 Full Moon Spells

 New Year's Eve, Day

 Samhain, Halloween

 Imbolc

 Thanksgiving

 Valentine's Day

 Yule, Christmas

 Ostara, Easter

 Health Spells

 April Fool's Day

 Home and Garden Spells

 Earth Day

 Protection Spells

 Beltane

 Travel and Communication Spells

 Mother's Day

 Money and Success Spells

 Father's Day

 Love and Relationship Spells

 Litha

 Grab Bag of Spells

 Lammas

 Mabon

Daily Magical Influences

Each day is ruled by a planet that possesses specific magical influences:

Monday (Moon): peace, healing, caring, psychic awareness, and purification.

Tuesday (Mars): passion, sex, courage, aggression, and protection.

Wednesday (Mercury): conscious mind, study, travel, divination, and wisdom.

Thursday (Jupiter): expansion, money, prosperity, and generosity.

Friday (Venus): love, friendship, reconciliation, and beauty.

Saturday (Saturn): longevity, exorcism, endings, homes, and houses.

Sunday (Sun): healing, spirituality, success, strength, and protection.

Lunar Phases

The lunar phase is important in determining best times for magic.

The waxing Moon (from the New Moon to the Full Moon) is the ideal time for magic to draw things toward you.

The Full Moon is the time of greatest power.

The waning Moon (from the Full Moon to the New Moon) is a time for study, meditation, and little magical work (except magic designed to banish harmful energies).

Astrological Symbols

The Sun	☉	Aries	♈
The Moon	☽	Taurus	♉
Mercury	☿	Gemini	♊
Venus	♀	Cancer	♋
Mars	♂	Leo	♌
Jupiter	♃	Virgo	♍
Saturn	♄	Libra	♎
Uranus	♅	Scorpio	♏
Neptune	♆	Sagittarius	♐
Pluto	♇	Capricorn	♑
		Aquarius	♒
		Pisces	♓

The Moon's Sign

The Moon's sign is a traditional consideration for astrologers. The Moon continuously moves through each sign in the zodiac, from Aries to Pisces. The Moon influences the sign it inhabits, creating different energies that affect our daily lives.

Aries: Good for starting things, but lacks staying power. Things occur rapidly, but quickly pass. People tend to be argumentative and assertive.

Taurus: Things begun now do last, tend to increase in value, and become hard to alter. Brings out an appreciation for beauty and sensory experience.

Gemini: Things begun now are easily changed by outside influence. Time for shortcuts, communications, games, and fun.

Cancer: Stimulates emotional rapport between people. Pinpoints need, supports growth and nurturance. Tend to domestic concerns.

Leo: Draws emphasis to the self, to central ideas or institutions, away from connections with others and emotional needs. People tend to be melodramatic.

Virgo: Favors accomplishment of details and commands from higher up. Focus on health, hygiene, and daily schedules.

Libra: Favors cooperation, compromise, social activities, beautification of surroundings, balance, and partnership.

Scorpio: Increases awareness of psychic power. Precipitates psychic crises and ends connections thoroughly. People tend to brood and become secretive under this Moon sign.

Sagittarius: Encourages flights of imagination and confidence. This Moon sign is adventurous, philosophical, and athletic. Favors expansion and growth.

Capricorn: Develops strong structure. Focus on traditions, responsibilities, and obligations. A good time to set boundaries and rules.

Aquarius: Rebellious energy. Time to break habits and make abrupt change. Personal freedom and individuality is the focus.

Pisces: The focus is on dreaming, nostalgia, intuition, and psychic impressions. A good time for spiritual or philanthropic activities.

Glossary of Magical Terms

Altar: a low table that holds magical tools as a focus for spell workings.

Athame: a ritual knife used to direct personal power during workings or to symbolically draw diagrams in a spell. It is rarely, if ever, used for actual physical cutting.

Aura: an invisible energy field surrounding a person. The aura can change color depending upon the state of the individual.

Balefire: a fire lit for magical purposes, usually outdoors.

Casting a circle: the process of drawing a circle around oneself to seal out unfriendly influences and raise magical power. It is the first step in a spell.

Censer: an incense burner. Traditionally, a censer is a metal container, filled with incense, that is swung on the end of a chain.

Censing: the process of burning incense to spiritually cleanse an object.

Centering yourself: to prepare for a magical rite by calming and centering all of your personal energy.

Chakra: one of the seven centers of spiritual energy in the human body, according to the philosophy of yoga.

Charging: to infuse an object with magical power.

Circle of protection: a circle cast to protect oneself from unfriendly influences.

Crystals: quartz or other stones that store cleansing or protective energies.

Deosil: clockwise movement, symbolic of life and positive energies.

Deva: a divine being according to Hindu beliefs; a devil or evil spirit according to Zoroastrianism.

Direct/Retrograde: refers to the motions of the planets when seen from the Earth. A planet is "direct" when it appears to be moving forward from the point of view of a person on the Earth. It is "retrograde" when it appears to be moving backward.

Dowsing: to use a divining rod to search for a thing, usually water or minerals.

Dowsing pendulum: a long cord with a coin or gem at one end. The pattern of its swing is used to predict the future.

Dryad: a tree spirit or forest guardian.

Fey: an archaic term for a magical spirit or a fairylike being.

Gris-gris: a small bag containing charms, herbs, stones, and other items to draw energy, luck, love, or prosperity to the wearer.

Mantra: a sacred chant used in Hindu tradition to embody the divinity invoked; it is said to possess deep magical power.

Needfire: a ceremonial fire kindled at dawn on major Wiccan holidays. It was traditionally used to light all other household fires.

Pentagram: a symbolically protective five-pointed star with one point upward.

Power hand: the dominant hand, the hand used most often.

Scry: to predict the future by gazing at or into an object such as a crystal ball or pool of water.

Second sight: the psychic power or ability to forsee the future.

Sigil: a personal seal or symbol.

Smudge/Smudge stick: to spiritually cleanse an object by waving incense over and around it. A smudge stick is a bundle of several incense sticks.

Wand: a stick or rod used for casting circles and as a focus for magical power.

Widdershins: counterclockwise movement, symbolic of negative magical purposes, sometimes used to disperse negative energies.

Spell Notes:

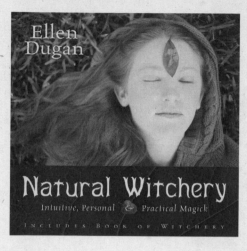